T0304840

CHASING SALAH

CHASING SALAH

The Biography

Simon Hughes

CONSTABLE

CONSTABLE

First published in Great Britain in 2024 by Constable

1 3 5 7 9 10 8 6 4 2

A CIP catalogue record for this book
is available from the British Library.

ISBN: 978-1-40872-115-5 (hardback)
ISBN: 978-1-40872-116-2 (trade paperback)

Typeset in Bembo by Hewer Text UK Ltd, Edinburgh
Printed and bound in Great Britain by Clays Ltd

Papers used by Constable are from well-managed
forests and other responsible sources

Constable
An imprint of
Little, Brown Book Group
Carmelite House
50 Victoria Embankment
London EC4Y 0DZ

The authorised representative
in the EEA is
Hachette Ireland
8 Castlecourt Centre
Dublin 15, D15 YF6A, Ireland
(email: info@hbgi.ie)

An Hachette UK Company
www.hachette.co.uk

www.littlebrown.co.uk

For Celeste and Vincent

Contents

Prologue: the long road

Mohamed Salah began his journey to Cairo for training sessions with a daily commute on a road with no name. In fact, it was more of a rocky path that connected the village of Nagrig to another road known only by two of the places it cut through, Tanta and Basyoun. In the height of summer, the heat was already searing when he set off but in the depths of winter, the sun was much lower in the sky and in this part of the Nile Delta the temperatures plunged, leaving dew on the fields of jasmine and white onion.

The first logistical problem for Salah, who was twelve when he began this lonely routine, was the reliability of the transport taking him to the nearest town on the first leg of the journey: the microbus. For anyone wanting to travel around Egypt on a budget, the microbus system is vital. Except, it is not really a system at all and is better described as an informal network, in which would-be travellers rely on sufficient fellow passengers turning up to cover the petrol and to make the driver enough cash to encourage him to get going. If you are the first person on board, there is usually a decent wait until the carriage is full. This has a knock-on effect for anyone boarding further down the road.

To get an idea of a microbus, imagine a sardine can with

1

tyres: they are not exactly comfortable or fragrant; smaller than a camper with two or three rows of three or four pleather seats, pressed up to the back of those in front. They are not for tall people and fortunately for Salah, he was rather small for his age, like a lot of the boys from the countryside. Whatever your height, it is impossible to complete a journey in a microbus without banging your head, due to the depressions in the roads, which drivers seem to attack even if they know they are there.

Salah had to be in Cairo for early afternoon. Cooperation from school was required, and he regularly left class at 9 a.m., having started his day only two hours earlier. If everything went to plan, it would take around three hours to navigate the 120 km of mainly backroads but this was not always the case. It meant he had to leave himself room for things to go wrong, especially on certain days, when the traffic was sometimes worse as he reached Cairo, or – as he learnt with time – on the days when it had seemed one of the drivers had been up late the night before, inevitably leading to tardiness.

There were four legs. On a good day, the first would take half an hour, the second would take one hour, the third another two hours, and the last between forty-five minutes and an hour. Even this did not account for breaks, waiting for the next microbus to arrive when he was late, or waiting for other passengers to turn up.

Like the microbus 'system', the 'terminal' at the end of leg one in Basyoun was not really a proper facility, but rather a gathering point at the rear of the town where insects attacked donkeys as the donkeys tried to seek shade beneath wooden carts. No one really knew how long the drivers had been working, but they seemed to like their rest; huddling around conspiratorially in a circle while puffing on rolled tobacco like it was an Olympic sport.

With the Qur'an crackling on the radio, the more vocal passengers reminded their driver it was time to go, but it is hard to imagine Salah, not yet even a teenager, as one of those. In familiar surroundings he was quietly confident, but all of this must have been incredibly unnerving, especially at first, as he travelled further and further away from the fresher air, stillness and isolation of Nagrig, and closer to the magnetism and mayhem of one of the biggest cities in Africa.

From Basyoun there was another microbus to the moody city of Tanta, where Salah was first registered to a football club. Western women have been warned not to visit Tanta, due to a number of attacks. In 2011, during the Egyptian revolution, the city was the scene of a bloodbath, as the army forced protesters back, shooting indiscriminately. Near the 'terminal', again an informal arrangement underneath an enormous concrete fly-over, there would later be a mural of Salah himself, painted on a wall next to a series of bullet holes, a reminder, for anyone who knows what they are looking for, of where Egypt has recently been.

To Cairo's Ramses Square, still a couple of hours away. Yet the city of Cairo itself is so vast that you enter the environs much earlier. Suddenly, the countryside gives way and human-ity is everywhere. It is hard to do the place justice through video, photography or even words. Perhaps only one word is needed: 'pandemonium', mainly because of the sheer number of vehi-cles and the impression that their brakes are directly attached to their horns. Amidst the din, behaviours are unfamiliar: no car boots seem to lock, so when a chassis hits an uneven part of the broiling tarmac, the boot bursts open, revealing whatever is inside – sometimes livestock.

There was still a distance for Salah to travel even when he reached Ramses Square – which is a real terminal and a place where it feels as though the whole world has descended. His club, El Mokawloon, was located on the other side of the city. And once he made it, through more choking traffic, once the city's pollution had got up his nose and was filling his lungs, and his fingernails had become familiar with crud, there was a walk uphill for twenty minutes or so after the drop-off point.

Finally, Salah had arrived. Though he believed it was worthwhile, that he was on to something, he never imagined where his dedication would eventually take him.

In 2019, I became one of the many journalists to try and recreate this journey, but as the road from Tanta to Cairo became more congested, I realised that being an adult with a guide, it was impossible to really capture what it was like for Salah. He had been by himself and in his own world as he stared at the changing landscape day after monotonous day, hoping his story would end differently to those of the other boys leaving the countryside in the pursuit of sporting success and fame and fortune.

The wages Salah took home from Cairo were not even enough to pay for the bus fares. His father, who made reasonable money out of Nagrig's jasmine fields, covered the difference. So much has changed in Egypt since, yet so much has not, as this book will explore. With the Egyptian economy tanking, the money from El Mokawloon would have been worth just £2 twenty years later when, in 2024, a thirty-two-year-old Salah was so talented, popular and marketable that he was earning close to a million pounds a week.

He was once just an anonymous kid from a place only a few people in Egypt had ever heard of. Yet since 2017, when he signed for Liverpool, the club that he subsequently helped return to its former glories, Salah has become one of the most identifiable footballers on the planet.

He is now to Egypt what Lionel Messi is to Argentina and Cristiano Ronaldo is to Portugal. In Europe, people have an idea of how big a star Salah is back home – but do they really get it? Both his and Egypt's own stories are unique. This is a country that has produced the most successful teams in the continent of Africa, and yet until Salah it had not produced a superstar like the Ivory Coast's Didier Drogba or Samuel Eto'o from Cameroon.

While the top European or South American nations might have two or three go-to players at any one time, Salah is the first Egyptian not just to thrive abroad but to become one of the game's greatest players. No Egyptian has generated the same level of interest both at home and across other parts of the world and that puts him under unique pressure. No European footballer would be expected to respond to the same level of scrutiny. For Egypt, Salah is alone. It is just him.

Egypt is a conservative but passionate, football-mad country. Egyptians tend to be attached to strong, male personalities, dating back to the pharaohs. Salah, however, does not fit easily into that profile. The relationship is therefore complex, even though he is the biggest name in Egypt and is followed by the most people, and everybody tends to acknowledge that.

Yet does he evoke the same sort of emotion as someone like

Drogba, a player who helped end a civil war? Many years later Drogba visited a bank in Abidjan and had to leave through the back door because a crowd was starting to gather. One man saw the escape and when he approached Drogba, he became so excited that he started to undress himself. There is an attachment to figures like Drogba because he makes people feel like they can relate to him. Perhaps this is what Salah lacks. He does not seem like a normal human being to some, maybe because he protects himself by putting layers between himself and others. If he makes mistakes, we never really hear about them. He doesn't appear to have natural flaws. His performance and yield are that good.

In Liverpool, he is the player whose records made the pursuit of the impossible seem realistic. His impact at the club was marked by the fact he reached a century of goals faster than any other player. By the end of his seventh season at Anfield, he had scored more times in the Premier League than any African and, at the time of writing in September 2024, his 214 goals overall meant he was close to becoming the fourth-highest scorer in the club's history, having already leapfrogged arguably its two greatest players, Sir Kenny Dalglish and Steven Gerrard.

While Dalglish cemented his status through his successes as a manager and Gerrard remains the longest-serving captain, like Salah, the pair were not out-and-out strikers. This makes Salah's record all the more remarkable: his 158 goals in the Premier League era are the most of any player since the formation of the competition in 1992. This means Salah also stands above Robbie Fowler and Michael Owen, even though he was a winger and they were centre forwards.

Across his time at Liverpool, Salah's forty-seven goals mark him as the club's all-time leading scorer in European competition. He has also won three Premier League Golden Boot titles. He would deliver when it really mattered, whether it was a penalty kick in the Champions League final or the fifteen goals in sixteen games against Manchester United. No Liverpool player in its history has scored more times versus their ferocious regional rivals.

Salah became so reliable in terms of availability and output, he was almost taken for granted. On two occasions, he was ignored for the Premier League Player of the Year, including in 2018–19 when he was the division's top scorer and finished the campaign as a Champions League winner. Did he get the recognition he deserved?

It probably does not help that he almost never gives interviews and when he did, he gives so little away about himself. What everyone sees is simply a good, industrious family man, who lives life cleanly and never seems to stop scoring. His consistency has meant he has been visible all the time and this has bred a feeling of familiarity. Yet his discretion has meant that, although he is always there, in plain sight, we barely really know him. He has never spoken to anyone publicly about his innermost feelings and I don't think he ever will because of how he styles himself and because of the potential consequences for such openness, especially in a country as authoritarian as Egypt, where he still has family.

It means that this book does not include an interview or exclusive commentary from Salah. By speaking to me, he would indirectly have been endorsing the content, which may have placed him in a difficult position – especially at home, where his every public remark is monitored by the state.

Yet by speaking to him, I suspect I would not have felt like I was getting any closer to the truth. I was also aware that cooperation had the potential to compromise journalism and, fundamentally, I wanted this book to be an extensive piece of reporting that explored his key relationships and explained the unique forces around him.

For many people close to Salah, speaking openly about him also brought complications: if they were still employed by Liverpool, it would require sanctioning by the club, which therefore reduced the amount of information they could tell me on the record. Some of these people were, after all, also protecting their own jobs.

Meanwhile, other sources were acutely aware of the heat that might come their way if they put their name to a quote that either someone with influence in Egypt or Liverpool, or indeed, Salah, did not like.

This explains why some of the more delicate topics involve the sort of off-record conversations that have been the basis for journalism since it started to play a functioning role in democratic society.

The dynamic meant that – like Premier League defenders, especially between 2017 and 2020 – I felt like I was always chasing him.

What became clear to me about Salah is that although he sees himself as an independent in the same way as Michael Jordan once did, he also takes satisfaction in his story resonating with people from the region he came from.

He would act as a bridge between two worlds and it is his hope that other Muslim footballers, especially from Egypt, would follow him.

Yet I'm not so sure they will. It takes a special ability and personality to ride above the distractions that he has had to deal with.

It is possible he is just a one-off.

Chapter 1

Egyptian king

Just to the south of Liverpool's city centre, the biggest arch of its kind outside China represents the oldest community from that country in Europe. The area strides Upper Parliament Street, where some of the Georgian townhouses have peeling signs that show the West African states and Caribbean islands that used to have a presence in the Liverpool afterhours scene. The district behind it is known by its postcode, and it is now more common in L8 to see shops with connections to the horn of Africa or the Middle East. The distinctions are a reminder that Liverpool is multi-ethnic rather than multicultural. There remains a sense of segregation because it is uncommon to see its foreign communities in other parts of the city, especially in the north, which is overwhelmingly white.

Liverpool's power grew out of its port, which was once the biggest in the British Empire outside London. Look around closely and there are reminders everywhere of Liverpool's past: statues, roads, buildings and docks are named after the men whose influence grew out of the slave trade, the industry that made some people in Liverpool very rich indeed.

The politics of Liverpool makes its identity more complicated. Though like a lot of places in Britain it was once dominated by the right, it has swung left since 1979, when the non-interventionist economic strategies of Margaret Thatcher hit the city hard. The idea of a 'managed decline' was floated at government level and by the end of her premiership eleven years later, the evidence in Liverpool, which felt stranded in every sense, suggested the policy had been carried out. Though Liverpool has identified with the left ever since, in truth it is better defined as a city in perpetual opposition. Within twelve months of New Labour rising to power in the late 1990s, it voted in a Liberal Democrat council that stood for longer than a decade.

All of this has fed into an outsider mentality and Liverpool has also been accused of exceptionalism. A lot of – but not all – Liverpudlians do not feel like they are a part of the national debate. When arrests were made following riots instigated by the far right in Liverpool in the summer of 2024, many of the men facing prosecution had addresses on Merseyside. This cold reality was a reminder that not all attitudes are the same. Simmering below the surface is a dark feeling that many in Liverpool prefer to ignore.

This snapshot underlines why the year of 2018 was a particularly special one in Liverpool. While the city centre was booming a decade after holding the title of European Capital of Culture, structures in wider parts of the region were creaking again after eight years of austerity. Liverpool was underfunded and some of the worst poverty could be found near the stadiums of its football clubs, Liverpool FC and Everton FC. Eleven of Liverpool's neighbourhoods had fused as the most deprived one per cent in the country, including Anfield and Walton, where many families, even those engaged in employment, were relying on food banks.

As it often had throughout the history of the city, salvation came in part from the success of one of its football teams. Liverpool FC were on the up under charismatic German manager Jürgen Klopp. Back in the Champions League for only the second time in eight years, the club was becoming relevant again on the stage that once made it so famous. At the start of the 2017–18 season, Liverpool had won the European Cup or Champions League five times – a record that made them the most successful team in England.

What was different about this team to those of the past was its expressiveness, in a religious sense, especially in an attack that would become one of the most feared in Europe. While an evangelical Christian from Brazil called Roberto Firmino joined Liverpool in 2015, he was flanked by two practising Muslims. The first to join in 2016 had been Sadio Mané, a Senegalese player who had since been photographed cleaning floors in a Liverpool mosque when he was not doing his weekly shop in a supermarket wearing a traditional West African tunic and sandals. Even though the more recent arrival was the most expensive transfer in the club's history, arguably less was expected from Mohamed Salah when he joined in 2017 because of his failure to make an impression at Chelsea during a previous spell in the Premier League.

Not even the recruiters at Liverpool predicted his impact when they recommended his signing to Klopp. But, by the end of his first season at Anfield, Liverpool were in another Champions League final thanks largely to Salah's forty-four goals in fifty-two games. The scale of this achievement had given the team a sense of invincibility: with him involved, anything was possible.

What followed was Salah-mania, reaching a point where it became routine for Liverpool supporters during the World Cup of 2018, regardless of race or religion, to gather at the city's Abdullah Quilliam mosque. Quilliam, a solicitor, had been a Methodist preacher until 1887 when, following a trip to Morocco, he became the first Christian in Victorian England to convert to Islam. Salah had scored the goal that sent his country to the tournament for the first time in twenty-eight years.

Liverpool's Irish Centre was only a few streets away and, though Ireland had not qualified, the tricolour flag flew from the windows of the mosque. Salah's goals as well as his reaction to some of those goals (he practised the *sujood* – the act of prostration that is part of Islamic worship), had helped lift a barrier of negative perceptions about Muslims that so many leaders and institutions could not.

A study by Stanford University in the United States revealed that the number of hate crimes on Merseyside fell after Salah's arrival at Liverpool. While there were 18.9 per cent fewer crimes than predicted, social media had seen a 53 per cent fall in anti-Muslim posts from Liverpool fans, who called him 'the Egyptian King' and claimed, 'I'd be a Muslim too,' when they serenaded him.

Salah had achieved this without saying anything inspiring. In fact, most of his words were bland. He'd simply scored goals for a really popular team that was winning again and, in that moment, reminded everyone of his faith by demonstrating a simple act that is usually performed by billions of people during prayer time every day of the week.

The goal that gave warning to the rest of the league that Salah was a different player to the one who left Chelsea after just nine hours of Premier League football came against Arsenal at Anfield in August 2017. The visiting team had a corner, but when Liverpool broke from the edge of their area, it was Salah carrying possession and it took him just 12.96 seconds to put the ball in the back of the net. Liverpool won that game 4–0 and a few months later, when the team scored the same number of goals at West Ham, one of them came from Salah. Again, it was delivered with blistering pace on the counterattack.

Given how quickly Salah made his mark at Liverpool, it is easy to forget that the partnerships around him evolved rather than arrived fully formed. Over the years that followed, Salah's name would be associated with Mané and Firmino in the same way that Liverpool's febrile supporter base remembered the surnames of partnerships like Toshack and Keegan, Rush and Dalglish, and more recently Torres and Gerrard. Yet, as Salah admitted much later, 'We could not do the pressing in the first season. It took time to do it properly. Our system – counterpressing – is not easy to adapt to quickly.'

This early part of Salah's Liverpool career featured indifferent outcomes. Having dismantled Arsenal at Anfield, Liverpool were then thumped 5–0 at Manchester City in a game heavily influenced by Mané's early red card for a high kick on Brazilian goalkeeper Ederson. The following month, they lost 4–1 at Wembley against Tottenham before throwing away a three-goal lead at Sevilla in the Champions League, where they ended up just about clinging to a draw.

In his first nineteen Premier League games for his new club, Salah started just seven beside Mané and Firmino, as Klopp used Philippe Coutinho, Daniel Sturridge and Dominic Solanke as part of his rotation. And when what became a famous three did start together, Liverpool won only three of the first seven games.

While these initial results did not indicate what the future might look like, what helped was the repetition of the training sessions, developing patterns. Often a three in attack became a five because the full-backs were allowed to express themselves. Meanwhile, with time, the midfield became less creative, more disciplined and awkward to play against.

Within this system, Salah became a bewitching red blur. By late November, he had scored fourteen goals in eighteen matches, more than any total recorded by a Liverpool player over a whole campaign since the 2013–14 season. His seven goals in four league matches led to his first Player of the Month award. He would later become the first player from any club to scoop the accolade three times in one season.

What was remarkable was the consistency that followed, with his worst goal drought lasting just one game before he reached thirty goals for the campaign. He would enter the history books again after his four goals against Watford meant he'd scored more times than anyone else for Liverpool in their debut season, moving past Fernando Torres. What was even more remarkable was the fact that there were still a couple of months to go.

Towards the end of that game, Salah played as a centre forward. It had not been a role Klopp envisioned him playing. At Roma, he'd played entirely on the wing because of the presence of a dominant striker in Edin Dzeko. Yet Klopp began to realise that in games where Liverpool had a lead, he could leave him in the centre, poised for a counterattack.

Despite the records Salah was breaking, Klopp wanted more out of him in a defensive capacity. Even after his first goal for

Liverpool in a pre-season friendly at Wigan Athletic, he preferred to focus on what he saw as an inability to defend. Against Watford, Klopp was appreciative of Salah's efforts in tracking back to prevent an opportunity opening up for the visiting team in the first half. 'He took each sprint like the hundred-metre final in the Olympic Games,' Klopp concluded.

Only legendary figures in Liverpool's history had matched Salah's numbers. His fortieth goal of the season, a figure previously achieved at Liverpool by Roger Hunt (1961–62) and the club's all-time leading scorer Ian Rush (1983–84 and 1986–87), meant his own status was secured beside such company inside just eight months.

Though neither Hunt nor Rush reached the milestone faster than the newcomer, it was difficult to gauge what Salah really thought of it all. The landmark was reached during a 3–0 victory over Bournemouth, after which he reluctantly agreed to be interviewed in Anfield's mixed zone for the first time by local journalists who had been waiting to speak to him since the start of the season. Salah stepped forward and spoke for more than three minutes, trying desperately to veer the conversation back to the role of his teammates and the simple importance of results over any personal achievements.

Twelve different Liverpool players had served him with an opportunity to score by this point, yet there were also eleven unassisted goals made possible by his own pace, his instinct, and as Klopp was increasingly pleased about, his pressing.

These numbers did not reflect everything, however. Salah was increasingly appreciative of the movement around him by teammates like Firmino. 'I think the way he plays it, gives us more chances to score,' Salah said enthusiastically, before moving on to the full-back usually found closer to the touchline. After Salah had finished speaking, Trent Alexander-Arnold appeared, describing training against Salah, as a 'nightmare because you're up against him. There's sometimes I don't really like him because he does that stuff to me.'

That 'stuff' wasn't showboating, but rather running at full speed, darting at opponents waiting for the slightest gap to appear before shifting his momentum to create an opportunity for himself. It had helped Salah close in on Rush's record of forty-seven goals in a season, as well as the Premier League Golden Boot. The latter seemed to be on his mind more than the target set by Rush. He would admit that some of his team-mates were now looking to pass to him, to try and help him beat Harry Kane and Sergio Agüero, the other forwards trying to win the award. It was the only issue Salah was asked about where the answer was firm, rather than deflective.

Do you want them to pass it more to you?

'Yes,' he said. 'They pass the ball anyway. I am happy to have this feeling, you know. You feel they want to support you and want to help you to score goals. That's a good feeling.'

It was a small insight into Salah's way of thinking. He wanted individual awards rather than club records. He liked feeling the support of those around him. Yet when it came to the Champions League, that mattered more than any personal accolade he might take. Salah knew that no Egyptian had ever lifted the trophy.

The chances of this happening increased when he scored twice against his old club Roma in a semi-final first leg at Anfield where Firmino and Mané helped complete a 5–2 rout. With the Italian press also wanting him to speak, he slalomed through the mixed zone again, leaving others to talk on his behalf. 'He deserves the credit, but I think he deserves even more to be honest,' his teammate Dejan Lovren said. 'Forty-three goals, guys. F***ing hell. Forty-three goals. F***ing hell.'

Lovren was an interesting character, a refugee forced out of Croatia as the former Yugoslavia disintegrated. He would grow up in Munich before returning to Zagreb where he launched his career. His outsider mentality meant he had something in common with Salah, a player who was treading new ground for so many reasons. They would become close friends.

Initially, Lovren described Liverpool as a team that had progressed through Europe despite its lack of 'superstars'. Then he seemed to remember what Salah was doing, a player whose forty-three goals in forty-seven appearances were supported by thirteen assists. For context, Lionel Messi had forty goals and eighteen assists for Barcelona in fifty appearances in 2017–18 and Cristiano Ronaldo forty-two goals and eight assists ahead of the first leg in the other semi-final between Real Madrid and Bayern Munich.

Lovren reappraised his assessment: 'Yes, he is the one,' the defender said. 'He is becoming the superstar. It looks easy what he does, but it is very difficult. I believe he should be regarded as one of the best three in the world at the end of the year.'

Instead, when the winner of the Ballon d'Or was announced in December 2018, Salah did not even feature in the top five nominees. Egypt's performance in the World Cup played a part, as the country was eliminated after only two games in the group stages.

Yet more significant was what happened in the Champions League final in Kyiv, where Liverpool lost 3–1 to a Real Madrid team inspired by Luka Modrić, who later in the summer captained Croatia to its first World Cup final.

Though France prevailed on that occasion, Modrić was voted as the best player in the world. It was the first time someone other than Messi or Ronaldo had taken the award since the Brazilian midfielder Kaka in 2007.

Yet Salah's sixth-place finish was remarkable in the context of Egyptian history because the country had never had a nominee in the category since it was launched in 1956. There can be no doubt, however, that he would have been higher had Kyiv turned out differently. Not only did Liverpool lose, but his night was over as early as the twenty-fifth minute after being yanked to the floor by defender, Sergio Ramos, who then landed on his arm.

Ramos – whose twenty-five red cards set a European record – somehow escaped punishment from the Slovenian referee, Damir Skomina. After Salah left the field in tears, everything that could go wrong for Liverpool did go wrong: while the team's German goalkeeper Loris Karius made two extraordinary blunders, Real's Welsh substitute Gareth Bale's first touch of the game was a bicycle kick, which flew past him.

Salah had been to hospital and back by the time the game was finished. As he sat in the bowels of the Olympic Stadium in pain and struggling to contain his emotions, Ramos and the rest of the Real squad were next door, celebrating.

Liverpool and Salah were devastated. On the basis of everything that had happened, the team was never going to win, nor was Salah going to receive the individual award that he deserved, given his impact across the entire season.

Yet the fervour around him was not dissipating. His shoulder injury now meant he was racing to be fit for the World Cup. After a €1 billion lawsuit against Ramos was launched by an Egyptian lawyer, a petition called on FIFA to take action against the defender for 'using tricks that defy the spirit of the game and fair play'. It received more than half a million signatures.

Ramos suggested 'everything is magnified' and claimed Salah, in fact, grabbed his arm first. 'I am only missing Firmino saying that he got a cold because a drop of my sweat landed on him,' he told the *AS* newspaper. Ramos also suggested he'd exchanged messages with Salah, but did not reveal the content of those messages.

Meanwhile, in the Indonesian capital of Jakarta, where nearly 84 per cent of the population are Muslim, a demonstration outside the Spanish embassy threatened to turn nasty until the country's military police showed up with their batons.

Salah had missed out on the game's most famous trophy as well as its most prestigious individual award but he was now a global superstar and during this period, his supporters were almost willing to go into battle for him.

Chapter 2

Scent of jasmine

When Mohamed Salah became famous in Egypt, most people in the country did not know where Nagrig was. Sometimes they misspelt it, even some of the journalists, who initially referred to it as Nagrid. That was not to say little was known about the wider governorate in which it sits, Gharbia, because it had produced notable people before.

An eight-kilometre westward walk through the fields from Nagrig is another village called Shubratna, where Lieutenant General Saad El-Shazly was born. Egyptian historians remember him as a brilliant military strategist who, in 1973, masterminded Directive 41, a plan that enabled the army to cross the Suez Canal and into the Sinai peninsula at the height of the Yom Kippur war.

From 2014 onwards, however, the region became more associated with its most talented footballer. Those journalists who left Cairo's dirt and noise behind them and followed the Nile downstream north were struck by just how far Nagrig was from any major town. It was hard to find and having crisscrossed agricultural roads and avoided the delta's many irrigation canals, there was a sense of achievement on arrival.

On closer inspection, however, Nagrig was indistinguishable from any of the other poor settlements nearby: a concrete slum in the countryside dominated by unplanned brick structures that seemed temporary but had been there for generations. An average scene on any of its dusty, unpaved streets would be chickens and cows roaming, presumably hoping to avoid the butcher hacking away in a doorway at indeterminate meat, while those people without jobs – the majority – hung around in the shade, smoking joints, staring into the middle distance. Like everywhere else, village life revolved around the mosque, but the most action was in the fields where the labour was harsh and virtually none of the product was being sold or used locally.

Instead, jasmine and onions were carted away to airfields and boats and transported to countries like Russia and France. Very few people in Nagrig see the benefit of its natural resources and it has been this way for a long time. In his outstanding book, *The Egyptians*, Jack Shenker tries to explain the relationship between the people here and what lies beneath them by citing the closing scene of the 1969 film, *Al Ard* (*The Land*), when an ageing villager stands up to his feudal overlord; his feet bound, his body tied to the legs of a horse ridden by a sheriff, yet he refuses to abandon his home, and it is 'difficult to tell', concludes Shenker, 'whether he is clutching the earth or the earth is clutching him'.

Only a few people have been able to do OK for themselves in Nagrig and more recently one of them is the mayor, Anwar Shetia, who welcomes anyone visiting the place on a writing trip by greeting them on the path that links the main road and the village itself, with a small entourage of helpers. When his mobile phone starts ringing, it is to the tune of the James song 'Sit Down', adapted to fit Salah's name by Liverpool fans. The player's father, Ghaly, has managed to avoid being caught up in the interest focused on his son in the football-crazed country and much of that is down to Shetia, whose civic duties now include being the official spokesperson for the whole family.

Shetia is a jolly fellow who clearly enjoys holding court from his perch on a chintz-covered armchair in what is an otherwise modest, whitewashed apartment in the centre of town. On the face of it, he cannot do enough for visitors but his answers are thin on detail. It suits the legend of Salah to portray the player as a boy who rose from impoverished surroundings to become one of the greatest footballers in the world. There is an element of accuracy in that because life in Nagrig is incredibly hard for most people, but in truth he came from one of the few lower-middle-income families in the village. While his father had a solid enough job with the ministry that deals in the jasmine supply, his mother – whose name has never been disclosed at the family's request – was obsessed about Salah's education and believed he was smart enough to carry on with his studies after leaving the school in Nagrig, which is now named after him.

Everyone in Nagrig understands the village is now associated with the most famous Arab footballer on the planet. Though there is pride in his achievements and many of its people see a meeting with outsiders as an opportunity to reflect the hardship they are experiencing, nobody seems to want to explain how the place and many places like it nearby reached this point.

That is because Salah grew up in an era where open opposition could get you killed, and not much about Egypt has changed. To understand Nagrig is to understand the history of the Nile Delta and the hold it has on the Egyptian economy and its national consciousness. To really get a grip of this, you have to move away from Nagrig and quietly ask questions of villagers in other settlements to find out why the poverty is so desperate.

Around the time Salah was hauling himself onto a succession of microbuses every morning to reach Cairo, in another village, not far from Nagrig, the tractors rumbled through the streets before dawn, followed closely by police trucks. The cavalcade was led by a squire from another part of the country who wanted to lock up the village's men for the illegal occupation of his land and stealing his crops. This, according to the villagers, was due to changes in the law that dictated peasants and farmers concede the fields they were working on, handing them back to hereditary landlords.

This landlord and his supporters were armed. Previously, the villagers had repelled his efforts by setting fire to his vehicle. This time, with Egyptian state apparatus behind him, the villagers had no chance. Dozens of men were rounded up and arrested, sent to jail without trial. Many fled via the fields in fear, never to return. This left the women and children, some of whom were as young as four when they were detained.

A Human Rights Watch (HRW) report detailed how officers broke into homes and stole valuables, kicking with their jackboots anyone who tried to stop them. Some of the women were bound together by their braided hair. The subjugation went on for months, with house raids happening after dark. The police were accused of planting drugs to force more arrests. Phone lines were cut and no one who remained in the village could communicate with the outside world. Meanwhile, cattle perished on the surrounding farms because no one was allowed to tend to them. The population shrank by three-quarters and never recovered.

According to the same HRW report, there were many other similar stories across Egypt in the mid-2000s, when President Hosni Mubarak reinstated an emergency law suspending constitutional rights, ostensibly under the banner of tackling terrorism. In 2007, the law would allow him to position police at the entrance to polling stations, intimidating candidates and the electorate, as Mubarak fought off threats to his power, especially from the popular but banned Muslim Brotherhood, a well-organised Islamic movement with links to Hamas. His opponents would call the election a sham – Mubarak won with 89 per cent of the vote.

As Salah grew up, Egypt was becoming more authoritarian. Mubarak would use his power to respond to resistance of any kind. The peasants and the farmers were not terrorists and hoisted black flags on the roads outside the villages like the one near Nagrig, to signify they were not going to allow Mubarak to sever their links to the land. The defiant flags did not flutter for very long.

Hosni Mubarak became president in 1981, eleven years before Salah's birth. He was born in Kafr el-Musalha, another unremarkable village in the Nile Delta, two hours closer to Cairo. Having committed his life to working his way up the ranks in the Egyptian Air Force, he entered politics under the presidency of Anwar Sadat, a military leader who collaborated with the spies of Nazi Germany during the Second World War, and became president in 1970.

During that decade, Sadat began the process of scaling back the reforms of his predecessor Abdel Gamal Nasser, who had wanted to reduce inequality and promote social justice. By comparison, Sadat was against collective welfare. Instead, he unleashed the Egyptian economy, enabling private wealth creation; an approach that fitted with a global trend moving towards an economic model of deregulated capitalism. In Egypt, this was called *infitah*, or, 'opening'.

Though *infitah* promised to deliver prosperity to all Egyptians after being launched in 1974, cooperatives were crushed and the huge parts of the Nile Delta nationalised by Nasser were returned to their original owners. As living standards tumbled, the landless were forgotten.

In Shenker's book about this period, the author details the effect of local corruption and a lack of investment in agriculture. Once one of the world's largest exporters of grain, Egypt became the third-biggest importer and national shortages of cereals quadrupled. An agricultural trade surplus of $300 million in 1970 turned into a deficit of $800 million inside seven years. Within three years of *infitah*, 80 per cent of Egyptians were worse off. Only a narrow top band of people had the disposable income to reap the benefits of new technology like televisions and refrigerators. 'Everyone else's life was wracked with insecurity,' Shenker writes.

Infitah came to define Sadat's reign and underpin that of Mubarak's, who was sitting next to Sadat on 9 October 1981 when he was shot and killed by one of his own soldiers during a military parade. Amidst strikes, looting and violence, Egyptians were pushing back, but Mubarak went further than Sadat, embracing the neoliberal orthodoxy espoused by Ronald Reagan in the USA and Margaret Thatcher in the UK.

Sadat's assassination came at a time when Thatcher was responding to rising unemployment and riots in Britain's inner cities by awarding the police a substantial pay rise, alone among workers in the public sector. Some of the more introspective figures within the organisation came to think of this as a bribe. Neoliberalism in Egypt would go further: piling nearly all of the country's resources at the top, claiming a 'trickle down' effect would benefit those struggling at the bottom. As it had in Britain, this required the state to discipline anyone who dared to challenge the system.

By the end of the 1980s, Egypt was on the brink of defaulting on a debt accrued by spending on military equipment from the USA. Yet in 1991, Francis Fukuyama, the American political scientist and economist, released a paper entitled 'The End of History?', later a book, in which he announced the triumph of western economic liberalism. If Egypt pushed back now, it risked being left behind.

In 1992, the year Salah was born, Mubarak instigated Law 96. It was dry-sounding but hugely significant for agricultural Egypt, especially in places like Nagrig. The new rules increased land rents threefold at a stroke and, by 1997, the Nile Delta had almost entirely been returned to the pre-Nasser owners or their descendants. Landlords were now able to charge farmers and peasants whatever they wanted and in some parts of the delta, there were rent rises of more than 400 per cent.

By 2001, the World Bank announced that Egypt's agricultural sector was now 'fully private'. Yet the country's economy was tanking. After a deal was struck with the International Monetary Fund in the May of that year, further deals were agreed with Africa's Development Bank in September and then the World Bank in November.

A fire sale of Egyptian assets followed. Mubarak promised to sell off 'a company a week' and he was almost true to his word.

By the end of his reign a decade later, 336 public institutions had been privatised. New favourable laws for employers meant they could now hand out contracts without any long-term rights, limiting the threat of strike action. A decade after the enactment of Law 96, one million families were left without land, accounting for a third of Egypt's rural population.

In Nagrig and the surrounding villages, the consequences were severe. One report from the United Nations (UN) documented 'abrupt impoverishment'. This meant extreme food shortages, the selling of assets and family breakups. Children were made to work where they could and young men tended to leave for the cities, heading towards Cairo's outskirts on microbuses, or further afield. Nagrig is just a two-hour drive from the Mediterranean Sea. Some of the villagers tried to cross it by dinghy and were unsuccessful.

Shenker concluded Egypt 'became a land of minority accumulation and majority degradation'. His view was supported by the UN in a human development report which described the last decade of Mubarak's rule as a period in Egypt's history that boasted the starkest inequality since colonial times. 'One per cent controls almost all of the wealth in the country,' the report read.

As Salah entered his teens, a quarter of Egyptians were jobless. Prospects were particularly bleak for those children born in the decade before Salah, with 75 per cent of those people looking for work. One in five Egyptians were surviving on less than two dollars a day. Salah was fifteen when the UN Human Poverty Index relegated Egypt to the bottom third of all developing countries. It was now a place where one in three babies suffered from malnutrition that would result in stunted growth.

★　　★　　★

The villagers of Nagrig remember Salah as an especially small child. He was also rake-thin but this did not affect his energy. He was incredibly fast and he seemed to run everywhere, in the same baggy jeans and the same baggy T-shirt; the clothes he wore to play football on the day the direction of his life changed.

A trial had been set up on a football pitch overlooked by Nagrig's mosque. Reda El-Mallah, a scout, had heard about a talented player from the village – not Mohamed Salah but a boy named Sherif. Salah was younger than the rest of the boys, who were essentially there to make up the numbers, affording Sherif the platform to showcase his talents. Salah, apparently, was a reluctant participant, but as soon as he received possession of the ball, he came alive. El-Mallah was impressed – more by Salah than Sherif. According to Mayor Shetia, Salah was already train-ing with Ittihad, a junior club in Basyoun, fifteen minutes away from Nagrig. El-Mallah decided within ten minutes that Salah was talented enough to go on trial at a bigger club in Tanta, the nearest city. Salah's father would later encourage his son to travel every day to and from Cairo even when he was finding it hard, but initially he took some persuading that Tanta was a good idea. His boy was shy, and at that point in his life, he'd never left the countryside.

Yet Salah went to Tanta, where the coaches could see his abil-ity but were not quite sure whether he was big enough to compete with some of the better-fed and sturdier city boys. El-Mallah was annoyed by the decision but he was undeterred. He took Salah to Othmason, Tanta's second club.

As he waited for his chance to play, Salah stood on the side-lines – in his baggy jeans and baggy T-shirt. When a ball was cleared from the pitch, he managed to control it using his chest.

One of the coaches was standing yards away and identified the action as unusual. Egyptian boys tended to be good with the ball at their feet in tight spaces but they were not as enthusiastic about using other parts of their body.

Shetia says Salah was different because the roads in Nagrig were not covered in tarmac, like they sometimes were in the cities. The rocks meant Salah often had to improvise. As I sat in front of him in 2019, the memory prompted Shetia to look out of one of the narrow windows of his apartment and point at what was below and the dense housing that reminded me of the favelas in South America. A lifetime later, Salah would be a world-famous footballer and then in a position to donate thousands of dollars a month to Nagrig, a village which all those years later still did not have a post office, maintaining its sense of isolation.

Shetia was a footballer himself and had played with one of Salah's uncles in his younger days. Like the other villagers of Nagrig, he was willing to show evidence of the place's struggles but was holding back on explaining exactly how it had got there.

Nagrig had certain privileges because of its connection to the country's greatest footballer. At the school named after him, a grant had meant girls no longer had to travel to the next town for their education. The state knew that from time to time people would visit and they wanted reporters to leave without developing a deeper sense of its history or the social problems that existed there.

Yet by 2019, there was virtually no money coming in from Cairo and the village's future relied on the generosity of just one person, a boy who used to run around in his baggy clothes. Nagrig's water supply was erratic and it was almost impossible to maintain the grass pitch which Salah had donated. This prompted him to gift AstroTurf, which in the sun burned the feet of players without adequate footwear. After donating more money for a sewage treatment works, Salah built a new medical centre, gifting two kidney dialysis machines along with other equipment.

Yet even if he wanted to, he could not turn Nagrig into the Sharm el-Sheikh of the delta. To do so would have been a problem for the government, in reminding much of the rest of the population what they did not have. The dynamic meant that Salah's charitable offerings had to be made discreetly.

'He does his best,' Shetia said, though it was difficult for Salah to return to Nagrig and see what he was contributing towards because of the interest in him. On one occasion, his address was leaked on Facebook and a thousand people turned up. As soon as he landed in Cairo, the state and the media knew about it. He was followed, watched and hounded. There were a suspicion his phone was tapped. Spies were everywhere.

Some of his family have been able to remain quietly in Nagrig. Having farmed the fields around the village when Salah was a child, his father's title with the Ministry of Health meant he was involved with the country's jasmine supply. By 2024 most of it was still going to Russia. Though the revolution of 2011 had led to the removal of Mubarak, it was just as the old president would have wanted it. The more things changed in Egypt, the more they stayed the same.

Chapter 3

Eyes and data

A lmost as soon as Mohamed Salah moved to Switzerland from Egypt in 2012, his potential was recognised by one of Liverpool's scouts. Paul Goldrick had studied Italian and French at the University of Manchester, before working part-time as a talent spotter for Manchester United. After moving to Milan, where he became a language teacher, helping the legendary player and manager Roberto Mancini speak English, he scouted Italy for Aston Villa, and from 2011 onwards, Liverpool, where his remit extended into Croatia, Serbia and Switzerland.

Goldrick had noted Salah's pace as a standout attribute. Basel played against Tottenham Hotspur in the Europa League during the 2012–13 season and Salah had performed well against Kyle Walker, one of the fastest full-backs in the Premier League. This made Liverpool enthusiastic about his future. Salah became famous as a right winger but for Basel, he often played more centrally and off the left. After knocking out Spurs, Liverpool's chief scout Barry Hunter watched him in the competition's semi-final against Chelsea, where he partnered Marco Streller in attack. Salah combined well with the tall, powerful forward and seemed to have a knack of understanding where the ball would fall.

Hunter went home to Reading and cut up some clips to start a discussion with other members of Liverpool's recruitment team. Above Hunter was Michael Edwards, who was moving up the ranks having been appointed as the club's director of technical performance in the summer of 2013, having previously worked as the head of performance and analysis. Edwards encouraged his staff to produce video content because it provoked debate. While one member of staff might have seen something positive with the naked eye, someone else might see the same moment slightly differently via video. It was always better for a scout to be able to show what they were talking about after being able to discuss it.

Edwards, Hunter and the head of recruitment, Dave Fallows, shared an office at Melwood, Liverpool's old training ground, where meetings about a single player with the club's manager Brendan Rodgers would sometimes last two hours. Edwards would later emerge as Liverpool's sporting director but at the time the title did not exist. This meant approaches to other clubs about players would be led by whichever figure knew the terrain best. In Salah's case, Fallows knew Basel's sporting director, Georg Heitz.

When Fallows flew to Basel only to find Salah out of the team, he knew Heitz well enough to approach him and ask about the player. Basel had other exciting youngsters like Aleksandar Dragović and Fabian Schär, defenders who would later earn moves to the Premier League with Leicester City and Newcastle United. Fallows concluded there was no point in playing games, and he told Heitz he was there for Salah. Heitz responded by telling him that he was clearly a huge talent, but he wasn't ready to move to Liverpool just yet.

There were no real plans to go for Salah the following season. Rodgers had told staff that he did not want to sign more back-up players and Salah was not considered ready-made at that time. Yet Liverpool continued to follow his progress. The reports coming back from Goldrick said that Salah always wanted to get into the box, with and without the ball. Though he wasn't a polished finisher, he created lots of opportunities for himself. He didn't always choose the safe option and with that came some apparent inconsistencies. He'd give possession away cheaply. He was also developing physically and his hold up play with his back to goal was sometimes an issue.

Fallows watched him in the Champions League against Steaua Bucharest, where he did not play as well as he had in other games. Yet Fallows noted that he worked hard and kept tracking back. It was also his view that he needed to do better protecting the ball. Fallows would attend games with Rodgers in England and abroad but at home, these scouting missions became more trouble than they were worth because Liverpool's manager would always get recognised. It was easier in a foreign country and when Basel played Schalke, Rodgers flew to northern Germany, only on this occasion with Hunter.

The 2013–14 winter transfer window was opening in a few weeks' time, but Rodgers did not have much money to spend. This meant Liverpool's options were narrow – accordingly, the pool of players available to him in the transfer market was the same. Fallows had been preparing for this challenge. Even if one of Liverpool's scouts wasn't at a Basel game over the previous months, either he or Hunter had watched his performances back on DVD. Though some of Basel's fixtures were available online, streaming services were considered unreliable. It was time-consuming work, involving much longer than the ninety minutes because of the difficulties with clipping different moments from a game. Liverpool did not have access to databases like WyScout or InStat, platforms that soon would make this process a lot easier.

Liverpool's analytics team would emerge as one of the most heralded in the world, but back in 2014 the department was in its infancy. Very little data relating to the Swiss league was available. The pursuit of Salah, therefore, initially involved traditional scouting, with men like Goldrick, Fallows and Hunter initially heading off and trusting their own eyes, and speaking to trusted contacts about targets like Salah.

Fallows went again to Basel on a trip that involved games involving other clubs. At a meeting near the city with Salah and his former agent, Sacha Empacher, he got the feeling that the player was ambitious. He wanted to play in a better league. There was a sense he wanted to go all the way to the top. Meanwhile, Fallows had got the impression from Heitz that Salah was a supple character who could settle quickly in unfamiliar surroundings. He was a good trainer. Though Fallows did not have a dossier hundreds of pages thick on the player's background, nothing suggested that Salah would have any problems fitting into the environment at Liverpool, a team which under Rodgers was unexpectedly pushing to win the league.

Fallows had seen good performances, average performances and not so good performances from Salah. Liverpool did not waver from him being anything but the club's top winter target, but he felt as though he had to convince him that he'd get a chance to shine. His reasoning related to the Liverpool squad being rather small.

Fallows stressed Salah would get a chance at Liverpool because the squad wasn't huge. When he mentioned how many players the club had on loan at other places, using Chelsea as a comparison, Salah told him that he was already aware of the depth at Anfield because he played the Football Manager simulation game, and he'd taken charge of Liverpool. When Salah told him, 'I have to sign lots of players,' Fallows could only laugh.

Salah was preparing to leave Basel in early 2014, when a spiky-haired lorry driver's son from Hampshire flew to Spain watching him at the Marbella Training Centre, where he was involved in a winter camp.

Michael Edwards was representing Liverpool, but anonymity contributed to him remaining on the touchline. His lack of fame meant he could access hotel lobbies where he was further able to develop an impression of the character of a footballer by watching mundane routines. In full intelligence-gathering mode, Edwards would get close to conversations, allowing him to better understand the culture the player was working in.

On the same trip, Edwards had got a sense of Emre Can's personality via this sort of clandestine approach. The Bayern Munich midfielder was on loan at Bayer Leverkusen, another club training at the centre. While Edwards would persuade Can to join Liverpool within six months, he liked the look of Son Heung-min, but the Korean international would instead join Tottenham in 2015.

Salah was also observed at an earlier camp in Davos, Switzerland, where he was again unaware of such surveillance.

He would eventually sign for Liverpool, but only four years later, and this was after rejecting the club for a spell at Chelsea, where he barely featured across twelve months before deciding to move on again.

Liverpool would return for the player, at which point the club had experienced a revolution where data was having a more prominent role in transfer decisions. Around early 2017, Salah was producing some 'interesting' numbers according to a staff source working at Liverpool, a club which had experienced significant turbulence in the decade since being acquired by American owners.

Tom Hicks and George Gillett completed a leveraged buyout from local businessman David Moores in 2007, but banks were closing in on the pair until a 2010 High Court ruling forced another sale to New England Sports Ventures (later renamed Fenway Sports Group, FSG). Two years later, FSG were still trying to understand what it took to run a football club, despite their success with the Boston Red Sox, a baseball institution. John W. Henry was the principal owner of FSG, but he would not charge someone from the organisation with the responsibility of running Liverpool at an executive level until March 2012, when Mike Gordon assumed the responsibility, albeit while operating from his home in Boston, Massachusetts.

There was, however, no official announcement about this development. It meant that Gordon, a Milwaukee native, could quietly learn about what was working at the club and what was not. A lot was not, and in the spring of that year, despite two cup final appearances, Liverpool were heading for a sixth-place finish in the Premier League. When Henry decided to hold a meeting at his Florida estate in Boca Raton involving most of the senior figures at Liverpool, Michael Edwards was somewhere near the bottom of the command chain. Yet Gordon quickly took a shine to Edwards because of their shared interest in data and their determination to show that a famous sports club could rebuild a winning culture without it being defined absolutely by money.

Gordon knew a bit about European football but he did not pretend to know everything. His background was in investments, working in equity research due to his fascination with analytics. He later became a hedge fund manager, controlling $9 billion in assets, including the ice hockey team Tampa Bay Lightning. Henry would recruit him to FSG in 2002, not long after the organisation's takeover of the Red Sox, and in the decade that followed, Gordon's stake increased.

Despite his influence at FSG, he had an office just around the corner from Fenway Park and he could easily walk to the creaking stadium in his baseball cap and jeans with nobody noticing him, and that was how Gordon liked to operate. Also flying under the radar was Edwards, someone who enjoyed his privacy while also relishing the challenge of keeping outsiders guessing at what he was up to. Edwards could be considered blunt to the point of rudeness by some but Gordon was relieved to have found someone who was willing to give him firm conclusions based around a language he understood: numbers and data.

Within a few months, Edwards' influence at Liverpool was felt, with the hire of Dr Ian Graham, a player performance analyst from a company involved at Tottenham Hotspur called Decision Technology. Edwards knew that Graham was becoming frustrated at Spurs, where he was regularly asked for his opinion about players but rarely felt as though he was having a meaningful impact. Thirty-thousand feet above the Atlantic Ocean, as the pair travelled together to the Sports Analytics Conference at Sloan University, Boston, Edwards planted the seed of the idea that it would be good to join him at Liverpool, promising they would eventually have a say in all departments at the club, not just recruitment.

Edwards himself had been a player performance analyst at Tottenham when Graham was there. It helped that Graham had also grown up as a supporter of Liverpool, a club which had built its success and fame around a traditional set of methods: the eye of a wizened, old-school scout like Geoff Twentyman and his relationship with the manager – in the first instance Bill Shankly – mattered most. Graham could see there was a rare opportunity to try something wildly different at the club, and he would become Liverpool's first director of research.

Nobody thought much about the appointment, and there was no announcement on the club's website. Perhaps inevitably at Liverpool, given the path the club had been on, Edwards experienced pushback after he was empowered by Gordon. Mel Johnson, one of the more traditional scouts, left the club, claiming that Liverpool were missing out on signings such as Dele Alli – whose enormous potential was instead recognised by Tottenham – because they were relying too much on their 'computer and stats-led' approach. Johnson insisted that football was 'not played on a computer', voicing his frustration at the amount of experience being tossed to one side. 'Some of these IT guys have come straight out of university and landed jobs at top clubs, despite having no football background whatsoever,' he complained.

It was true that Edwards was degree-educated, having graduated from Sheffield University. Unlike Graham, however, he did have a background in football, having left the south coast of England as a teenager to join Peterborough United's youth academy on a two-year apprenticeship. Though he was not considered to be the most gifted player in the team, he was a hard worker and reliable, mostly playing at right back but some-times in midfield.

One day a week, he would travel to Cambridge to study leisure and tourism. Following his release from Peterborough, his degree in business and informatics allowed him to under-stand better how computer data corresponded with people in the real world. Yet he seemed destined for a career in teaching until an old teammate from Peterborough, Simon Wilson (who studied in Liverpool and played for non-league side Marine following his own departure from the club), recommended him to his employers, data specialists Prozone. They had a contract with Portsmouth, whose owner, Milan Mandaric, was keen on data while, initially, manager Harry Redknapp, a traditionalist, was less so. Yet when Redknapp moved to Spurs four years later, he took Edwards, who he always called 'Eddie', with him. The opportunity to join Liverpool coincided with Edwards' wife being offered a job in the north-west of England.

From afar, Edwards had heard about the exciting things FSG had achieved at the Red Sox through data. He was given the sales pitch by Damien Comolli, the Frenchman formerly with Spurs who became the first senior appointment of the FSG era at Liverpool when he was made director of football strategy in 2010. Comolli would last sixteen months in the role – fired, on the face of it, because record signing Andy Carroll failed to justify his price tag. He had arrived from Newcastle United for a record fee in a deal that was done under pressure and in response to the sale of Fernando Torres to Chelsea for a British record fee earlier on the same day. Comolli would spend the subsequent months trying to find the wingers that could supply the crosses for Carroll, a six-foot-three centre forward, to flourish.

Though the process made sense, given Liverpool's outlay on Carroll, it did not involve a great deal of consideration for data because the department simply wasn't there. Graham only arrived at the club after Comolli was fired, a decision that came within a month of the summit in Florida called by Henry. Edwards did not immediately fill the space but he was becoming more influential behind the scenes. He has since been cast as someone who shirks the limelight – he has never done an interview with any media outlet. Yet there is another side to Edwards; those who have worked with him often speak of his ruthlessness. 'Underestimate him at your peril,' said one former Liverpool staff member.

Certainly, Edwards had no compunction telling people with more high-level experience in football that they were wrong or they were no longer wanted. Yet it was unfair to claim that Liverpool had totally given up on old scouting methods under Edwards, as Johnson implied, because players still had to pass the 'eye test'. By the time Salah was signed, for example, both Edwards and the club's head of recruitment, Dave Fallows, had watched him on dozens of occasions.

A culture war is perhaps too extreme a description, but it eventually became a battle between personalities and egos when the first managerial hire of the Gordon era, Brendan Rodgers, came up against Edwards. He would prove to be the manager that missed out on Salah the first time around because the player wanted to experience playing for José Mourinho at Chelsea instead. Within twelve months, Liverpool's results were not good and Rodgers was under huge pressure.

Gordon wanted Liverpool to be collaborative, with everybody involved in recruitment taking responsibility for successes and failures. Yet some of the players Edwards had recommended were not delivering and it was mainly Rodgers taking the heat because he was the one having to answer questions about them. When Rodgers said that he wanted to live and die by his own decisions, Gordon warned him that only he would carry the can if they went wrong. In October 2015, after a 1–1 draw in the Merseyside derby left Liverpool tenth in the league table, Rodgers was sacked.

In the three years since arriving at Liverpool, Ian Graham had mainly worked from his home in the south-west of England, close to the border with Wales – the country where he was born, in the valleys around Swansea. This was Rugby Union territory but Graham spent some of his childhood playing on the *Sensible Soccer* computer game, developing a fetish for numbers, imagining that he would become a scientist of some kind; a focus that increased after completing a PhD at Cambridge, where he graduated as a doctor of theoretical physics.

Graham did not see a future in football in 2005, when analysis of the sport tended to be populated by ex-players themselves and data was treated with suspicion or hostility. Decision Technology would become the first company of its kind to get a foothold in the game. While the firm's contracts took Graham into Tottenham, it also had a deal with *The Times* newspaper, where he contributed to a column called 'The Fink Tank' after its writer, Daniel Finkelstein, the Chelsea fan, politician and future Conservative lord.

In 2023, Graham told the Spanish newspaper *El Pais* that it took him an entire day's work just to watch one game. 'I can't trust my eyes,' he reasoned. 'Until I see all the data, I do not feel like I can understand the game well at all.' It was this sort of focus that led to a conversation with Jürgen Klopp upon their introduction, following his appointment as Rodgers' replacement, when Graham told the German that his Borussia Dortmund team had been unlucky to lose two games the previous season, even though he'd only crunched the numbers without watching them live or even watching them back.

Klopp had been the obvious candidate to follow Rodgers. He had achieved at Dortmund what Liverpool wanted, having won two Bundesliga titles despite lacking the financial muscle and appeal of the biggest team in everyone's way, Bayern Munich. For Liverpool and Klopp, the scale of the challenge was even greater because Manchester City, Manchester United, Chelsea and Arsenal were ahead of them when Klopp arrived. Yet he had the personality to manage Liverpool. He was charismatic and forceful. He created exciting teams, mainly with young players. You could not take your eyes off Dortmund. You could not take your eyes off Klopp.

Graham had a hand in all the football-related decisions at Liverpool because the club now tested everything by data. He assessed each of Klopp's seasons in charge of Dortmund, noting he placed a significant physical demand on his players. As the years passed and the players got older, it was a simple fact that some of them were finding it harder to run as far and as fast as he wanted. It was Graham's view that Liverpool would need a world-class medical team to support Klopp's squad. When the time came for it, Edwards would have to be ruthless in cutting loose those who were no longer capable of meeting Klopp's key expectations.

It became clear to Liverpool's owners upon meeting Klopp in the autumn of 2015 that, although he did not implicitly understand how to use data, he respected the value it could offer him in reaching conclusions. Most importantly, he was willing to work collaboratively. At Dortmund, and across Germany, it was already common for a manager to work beside a sporting director. Though Edwards did not yet have that title at Liverpool, it was always Gordon's plan to introduce him as a more senior figure. Unlike Rodgers, Klopp was secure enough in himself not to feel threatened by someone who was constantly assessing the performance of the players and the team and, by extension, to some degree, the manager and the environment he was creating.

Edwards had an office at Melwood, Liverpool's old training ground, just down the corridor and on the right from Klopp's. The pressure of running Liverpool would eventually impact the balance of power between the pair but during the club's rise between 2015 and 2020, Klopp described Edwards as 'a very thoughtful person. We don't always have to have the same opinion from the first second of a conversation, but we finish pretty much all our talks with the same opinion. Or similar opinions.'

Edwards was not ultimately Klopp's boss but he was Graham's. Beside the head of research in the chain of command was the head of recruitment, Fallows, and the chief scout, Barry Hunter, both of whom were brought to Liverpool as Edwards' position became clearer. They arrived in late 2012 after being placed on gardening leave by their former club, Manchester City. It was a delay that impacted upon the decisions that were made in the transfer market that summer because it allowed Rodgers, newly appointed as manager, to influence more of what was happening. Mixed results followed. Gordon was keen to redress the balance.

Like Edwards, Fallows was university educated, having studied at Leeds, and like Edwards, he'd handled Prozone's contract with a Premier League club before he was headhunted. In Fallows' case, the offer came from Bolton Wanderers, where Sam Allardyce was one of the first British managers to welcome the use of data. When Allardyce moved on to Newcastle United, Fallows joined him, tasked with the responsibility of watching opponents and player performance.

In 2008, Manchester City became one of the richest clubs in the world following Sheikh Mansour's takeover. There, Fallows was hugely respected not only for his talent but for his modesty and diligence. He would leave for Liverpool with staff sensing that the directors at City did not fully appreciate what they were losing. Some of the measures he brought in would only benefit the club after his departure.

There was a similar feeling about Hunter, a former Northern Ireland international who captained and managed Rushden & Diamonds as they pushed through the lower leagues in the early 2000s thanks to the investment of a rich owner, the man behind the Dr Marten's boot empire, Max Griggs. At City, it had seemed Hunter's role as the club's scouting co-ordinator for Europe was under threat when Italian Roberto Mancini became manager. A lot of his work was in Italy, yet Hunter impressed colleagues by taming some of the instincts of Mancini, a manager who would deliver City's first title in forty-four years but fell out with many people during his time in charge. Across Serie A, clubs, scouts and agents never lost sight of Hunter's role: if you wanted to access City, you had to go through him. Had

Mancini been able to take over, some of the structures implemented by Hunter might have been lost.

Fallows and Hunter had some but not all control over City. Liverpool were promising them greater influence. Their arrival at Anfield would arguably light the touchpaper on the relationship between the clubs in the seasons that followed, as they became rivals both on and off the pitch.

Over his five years at Liverpool, Graham had devised a metric there that he thought allowed him to see the invisible. Graham felt it was unfair measuring a player's value to a team purely on goals and assists, because it did not account for the moving parts around him. What if the same player was put in a different environment, like the one at Liverpool – would he do better? For example, 'Goal probability added' allowed Graham to assess how likely a player would contribute a goal or assist when receiving the ball in a certain area of the pitch, albeit without being under pressure. He would assess such scenarios over hundreds of games in some cases.

The metric showed him that Salah regularly got the closest of Liverpool's targets to scoring. Though he did not have detailed records from the player's time in Switzerland, he was able to assess his performances in the Premier League with Chelsea and Serie A with Fiorentina and Roma. It was his view that, even at Chelsea, he didn't do too badly, though the sample size he was looking at was small. Graham would describe him as a 'mid-level winger' at the age of twenty but five years later, he was emerging as one of the best players around in his position because the disappointments of Chelsea did not set him back.

For Graham and for Liverpool, it was fortunate that no other

Premier League club was very interested in signing him. In the eyes of many people, Salah had failed at Chelsea and '. . . no sporting director wants to touch a failure'. José Mourinho would argue that Eden Hazard was in his way and Graham agreed. 'If I had been the Chelsea manager, I would also have put Hazard ahead of Mo,' Graham told *El Pais*. 'So, it's not that Mo did something wrong. There was a reasonable excuse for him not to play.'

Though it was useful in supporting arguments, Graham admitted that data did not offer the 'complete picture'. It had been Edwards' job to use the data and video analysis and assess whether Liverpool had the financial capability to sign players. He was also looking at personality. According to Graham, Edwards had told him, 'Mo Salah was the most professional and dedicated footballer he had ever met. He was desperate to be successful in the Premier League and prove everyone wrong.'

When Salah was at Chelsea, Liverpool's scouting department stopped following his progress, mainly because he wasn't playing. Yet the club also felt that even if they wanted to sign Salah, Chelsea were unlikely to sell him to them. In 2013, Liverpool had brought Daniel Sturridge from Stamford Bridge and he had since established himself as the first choice number 9 for England. Why would they risk making the same mistake?

Instead, Salah went to Italy, to Fiorentina and then AS Roma. Naturally, this brought him back into Paul Goldrick's sphere of interest. Initially, it was noted back on Merseyside that Salah was struggling to complete matches, adding to the sense developed at Chelsea that he wasn't robust enough physically, certainly not as he would become. He would relaunch his career in Florence, but in ten Serie A starts, he was subbed off in seven of them. The following season, in 2015–16, he started thirty-two league games for Roma but finished only eighteen. The season before he finally joined Liverpool, he made twenty-nine starts and remained on the pitch until the final whistle on only fifteen occasions.

Goldrick, however, told Fallows and Hunter that Salah was becoming stronger. His stamina was increasing. This was evidenced by the fact he was affecting games more as they reached their conclusions. In a Roma shirt, he was also finishing seasons strongly.

Liverpool started to think again about Salah due to the team's struggles when Sadio Mané departed for the Africa Cup of Nations in January 2017. Suddenly, Liverpool lacked pace in attack and without the Senegalese, Liverpool's replacements were not penetrating the box as much. With Mané out of the team, Edwards, Fallows, Hunter and Mike Gordon agreed that Liverpool had to be almost perfect to win games. Rather than being a threat on the counterattack and getting a goal out of nowhere, the team had to pass opponents off the park. And this wasn't really the style of football Klopp was comfortable with.

The recruitment team started to look at what options were available to them that changed this dynamic. In Rome, Salah was starring in a team heading towards qualification for the Champions League by finishing second in Serie A. Much of their success was hooked from the relationship between Salah and the centre forward, Edin Dzeko.

It was Fallows' view that the Bosnian had similar characteristics to Liverpool's number 9, Roberto Firmino. Fallows had been involved in the process that brought Dzeko to Manchester City in 2011, so he knew all about his abilities. Though Dzeko was taller, he was considered outstanding with the ball at his feet. His clever movement, dropping deeper, afforded Salah the space to run into. Might the same trick work at Liverpool?

Much of the debate that followed involved Salah's position. In Mané's first season at Liverpool, he played off the right wing. Salah's arrival would potentially mean Mané switched sides. In the end, it would be Klopp's decision and he still needed persuading of any potential plan. Out of sight, Goldrick, whose work Hunter had respected from his time at City when they were both on the Italian circuit, intensified his research. Goldrick was known for his integrity and diligence. Sometimes in the pursuit of information, scouts risked giving their own game away. This meant he did not push his contacts particularly hard about Salah, fearing someone might twig how interested Liverpool were. In conversations, he would carefully ask questions without being too explicit. Initially, he would chat to agents with Roma players about broader issues, leading them to a point where they might naturally disclose information about Salah.

Italy tends to be a country where things end up in the press whenever something happens in a dressing room. It means there is lots of open information. Goldrick was thought of as a master of going beyond the news. He would provide Liverpool with daily updates of hidden, developing situations involving players and the clubs they represent. He knew, for example, that in the summer of 2017, Roma would need to sell a player for a lot of money to comply with Financial Fair Play regulations. Given that Salah had just two years left on his contract, Roma could not afford to let him run it down.

Edwards was now in a more prominent role at Liverpool. As sporting director, he and Fallows arranged a summit with

Roma's sporting director Monchi, as well as the club's CEO Mauro Baldissoni. En route, the visitors from Merseyside rendezvoused with Goldrick nearby, and the latest developments were shared. On Goldrick's advice, the meet happened in Milan rather than Rome, and at a nondescript legal office linked to Baldissoni, rather than a restaurant. The arrangement stopped anyone from photographing them.

The subsequent negotiations lasted between three and four hours. Monchi, who at this point was regarded as one of the smartest sporting directors in the world following great success in Spain with Sevilla, could only speak broken English and this meant some of the conversation went through Baldissoni. Despite the language barrier, Fallows was impressed by Monchi because of his decisiveness. Roma needed money, Liverpool wanted to buy: there was no messing around. Neither party was playing a game.

Yet Edwards warned Monchi that there were limits to what he was able to agree to. Edwards used the fee Liverpool had paid for Andy Carroll in 2011 as a reference point. The forward was signed from Newcastle United in the last hours of the winter transfer window for a record £35 million. Edwards did not want the deal for Salah to be over that amount, placing more pressure on the player. It was later reported by some outlets that Liverpool paid £36.5 million for Salah, thus breaking the Carroll record, when, in fact, it was £34.3 million plus bonuses. Either way, it wasn't like Liverpool had obliterated their transfer record.

There were other gatherings of significance during this period. A few months earlier, Fallows had flown to Dubai with Edwards to see Salah's representative, Ramy Abbas. Nobody at

Liverpool had a relationship with him and it was considered important to try and build a rapport and show respect by going out of their way to reach him. The trip was memorable for the fact Fallows and Edwards did not see any sunshine. They arrived in the evening when it was dark, met with Abbas for a few hours at a restaurant on the top floor of a tower, then flew back very early the following morning. Neither Edwards nor Fallows even got to wear their t-shirts.

Abbas was a straight talker but he was impressed with Fallows, who he thought was likeable because of his humility and knowledge. Abbas could see that he was a fan of the game, and he quickly understood that he knew an awful lot about his client, maybe even more than Abbas himself.

Though Abbas mentioned interest from Paris Saint-Germain and Atletico Madrid, it was Edwards and Fallows' view that Abbas was not the sort of character to actually court the interest of just anyone who picks up a phone and made him a tempting offer. The delegation from Liverpool flew home reassured by Abbas' promise that he would keep them updated with any developments and not mess them around.

Now all Edwards needed to do was to persuade Klopp that signing him was the right idea. It was agreed at Liverpool that Edwards had the power to veto a bad idea presented by Klopp but he would never pursue a deal for a player the manager did not want to sign.

It helped that Klopp had first seen Salah's potential during a pre-season friendly between Basel and Dortmund in the summer of 2013. His performance would prompt some discussion with his coaching staff after the match. 'We didn't know him,' Klopp would later admit. 'It was: "What the f★★★?!" It was unbelievable.'

Yet as 2016 turned into 2017, Klopp thought more favourably about Julian Brandt, an attacking player from Bayer Leverkusen who members of the scouting team had been told was not as enthusiastic about moving to the Premier League because of concerns about his place in the German national side. A World Cup was approaching. Was adjusting to a new country and a new league wise preparation?

Whereas Liverpool's previous manager Rodgers was willing to have discussions about a player over long meetings at Melwood, Klopp's approach involved less formality. Though Edwards would deal with him on a one to one basis, and Hunter and Fallows would sometimes join them to run through clips. More often than not, the four men would chat casually in the club's canteen about possibilities.

Klopp was keen on a bigger name, but Fallows especially doubled down on his view that Salah would be a success at Liverpool. Though Klopp was positive about him, he had other ideas – but Fallows decided it was unwise to present alternatives. From his experience, the more names you mention, the more confused a manager becomes, crowding his mind. Klopp could see Fallows was not budging and Fallows would insist over and over again that Salah was exactly the player he needed. Fallows had been watching him for years and he knew that he was desperate to prove himself in England after what happened at Chelsea. He was hungry. It was not often this sort of opportunity came up.

In Basel, Salah had impressed in each of the attacking roles he was assigned to, but in Rome, he had a fixed position and this helped Liverpool get a better grasp of what he might do for them. Over the previous three years, his tactical understanding had improved dramatically. Most of the questions about him had been answered. Certainly, his use of the ball was better: and this was the sort of thing that usually got a player substituted or dropped by a manager. What stood out the most, though, was the number of times he managed to get into the box. Some of this was because of Dzeko's movement. Yet his desire to affect the game was extraordinary. Fallows had never seen anything like it before and he's never seen anything like it since.

'They wanted to do it earlier so that nobody could jump in,' Klopp reflected in 2017. 'Michael Edwards, Dave Fallows and Barry [Hunter], they were really in my ear and were on it: "Come on, come on, Mo Salah, he's the solution!"'

Upon signing for the club, Klopp had suggested that Salah had the 'perfect mix of experience and potential', reasoning that his previous frustrations in the Premier League had become a strength because he arrived on Merseyside with more wisdom, knowing exactly what it took to flourish. 'He also has pedigree in the Champions League and he is one of the most important players for his country,' Klopp added. 'His record in Italy has been outstanding and he possesses qualities that will enhance our team and squad. I have followed him since he emerged at Basel and he has matured into a really good player. His pace is incredible, he gives us more attacking threat and we are already strong in this area.'

Most importantly for Klopp was Salah's hunger. 'He is willing and eager to be even better and improve further. He is an ambitious player who wants to win and win at the highest level; he knows he can fulfil those ambitions with Liverpool.'

Salah would do his own interview at Melwood for the club's

television channel, where he typically gave away very little about himself. To those listening, it seemed as though he wanted to let his feet do the talking. Waiting for him upon his arrival in the old press room was Fallows. His private jet had landed late into John Lennon Airport.

'Just checking you haven't signed for Chelsea,' Liverpool's head of recruitment joked.

Salah's medical took place opposite a Sainsbury's supermarket, at the Wilmslow Hospital on Alderley Road in Cheshire. He would move into a nearby property on the same luxury estate in Prestbury as former Manchester United manager Sir Alex Ferguson. Soon enough, one of his neighbours was Alex Oxlade-Chamberlain, another new summer signing from Arsenal.

Initially, it was the recruitment of Oxlade-Chamberlain rather than Salah that gave the existing players the confidence the Klopp era was heading in the right direction. He showed that the club was becoming a more appealing destination than some of their rivals.

Less was known about Salah. Though he'd relaunched his career in Italy, only vice captain James Milner really paid attention to what was happening in other leagues across Europe. Salah had done extremely well at Roma but Serie A was a different beast to the Premier League. Was he really capable of returning to a competition where he was considered a failure and change people's opinions? Overall, neither the arrival of Salah or a midfielder who had yet to deliver on his enormous promise under Arsène Wenger were considered to be transformational.

The feeling was different when Virgil van Dijk joined from Southampton later that year in a world record fee for a defender, before goalkeeper Alisson Becker arrived in a world record fee for a goalkeeper from AS Roma the following summer.

When Liverpool players chatted to their teammates who'd played with Salah at Chelsea, it was mentioned that he was raw but fast, and confident but quiet. It had impressed some of the Chelsea players that Salah backed himself to leave and relaunch his career elsewhere due to a lack of game time. It would have been easier for him to sit on his backside and watch the money roll in but Salah was clearly impatient to make a name for himself, even if it seemed he was not quite ready for a Chelsea dressing room filled with significant egos and personalities.

Still, none of the Liverpool squad really knew what to expect on the first day of pre-season training at the start of July and this extended to the staff, for whom his physical state immediately generated conversation.

'He was in an unbelievable shape,' said one figure.

'Phenomenal,' said another. 'Prepackaged for Premier League football.'

What struck both the players and his staff was his speed. 'It was insane,' said one of the staffers. 'There were a couple of moments in the early training sessions where passes were misplaced and it seemed as though the ball would run out. But Mo was blisteringly fast; he had the ability to turn a bad pass into a useful one.'

After two friendly matches with Tranmere Rovers and Wigan Athletic, Liverpool won the Asia Trophy in Hong Kong, beating Crystal Palace and Leicester City. The trip to the Far East was central to the club's marketing strategy and shirt sponsorship agreement with Standard Chartered. With the rains disrupting some of the sessions, another camp held in southern Germany had extra importance, where Klopp had an opportunity to push the players to their limits.

Photographs of the Liverpool squad enjoying dips in Bavaria's Tegernsee lake followed, before bike rides into the mountains where Alpine houses dotted the lush landscape. Everybody seemed to be having a great time, but this hid the severe reality of the testing week described by separate members of staff as 'monster' and 'brutal' for the players, ahead of tough friendlies on successive days against Bayern Munich and Atlético Madrid. Liverpool stayed at the luxury Uberfahrt hotel and trained at FC Rottach. By the end of the week, the pitch was so worn that, according to the German newspaper *Bild*, when Liverpool tried to use the facility again six years later, they were turned away.

Klopp acknowledged that the sessions were tough. Some of the players vomited due to the amount of running. Yet he believed if they could get through this, they'd find competitive matches a lot easier. Some of the staff considered this to be particularly unscientific but could see the potential psychological advantages of such an approach.

There were triple sessions daily involving two of football and one of running, including the day before Liverpool faced Bayern at the Allianz Arena on Saturday evening. 'It was mental,' says one member of staff who wondered whether Klopp had taken it too far.

Though the camp tested the limits of the players, it also tested the limits of the staff. They were shattered both physically and emotionally. Two sessions were held during the day, after which some were too tired to even eat when they returned to the hotel. It was at that point that the staff would have to set up the content for another session starting at 7 p.m.

The conditioning of those who could manage it improved. Yet the process paid little respect to the periodisation of each player's load. The opening weekend of the Premier League season was just a week away – it felt like a risky approach. The concern was registered with Klopp. His power was growing and everyone knew that, including the staff and the players.

Previously, Klopp had switched training sessions to a time later in the day, much to the inconvenience of the squad, who liked spending time with their families in the afternoon. When captain Jordan Henderson was dispatched to discuss the issue with Klopp, he was told that anyone who had a problem should knock on his office door at Melwood. Nobody followed up.

In the first game of the Audi Cup, Liverpool blew Bayern away, scoring two first-half goals before completing a 3–0 rout in the second half. The performance indicated what Salah, Roberto Firmino and Sadio Mané were capable of when they combined. Throughout the game, both Salah and Mané were able to pounce on the space left when Firmino dropped into a deeper position. Though Klopp's Liverpool started out as a 4-3-3 and are remembered for that because of the way they executed it so well, Firmino was a number 9 and a number 10 rolled into one. Often, Liverpool would become a 4-3-1-2, using the pace of Salah and Mané to devastating effect on the counterattack, cutting infield. Salah would score Liverpool's second goal in Munich with a rare header following a rebound. Yet it was Mané's opener that encouraged Klopp the most because Firmino had pressed and suffocated the Bayern defence into a mistake.

The following morning, the *Liverpool Echo*'s front page ran with the headline, 'BRILLIANT REDS BATTER BAYERN.' On the back page: 'POETRY IN MUNCHEN'. The result against the German champions in their own ground was eye-catching and brought a new sense of excitement ahead of the season's opener at Vicarage Road against Watford.

Yet there was a casualty from this victory and the week spent in Bavaria. At half-time in the Allianz, Adam Lallana, the ball-playing midfielder, reported that he had a pain in his thigh. Lallana reasoned that had the game been a Premier League fixture, he'd have probably carried on without telling anyone about it. As a precaution, Klopp was to be advised, Lallana should come off and upon returning to Merseyside, he'd be booked in for a scan. But Klopp flew into a rage when this was suggested and a full-scale row followed, one that involved Lallana, in front of the rest of the squad about the content of the training sessions leading up to the two friendly matches.

Lallana did not return for the second half but when he was scanned, it was established that he'd sustained the highest-grade tear possible on the central tendon of his thigh. The club consulted a specialist, trying to find out whether he'd need an operation to stick it back together. Though Lallana managed to avoid that, it led to nearly three months on the treatment table.

'Nearly all of the players suffered that week,' recalled one staff member. 'If Mo was one of them, he didn't show it.'

Salah's arrival at Liverpool coincided with someone else trying to get away, an attempted escape involving a mysterious undiagnosed injury, which brought disruption to the squad's preparations for the season after returning from Germany.

At Melwood, Liverpool's players were getting ready for another tough training session when Philippe Coutinho entered the dressing room with a face like thunder. This was unusual because the Brazilian midfielder was usually such a positive character.

Later, on the grass of Melwood, his teammates were astonished at the number of times he gave the ball away. Some of the players wondered whether he was deliberately trying to sabotage the session, his effort was that bad.

Coutinho had joined Liverpool from Inter Milan in 2013, emerging as the team's star player before Salah's arrival. With the number 10 on his back, Coutinho was one of the driving forces behind the club's assault on the Premier League title under Rodgers in 2014. This brought attention from other leading clubs across Europe and for the next three seasons, Barcelona monitored him closely, sending scouts to Merseyside for most games.

In July 2017, while the Liverpool squad was in Hong Kong, FSG rejected an opening bid of £72 million from Barcelona for Coutinho, insisting he would not be leaving the club at any point during the summer. When Barcelona came back with an increased offer of £90 million, only to receive the same response, Coutinho took matters into his own hands.

Suddenly, he complained of a back injury, though a scan cleared him of any problems. Some of the staff believed that the extreme nature of the week in Bavaria gave Coutinho an opportunity to claim something was wrong following injuries to other players, but Klopp was able to see right through what was going on.

Though he loved Coutinho as a player, he felt that his Liverpool teammates relied on him too much, particularly when they were looking for someone to get them out of a hole. This, thought Klopp, made Liverpool too predictable: if Coutinho wanted to go, and he got the money that he wanted, the money could help transform other areas of the team.

Klopp's stance hardened when he discovered that Coutinho had approached Jordan Henderson and James Milner to discuss his problems in one of Melwood's anterooms. Coutinho believed that the senior players would understand why he wanted to go. Barcelona had won five of the previous six La Liga titles. The best player on the planet, Lionel Messi, wanted him there. Barcelona were promising that Coutinho would become a central part of a team rebuild while his wages would increase more than threefold, from £150,000 a week on Merseyside to £470,000 a week in Catalonia.

While Barcelona had won the Champions League two years earlier and had since progressed to its latter stages, Liverpool were appearing in the competition for only the second time in nine years. Coutinho begged Henderson and Milner to help him change the club's mind. When Klopp found out the Brazilian had brought other people into the discussion, he was furious. He understood that football clubs are working environments like anywhere else in the sense that, when someone doesn't really want to be there and lets it be known, mood spreads quickly and productivity levels decrease. Others – friends – can also become unsettled.

FSG were now in a tricky position. Klopp was happy to cut the player loose. The player certainly wanted to go. Yet the owners had already suggested he was going nowhere and letting this happen now would make them look weak publicly – especially in the minds of some of their fiercest critics, who believed they were more interested in making money than achieving success. If they suddenly sanctioned such a deal, other players would know what to do if they ever wished to leave: disrupt and get what you want.

Liverpool decided to keep up with the pretence that Coutinho was injured, to promise him that a deal with Barcelona could be done in the next transfer window if the money was right, and in the meantime, attempt to refocus his mind gradually, reintegrating him into the squad. This would limit the attention on him and, in theory, increase the chances of Liverpool's season beginning with fewer distractions.

Before finally leaving for Barcelona in January 2018 in one of the most expensive transfer deals of all time, Coutinho played twenty more games for Liverpool but he would not return to the team until September. In fact, he played for Brazil against Ecuador in World Cup qualifying games, scoring a goal, before he represented his club side again in a chaotic 2–2 draw at home in the Champions League with Sevilla.

Progress in the group stages of the competition was not without its bumps, and Liverpool needed to win their last game at home to Spartak Moscow to ensure progression to the knock-out rounds. Coutinho, as captain, gave a dazzling performance, as Klopp fielded a front four that included Salah, Mané and Firmino, with each player scoring including Coutinho, who grabbed a hat-trick in a 7–0 victory.

Klopp seemingly knew where Coutinho's career was heading because he refused to bite on suggestions that he'd found a 'fab four' forward line in Anfield's pressroom afterwards. Coutinho was three weeks away from leaving the club in a move to Barcelona costing £142 million.

After FSG had issued a series of denials about the prospect of this happening, at least in the summer, it was left to Klopp to explain on Liverpool's website why the transfer had been sanctioned. 'Philippe was insistent with me, the owners and even his teammates this was a move he was desperate to make happen,' Klopp said, the key word being: 'teammates'.

Back at Melwood, Klopp gathered the squad in the dressing room, telling them that though they'd lost a friend and a fine player, it was their opportunity to stick two fingers up to anyone who thought they relied on him. This suggestion clearly annoyed Klopp, a manager who had always pressed upon the importance of the team structure before any individual.

With a tough Christmas schedule now behind them, Salah had already scored twenty-three goals for Liverpool – a career best for any season to date, and the campaign was barely halfway through. He was not yet a hero but he was becoming a reference point for the team: the player others looked towards to make a difference when it mattered.

Though Klopp tried to avoid such reliance, there remained space for a main man, at least in the hearts and minds of the Liverpool fans, who were becoming more and more optimistic about the future under Klopp. On the terraces of Anfield, Salah had already established a new nickname for himself. To Liverpudlians, he was already the 'Egyptian King'.

Chapter 4

Football in Egypt is dangerous

When a small fire started below deck on a ferry oversubscribed with 1,400 mainly Egyptian workers travelling home from Saudi Arabia in the early hours of 3 February 2006, many of the passengers assumed the boat would turn back because it was only half an hour out of the port of Duba. Instead, the *Al Salam* pushed on through the waters of the Red Sea amidst high winds and, as the flames started to spread, it became clear that there were not enough lifejackets or lifeboats aboard. Within a couple of hours, more than a thousand Egyptians had lost their lives, amongst them worshippers returning from Mecca.

The ferry's owner was a senior Egyptian lawmaker. An investigation later concluded that the vessel had not met minimum safety standards but the owner and his son through 'wicked collaboration' ensured it sailed anyway. Though he was charged with manslaughter, the Egyptian authorities allowed him to escape to Britain. In absentia, he was acquitted, and though that decision was later overturned, he has never returned to Egypt.

The tragedy happened at the tail end of Hosni Mubarak's presidency, with the country in an economic mess. Fortunately for Mubarak, the Africa Cup of Nations (AFCON) was also reaching a thrilling finale in Egypt, a country that was focused on its attempts to win the competition for only the second time in twenty years. The day the *Al Salam* sank, the hosts were playing the Democratic Republic of Congo in a quarter-final tie held in Cairo in front of 74,000 fans. If Mubarak was tempted to withdraw from his plans to attend the game and go to the Red Sea port of Safaga, where distressed families were awaiting news of their loved ones, he did not show it. It was as if one of the worst maritime disasters in Egypt's history had not happened. Instead, he attended a morning training session in Cairo before heading to the VIP section of the stadium, where he was photographed celebrating as Egypt thumped their opponents 4–1.

Egypt became champions after narrowly beating Senegal in the semis, then Ivory Coast on penalties following a goalless final. Mohamed Aboutrika, the team's most revered player, would score the vital kick, and as the president handed out the medals and then the trophy to the winning captain, Hossam Hassan, the veteran forward responded by kissing the president on the forehead.

Within a week of the *Al Salam* capsizing, the country was in full party mode. It would prove to be the trigger point to an era of unprecedented success in Egyptian football. While the national team would become the first African nation to win three AFCON titles in a row, following further triumphs in 2008 and 2010, Egypt's most popular club side, Al Ahly, brought home three African Champions League titles between 2005 and 2008.

Given the grinding economic and social conditions many Egyptians were living in, Mubarak realised the hype around football was a useful distraction and it became a functioning part of his soft power. British conscripts had introduced football to the country in the late nineteenth century, only for the sport to be embraced by the pro-independence movement as a vehicle for nation building. This contributed towards the formation of a club that became one of the biggest in Egypt. Al Ahly was established in 1907 in an attempt by nationalists to improve the physicality of Egyptians. At its formation, it had an Egyptian-only membership policy and the club came to embody the rebellion against colonisation. Following Egyptian independence in 1952, Al Ahly became tremendously popular not only in Egypt but all over Africa and the Arab world and, in some ways, the club's successes over many years filled a gap due to the lack of success delivered by the national team.

Mubarak's authoritarian regime had controlled Egypt for nearly nine years by the time the country qualified for only its second World Cup in 1990. Though Egypt did not get out of a tough group that included reigning European champions the Netherlands, as well as England and Republic of Ireland, the excitement around the tournament made Mubarak understand how useful football could be. What followed was a boom that caused the structures in Egyptian football to change radically. Suddenly, money was independently being ploughed into a game that was becoming more professionalised. Amid rising transfer fees and salaries, the leading clubs were striking advertising deals and marketing themselves better.

All of this meant Egypt's smaller clubs were struggling to compete. Mubarak ensured they were not left behind by putting some of these clubs under the control of major companies with links to the state, which made it easier to channel revenue. El Mokawloon, the club run by one of the biggest construction companies in the region, and the one which Mohamed Salah played for decades later, was already one. Quickly, the Egyptian league became the strongest in Africa and amidst the success of the national team and the rise of television, with an abundance of talk shows that mixed sport, music and some politics, football was stirring some very powerful emotions indeed.

Mubarak, however, did not foresee what this would mean for the game's supporter bases at ground level. Football in Egypt became dangerous. From 2007 onwards, some fanbases developed an 'ultra' wing, a culture that had spread from southern Europe and into Morocco and Tunisia. By the time it arrived in Egypt, lots of these supporters were against the police and the media. For many Egyptians, football had become a sport consumed on television, but it wasn't the case for the ultras, who arrived in the stadiums like invading forces. They were independent, alternative, well organised and ultimately posed a challenge to Mubarak because he could not tap into them. Quickly, the ultras were ostracised by the media and became a focus of police attention.

It is felt across Egypt that the country's football boom ended in 2009, when the national team missed out on qualification for a first World Cup appearance in twenty years by losing to Algeria amidst violent scenes. Egypt had reached Italy in 1990 after knocking Algeria out in a game which left the Egyptian team doctor losing an eye after being attacked with a broken bottle. The former African Player of the Year, Lakhdar Belloumi, denied any involvement but after being convicted in absentia, he remained on an Interpol arrest warrant until the two governments met ahead of the World Cup two decades later.

The summit diffused tensions ahead of the first leg in Algiers, which Algeria won 3–1. With Egypt now needing at least two goals to progress, pressure in the Egyptian media cranked up a few levels. *Shoot*, the most popular weekly football newspaper in Egypt, published a front page which depicted a scene from the film *300* where the Spartans held off an attack by more than 100,000 Persian soldiers. Beneath the faces of Egypt's footballers, leading the charge with the country's red, white and black flag was the three-time AFCON-winning coach Hassan Shehata and a headline of 'ATTACK' smeared in blood.

Upon arriving in Cairo, the Algerian team bus was stoned and three players were injured. Even though a representative from FIFA witnessed the attack, local media reported that the incident had been fabricated in an attempt to get the second leg cancelled. A 2–0 victory for Egypt was followed by more conflict outside Cairo's International Stadium, before the violence spread as far as Marseille in France, where Algerian immigrants attacked Egyptian businesses.

Algeria would narrowly win the subsequent play-off, held on neutral territory in Sudan. Though the tie seemed to go off without incident, Egyptian state media channels reported that some fans had been attacked by Algerians with knives. This prompted Mubarak to threaten an invasion of Sudan to protect the affected Egyptians. The Sudanese government reacted by summoning the Egyptian ambassador, claiming the reports in Egypt were exaggerated.

Mubarak had marginalised intellectuals and Islamists, turning them into his biggest critics. For them, the obsession with football was vulgar and making the nation focus on the wrong things. An appearance in the World Cup was the natural next step for the president's Egypt but for the increasing number of his opponents in the country, their failure to proceed proved it was difficult to sustain the hype around football.

'Football was no longer a background noise but entangled in a revolutionary transition,' wrote Carl Rommel, a social anthropologist from Sweden who was living in Cairo at the time. Rommel would publish a book, *Egypt's Football Revolution*, in which he detailed how the ultras played a significant role in the overthrowing of Mubarak two years later. His creaking system was slow to react to the 'Arab Spring' of revolutions spreading eastwards from Tunisia in late 2010 and, by the time Egypt's revolution started in Cairo's Tahrir Square with its occupation by 50,000 protestors, many of the participants had already experienced fighting the police due to their activities with the ultras of clubs like Al Ahly. 'There were two groups that were crucial for the Egyptian revolution to succeed, the Muslim Brotherhood and the Al Ahly ultras,' wrote Stephane Lacroix, a French expert on political Islam. 'The ultras were the most important.'

With the police disappearing following Mubarak's resignation, the ultras were now empowered and could largely do what they liked inside stadiums; this led to them becoming more provocative than ever before. The mood would change again within a year, however, after seventy-two Al Ahly fans were killed in Port Said during a game with local club Al Masry. Though initially the authorities tried to claim this was the result of violence, panic and an unfortunate closing of the stadium's gates, it was later established that Al Ahly fans were deliberately killed. Though twenty-one Al Masry ultras were sentenced to death, across Egypt it was suspected ideological and political motivations were behind the carnage, with newly elected parliament members and the security services accused of instigating and then allowing the violence to play out as payback for the revolution.

The Muslim Brotherhood had replaced Mubarak's autocracy in the first democratic elections in decades but by 2013, with Egypt's domestic league suspended and all matches now being played in closed stadiums, the Brotherhood was quashed by Abdel Fattah el-Sisi, who returned Egypt to being a one-party state as president.

After 2011, football would lose its position at the centre of the country's culture, with Egyptians becoming cynical about the game's role in society, if not turning away from it altogether. During this transition, Mohamed Salah was developing a reputation in the game because of his achievements outside Africa. The suspension of the league after Port Said led to the arrangement of a series of friendly matches in Europe, as the country's under-twenty-three team prepared for the 2012 Olympics in London. Salah took the opportunity, and five years later, as he emerged a legend at Liverpool, he would fire home the penalty that sent Egypt to its first World Cup in twenty-eight years.

Instantly, Salah became a national hero, achieving something even the greats of the 2006–10 period could not. Yet much of Egypt now realised how much of a dangerous, corruptive and corrosive influence the sport could be. The memory of Mubarak remained fresh, little had changed since, and fewer Egyptians were willing to be consumed by the distraction of a sport. The country's struggles and its subsequent paranoia would therefore impact on the way Salah was viewed. Though he was loved, there was a mixture of ambivalence and suspicion towards the game he played. It was not an easy time to become the most famous Arab footballer on the planet.

★   ★   ★

Back in the mid-2000s, Mubarak's political tentacles had been carefully and tightly wrapped around some of Egypt's leading football clubs. At El Mokawloon, a granite-jawed businessman called Ibrahim Mahlab was the club's president. Since 2001, he had also acted as the CEO of a huge construction firm by the same name which in English is translated as Arab Contractors.

Mahlab had emerged as a significant person in Egypt. His appointment came after Mubarak removed the company's previous CEO, Ismail Osman, a second-generation relative of its founder, Osman Ahmed Osman, who was behind many of the country's most significant building projects, including the Aswan Dam.

Though the company had been nationalised by Nasser and remained under the control of state ownership when Sadat came to power, it was able to take full advantage of his economic liberalisation by establishing a string of connected private firms.

Arab Contractors proceeded to build each of Egypt's major international airports and develop the Cairo-to-Alexandria desert road. Osman's influence would grow and, by the late 1970s, he was considered the second most powerful man in Egypt behind Sadat.

Mubarak spotted the threat and on his rise to presidency, stopped Osman from investing in any more private projects. By 2001, the company was struggling and when Mubarak removed the last Osman from its board, Mahlab came in, a person who was appointed to parliament by Mubarak shortly before the revolution.

When the Muslim Brotherhood were overthrown two years later, Mahlab returned to politics as the country's minister for housing before briefly emerging as prime minister under the new military regime, vowing to 'work together to restore security and safety to Egypt and crush terrorism in all corners of the country'.

It was around this time that former president Mubarak was found guilty of fraudulently billing the government for personal expenses, such as the five villas his family had in the seaside resort of Sharm el-Sheikh. One name missing from the indictment sheet was Malhab's, even though Arab Contractors were named as the state construction company deeply involved in authorising the payments for Mubarak's personal use.

Some of the bolder sections of Egypt's media reported that the legal move against Mubarak was an attempt by the military government to distance itself from the past and mollify a public that increasingly wanted something to be done about corruption, as the country slipped back into becoming an authoritarian regime, one not altogether different from Mubarak's rule.

Under the military, Malhab made some significant decisions, one of which made the news in Europe. In 2014, he put in the calls that prevented Salah from having to return to the country to complete military service, an outcome that was not as close to being guaranteed as many outside Egypt might assume, considering the importance of a duty which could have at the very least interfered with his career in Europe, if not shorten it by three years altogether.

Mahlab is not thought of as one of the most influential figures in Salah's life but perhaps he should be. His statecraft ultimately helped keep the player abroad, and in plain sight and minds of other clubs thinking about taking him away from Chelsea. None of these clubs would consider investing in a player who might not have been available for them for any period, especially one who was instead spending his time polishing his jackboots in a desert camp.

It is thought this was not the first time Mahlab had influenced the direction of Salah's career, though eight years earlier, from his new lodgings on the outskirts of Cairo, it would have been understandable if a teenage Salah was not aware of the impact Malhab was having on his own trajectory, and that of other boys like him from the countryside.

Back in 2006, El Mokawloon had a problem with Salah because he was not training or performing to the levels the coaches thought he was capable of. The story goes that Regab Refaat, the club's head of youth development, asked Mahlab to build an apartment block so that players like Salah would stay in Cairo rather than having to travel all the way back to places like Nagrig every day.

For Refaat, the journey from Nagrig to Cairo was not even a consideration until it started impacting Salah's development. There were a lot of kids like Salah, spending endless hours bussing it from the delta in the pursuit of a dream. Though his sacrifice might have seemed extraordinary for non-Africans, it wasn't an unusual journey to make for an Egyptian boy from a modest background.

Refaat came to rate footballers from the countryside over those from the city because they tended to make more sacrifices and were ultimately hungrier for success. As soon as Refaat identified Salah's talent and could see he was being held back by this gruelling process, he had to act. Initially, Refaat suggested Salah stayed in Cairo for two nights a week, allowing him to rest properly after training sessions rather than travelling all the way back to Nagrig. When that didn't work, Refaat approached the president for extra funding, which would also allow Salah to receive education, food and medical assistance.

To Refaat, Salah was initially just one name on a list of forty players recommended for trial in Cairo by the coaches at Tanta-based Othmason and a number of other clubs with connections to El Mokawloon across the Nile Delta. Yet Refaat, who was responsible for setting up a relationship between the Othmason youth team and his own club, quickly became very excited about the intake of players born in 1992 and 1993.

On first inspection, Refaat liked two things about Salah: his acceleration and how powerfully he could kick the ball with his left foot. This surprised Refaat: Salah was so light and there was barely any muscle strength in either of his legs. Refaat told the coaches at El Mokawloon to keep a close eye on Salah and after a couple of months, his salary was increased by a small amount to mark the progress he was making.

The first records of Salah's involvement at El Mokawloon are preserved in the cabinet at Refaat's apartment in Almazah, one of Cairo's wealthier districts, not far from the city's airport. He simply notes in 2004, 'The player Mohamed Salah has joined the team.' The next mention is two years later when, at the time Salah was aged fourteen, the notes showed that he mainly played as a left back in a side that went the whole season unbeaten to win the Cairo championship.

Salah remained small and thin when some of his teammates were experiencing growth spurts. One of the coaches suggested that he might get left behind and overtaken by other, more physical players and Salah responded by going to the gym for the first time in his life. 'He was tougher than a lot of people thought,' concluded Shefif Alaa, one of his old teammates. 'They underestimated him.'

Eventually, Salah became one of that same coach's first picks and playing at left back did not stop him from delivering important moments. In 2007, the fifteen-year-olds of El Mokawloon recorded an eye-catching win over Zamalek where they had to defend for long periods of the game but secured a victory when Salah seized possession on the edge of his own box before dribbling around a few players and charging into space. After the goal that followed, he was called up to train with the first team but he still played with the under-sixteens for a period which, according to Refaat, was a decision designed to keep him 'humble', even though Refaat suspected the promotion would not see him get above his station.

Keeping him focused also involved the sort of strict discipline that Salah experienced at half-time in one game where, according to teammates, he played particularly badly. Another coach, Hamdi Nouh, came down hard on him and Salah was crying as he returned to a pitch on which he would score a hat-trick after being moved into a more advanced position.

There are lots of coaches in Egypt willing to claim they played a defining role in Salah's development and Said El Shishiny is another one of them. He claims it was his decision to play him for the first time on the right wing, the position that became his own upon moving to Europe despite being left-footed. El Shishiny admitted that he was unusually well stocked at left back and, given Salah's attacking instincts, it seemed like a good idea to get him into an area of the pitch where he could turn and shoot quickly.

Initially, Salah would often miss. El Shishiny remembers a game against ENPPI, where the team won but Salah failed to capitalise on three chances. In the changing room afterwards, he was crying again. When El Shishiny asked why he was so upset, Salah told him it was because he did not score. El Shishiny looked around and everyone else was celebrating. He had worked with young boys for a long time and concluded that Salah's reaction wasn't because he was selfish. It was simply because he hadn't met the standards he'd set for himself and, having already trained with the first team, he had a better idea of what he had to do to stay there. El Shishiny reassured him that the next season he'd end up being the team's top scorer. He was right. Salah finished with thirty goals.

Mohamed Radwan is an El Mokawloon man to the core, having spent his entire playing career in the team's midfield before emerging as a coach, managing the club four times. In the middle of the second of those spells, he decided to watch the club's under-sixteens against Al Ahly. His assistants wondered why he'd be interested in players who were so young but Salah caught his attention. He was fifteen years old, talented but physically underdeveloped compared to other players his age. Radwan invited him to train with the first team and put him on a special diet and in training programmes.

Radwan had seen lots of boys like Salah, those from the countryside who suffered from malnourishment under Mubarak. The majority of them were unable to improve their situation. Many lacked the confidence to thrive beyond the countryside in a world they barely understood. Though Salah believed in himself, he was daunted by the prospect of representing El Mokawloon's first team. Radwan decided to use him in a game against ENPPI, even though he was just fifteen. When he asked Salah whether he was ready, he responded emphatically, 'No, sir.'

Radwan, who referred to Salah as '*Hadi*' (or 'village boy'), told the *Daily Mirror* in 2018 ahead of the Champions League final in Kyiv, 'You would tell him to do something and all he kept on saying at that time was, "Thank you, Coach."'

Radwan could see that Salah was apprehensive but he played him anyway and he became the youngest player to appear in the Egyptian top flight. Yet his progression would not be consistent: for the next couple of years, he mainly played with his own age group and it wasn't until another coach arrived, Mohamed Amer, that the Egyptian public really started to notice him.

That was largely because after a game against Zamalek, Amer, whose playing career was mainly spent with Al Ahly, boldly told journalists that within two years Salah would be considered the Egyptian Messi. By that point, Salah's decision making was improving. Amer concluded that this could often be a problem with fast players because they thought they could simply beat opponents all the time. Salah, though, was interested in the tactical side of the game. Amer also thought that his grounding as a left back helped him understand that mindset when he switched to the right wing.

Often, according to Amer, the fastest players did not know how to use their pace. It was particularly a problem for young-sters, but Salah seemed to understand at which points the oppo-nent was at his most vulnerable. The 2010–11 season was his first full campaign as a regular in the senior setup at El Mokawloon and, often, Amer used him as a substitute when the other team was tiring.

Amer also liked the fact that Salah wanted to get close to the team's senior figures and learn from them. In El Mokawloon's case, the star was Mohamed Samara, a player who was working his way back to fitness after an injury on the day Salah scored the first hat-trick of his senior career in a 4–0 victory over El Dakhleya. Salah wanted to show Samara gratitude for the guidance the twenty-eight-year-old had given him by celebrating each goal with him. By the third goal, teammates knew what Salah was going to do and tried to block his path, a moment at which everyone laughed.

Samara was born in Cairo but chose to represent Palestine. He would educate Salah on the politics of the region and on the morning Samara turned twenty-nine, he found a gift waiting for him in the dressing room. Samara had not mentioned his birthday to any of his teammates but Salah had found out. Even though he wasn't getting paid vast amounts of money by El Mokawloon, Samara concluded he was generous – the Fossil watch and aftershave were not cheap.

Salah was still living in the apartments built by Mahlab and this meant he spent most of his time with his team- and room-mate of five years, Ali Fathi. They would find ways of challenging each other. Sometimes whoever won the most games on the PlayStation they'd bought together would buy dinner. Fathi would often be Real Madrid and Salah was Barcelona, then managed in real life by Pep Guardiola. A friendly sense of rivalry extended to the training pitch during five-a-side matches. Dinner would be arranged by whichever player scored the fewest goals with their right foot. Both Fathi and Salah were left-footed.

After becoming a first team player, Fathi says Salah really

began to understand the importance of his physical condition. For years, the coaches had attempted to bring in line what they considered to be his weakness: though he was fast, he was sometimes easily knocked off the ball. In the first team, Salah got angry whenever that happened. It led to him enrolling at a private gym. Even though he was already very fast, he told an instructor that he needed to improve and that meant lots of exercises for stamina and acceleration.

Fathi believed the diet of Egyptian footballers tended not to be very good and this explained why some found it hard to adjust to the standards in Europe. Fathi had experience of this after joining CD Nacional in Madeira, where he competed in the Portuguese top flight. Salah's mindset was European before he'd even left Egypt. According to Fathi, Cristiano Ronaldo wasn't Salah's favourite player but he looked at his body and realised he had to transform himself if he was ever going to succeed outside Egypt, a challenge he spoke about regularly.

This led to him spending at least half an hour lifting dumb-bells in El Mokawloon's modest and underused gymnasium after every training session. Most of the coaches did not really understand gym work, so Salah watched YouTube videos and followed his own programme.

Amer was aware of what Salah was doing but he never spoke to him about it because he liked his players to be independent and make their own decisions. Amer had spent some of his playing career with the giants of Al Ahly and concluded that Salah trained with the dedication of an Al Ahly player. Except, Al Ahly never showed any interest in signing him, and he was publicly rejected by Zamalek's president, who thought his game was not rounded enough. Refaat believed Salah was fortunate that neither club came for him, because of the pressure they put on players to join. Though Salah dreamed of Europe, the pay in Egypt was competitive and the major clubs made it difficult to say no. Older players, meanwhile, tended to do better at Al Ahly and Zamalek because the coaches trusted them over youth.

Looking back in 2018, Salah admitted his life could have turned out very differently had he gone to one of Egypt's big two. Maybe a transfer to Europe would have been less important; maybe it involved a bigger ego: 'What if I had joined Zamalek? I think if I had signed for Zamalek I would not be where I am now. Al Ahly and Zamalek do not allow their players to leave easily, so I believe I would have stayed in Zamalek for not less than four years.'

Despite his connections with Al Ahly, Amer did not recommend Salah to his former club but that was mainly because he was trying to get El Mokawloon out of a relegation battle. The club was spared such ignominy by political events outside its control. After the revolution in 2011, there was a long break between games. Then after Port Said a year later, the league was suspended altogether for what initially seemed like an indefinite period.

A bloody revolution and a horrendous stadium disaster had the potential to disrupt the careers of all Egyptian footballers. The uncertain political outlook after the revolution meant Zamalek and Al Ahly were spending less money on players. With the gates of stadiums locked even after the league resumed play following Port Said, revenue streams were decimated. Both of these mighty clubs were previously able to offer the best

Egyptian footballers big wages to stop them leaving for Europe. Suddenly, the landscape had shifted.

In the space of eight months, Bob Bradley went from preparing the United States national team for a friendly that never happened in Cairo because of the Arab Spring, to becoming the first new coach of Egypt following the revolution. Not long after his appointment, the worst stadium disaster in the country's history followed and the domestic league was cancelled. Then the headquarters of the Egyptian Football Association was burned down.

Yet Bradley, a tough New Jerseyan, was never tempted to walk away from a role that he knew was going to be challenging, even after he described Port Said as a 'massacre', a word which prompted some Egyptians to think he was criticising the country's regime. At a press conference, arranged hastily by the Egyptian Football Association (EFA), Bradley denied his comments related to his view of the forces running Egypt.

It was a tutorial in the blurred lines between football and politics. He would quickly understand that nothing was as it seemed on the surface in Egypt. What lurked below was often far more relevant. For example, he would learn that inside the EFA itself, there were four boards and each one was riven with factions.

With the league shut down so soon after his arrival in the country and nearly all of the players available to him based in Egypt, he would lean on advice from his assistant, especially in those early months. Bradley felt as though having Diaa Al-Sayed around allowed him to bridge any cultural gaps. His presence brought a better understanding of the backgrounds of players like Salah. Al-Sayed knew how to talk to them and challenge them. On first inspection, he saw Salah as 'humble, motivated and ready to learn'. Al-Sayed had a grasp of what was coming through because he was also Egypt's under-twenty coach. In 2011, he had taken Egypt to the U-20 World Cup in Colombia and a team that included Salah did well, progressing with seven points from a group that included Brazil. In the first knockout round, they were unlucky, losing 2–1 to Argentina in Medellín.

Their performance showed Bradley that some of Egypt's younger players were capable of holding their own on a stage that included some of the most exciting talent on the planet. Upon returning from the tournament, Salah made his senior international debut somewhat inauspiciously in a 2–1 defeat to Sierra Leone after being called up by Bradley's predecessor, the caretaker manager Hany Ramzy.

Bradley could tell straight away that Salah appreciated he had to sharpen up certain parts of his game and this involved a lot of extra work, which he appeared to relish. If he was concerned about the suspension of league fixtures and the effect that might have on his career, he didn't show it. Like the rest of the players, Salah wasn't getting paid but he used the time to work on his shape in the gym. Bradley held several lengthy training camps and he could see Salah's physical development more clearly because of the breaks between their meetings.

Egypt were having a hard time getting friendlies due to the political situation. This meant some of the 'home' fixtures were instead played in neutral venues like Khartoum, Sudan. There were other games in Tripoli and Beirut. Nearly always, the stadiums were empty due to security concerns.

According to Bradley, Egypt's players, however, could not wait for the international get-togethers because it afforded them the time to socialise and distance themselves from the political turmoil. There was also the focus of the games and the release of energy with plain old competitive exercise. Egypt raced through their qualifying group for the 2014 World Cup, winning all six of their matches.

Salah was becoming a key player. In Guinea, he scored a stoppage-time winner to secure a 3–2 victory. Then in Zimbabwe, he scored a hat-trick in a 4–2 win. Away to Mozambique, he scored the only goal of the match and he then helped Egypt secure their 100 per cent record by scoring his sixth goal in qualifying in another 4–2 win. He finished this section as Africa's joint top scorer.

Adam Al-Abd was a defender with Championship side Brighton and Hove Albion. He qualified to play for Egypt through his father and he would represent the country seven times during this period. Before landing in Cairo, he did not know any of his teammates but he says Salah made the strongest impression.

'Bob [Bradley] finished every session with small-sided games. Mo would bang in five or six goals within a few minutes. I would think to myself, Christ, how good is this lad? But I also thought, Who is going to spot him in Egypt? And, is anyone going to really give him a chance even if they like what they see? He was still quite small and skinny but his pace was frightening.'

Al-Abd went back to Brighton and spoke about the standard of players in Egypt. Brighton later became a Premier League club that successfully navigated some of the more obscure transfer markets but it was almost impossible to sign someone like Salah in the early 2010s because of work-permit requirements that dictated he needed to have played in 75 per cent of Egypt's fixtures over a two-year period.

The rules were different in Switzerland, a non-EU country. From afar, Basel had been following Salah's progress since the U-20 World Cup in Colombia. Their interest in him intensified following a friendly match in March 2012 with an under-twenty-three team scheduled to represent Egypt at that summer's Olympics in London.

Since returning to Egypt from South America, Salah had been on short trials in Germany and Belgium. One of his agents at the time, Sascha Empacher, was left with the feeling that European scouts and coaches didn't really trust Egyptian players, who tended to need more time to settle when moving abroad compared to other African players. This, according to other agents who have worked with Egyptian players, was because of the strength of the country's identity, which was defined by its location. Though Egypt is in Africa, it is the gateway to the Middle East, a region which it is closely connected to culturally. 'Egypt is like no other place on Earth,' said an agent who tried to use the market since Salah's success but found working with Egyptian clubs difficult because of the layers of management and bureaucracy, which made it harder to reach decisions quickly.

Playing with the under-twenty-threes against Basel at the club's training ground, Salah was introduced as a second-half substitute but he scored twice in a 4–3 win. Rudi Zbinden, Basel's chief scout, was already aware of the player's potential because of a report filed by one of the Buenos Aires-based scouts he'd dispatched to Colombia six months earlier. Basel were preparing to sell Xherdan Shaqiri to Bayern Munich and in the conversations around the left-footed forward's potential replace-ment, Salah's name came up. Basel's sporting director Georg Heitz had chaired those meetings. 'Our scouting department were very impressed,' Heitz told the *Liverpool Echo* in 2017. 'But then you think, Well, he's Egyptian and we don't know many success stories of Egyptian players coming to Europe. We thought it was a risk to sign him at that point.'

Salah would pass the all-important eye-test. 'You could see the talent after five minutes on the pitch,' Heitz reflected. 'Not only was he quick, but he always had his head up.' Though Heitz claimed Basel decided to sign him there and then, Salah was invited to train with Basel for a week. 'We could get an impression about his character and his will,' Heitz added. 'It was very clear that he was so ambitious. He wanted to be successful in Europe. We did not have any doubts.'

Zbinden remembered the period slightly differently. He said the conversation about Salah ramped up after Empacher approached Heitz about him, asking for a trial. Heitz had never heard of the player, so he went to Zbinden and asked whether he had anything on file. When he looked through his notes, he saw a 'glowing report' from Colombia.

In the meantime, Bradley was becoming more involved in the futures of his players. He was concerned about the league shutdown and the impact that was having on their develop-ment. With that in mind, he would meet with Empacher and then Heitz after establishing that Salah was keen on trying something different.

Though Salah did well playing against Basel, Zbinden was concerned by what he saw in subsequent training sessions. From the footage he'd watched from Egypt, he'd already developed concerns about Salah's final ball – whether that be a pass, a cross or a shot. Salah would get into good positions because of his pace but Zbinden wasn't sure he could deliver when it mattered. It did not help that all the conversations Heitz had about the player with his contacts in Egypt were positive. Surely, he concluded, Salah was not already the perfect player?

Of course he wasn't. Both Zbinden and Heitz agreed that it was unfair to come to any quick conclusions. They had not seen him play live in Egypt, where he would have been at his most comfortable and he'd arrived in Switzerland speaking only a few words of English. Yet Zbinden says both his and Heitz's enthusiasm increased on the fifth day of the trial. 'In the very last training session, a five-a-side, he exploded,' Zbinden recalled. 'He dribbled, he scored goals. Heiko Vogel – the Basel coach – and I just looked at each other and said, "Ah, he is the guy from the videos, after all": the guy we wanted.'

Heitz believed Salah was worth three million Swiss francs (£1.5 million) but the deal suddenly became complicated. He had received a fax from El Mokawloon which gave them permission to proceed with negotiations with the player, only for the club to try and restructure the finances, which meant he had to begin negotiations all over again.

With the deal in motion, Heitz estimated it would take Salah at least six months to adapt to Swiss football, never mind the country. Yet he would make an immediate impression on his new coach. Salah's goal in the first ten minutes of a pre-season friendly with Partizan Belgrade in the same Tegernsee resort in southern Bavaria where he would later spend his summers training with Liverpool, would prompt Vogel to substitute him at half-time.

When Heitz asked him why he'd made the decision, Vogel replied: 'I needed to take him off, he's too good and I'm afraid he might get injured.'

Before his Basel career really got going, Salah was off to the Olympics. Hany Ramzy was in charge of a team that would come to form the backbone of the senior side over the next ten years. Though most of the squad were fasting during the competition because of Ramadan, Egypt reached the quarter finals. In Cardiff's Millennium Stadium, Salah scored in a thrilling match against Brazil, which ended in a 3–2 defeat. The other scorer that day was Mohamed Aboutrika, who'd reversed his decision to retire from football altogether after cradling a fourteen-year-old supporter in Port Said as he died in front of him. The teenager's last words were, 'Captain, I'm glad to have met you.'

For Salah, Aboutrika's return to the squad gave him the opportunity to spend nearly a month with the figure who had become an icon of the Arab Spring. When the pair were in Bradley's company, the American could see how much Salah idolised him. 'Mohamed couldn't get enough of him,' Bradley concluded. 'He wanted to learn what it took to become arguably the greatest player in Egyptian football history.'

After the defeat to Brazil, Salah scored again in a 1–1 draw with New Zealand at Old Trafford, a ground where he would later enjoy great success with Liverpool. This rendered the third group game against Belarus at Hampden Park in Glasgow crucial and Salah's opener inspired a 3–1 victory that propelled the country into the knockout stages, where they lost 3-0 to Japan.

For Egypt, an even bigger match was looming. After the success of the qualifying groups, Ghana stood in the way of a first World Cup appearance in twenty-four years. This was Salah's first opportunity to prove he was capable of inspiring the nation to even greater heights than the players that secured three Africa Cup of Nations titles back to back. After the revolution and Port Said, it cannot be overstated what this would have meant for Africa's most successful football country, albeit one that had never flourished on the greatest stage of them all.

Ahead of the game, Bradley suggested he was 'perfectly happy' to be playing Ghana, even though they had reached the quarter finals of the World Cup in South Africa in 2010. The two-leg tie meant Egypt avoided Algeria and Tunisia. 'The match will be just about football. There will be no politics and less emotion that can sometimes have a negative effect on the team.'

In the first leg, held in the Ghanaian city of Kumasi, Egypt lost 6–1. Bradley compared the state of the shock from that result to Brazil's 7–1 trouncing to Germany in the semi-final in the tournament that followed. In the dressing room afterwards, all he could see were ghost-like faces. Back at the hotel, he told the players he loved them, that they weren't themselves in Kumasi; the toil of the previous years and the pressure they were facing had finally got to them. He admitted he did not know whether he'd be in charge for the return leg.

Bradley survived – but only temporarily, because he left his position after overseeing a 2–1 victory in Cairo a month later, a result which meant Egypt were eliminated 7–3 on aggregate. Bradley had arrived in the country at one of the most difficult times in its history and he said Egyptians tended to recognise that. They were grateful that he stood loyal to his position, even as the political situation became more volatile.

Bradley saw Egypt as a complicated place. He concluded he

could not begin to understand all of its problems. He saw it as his responsibility to try and bring the country's footballers together. 'My focus was all on the players,' he said. 'I tried to connect them at a time the whole place was divided. We had to show unity.'

He wondered whether Egyptians had lost faith in leadership figures. In the years that followed, Salah would assume an unofficial leadership position as he became one of the best footballers on the planet and the most famous sportsperson in the Arab world. While that would bring adulation, he would also inherit the pressures of a society that was more cynical of so-called greatness than it had ever been.

Chapter 5

The Blues

In the last eight months of his Basel career, Salah played four times against Chelsea, scoring in three of those games. The first and second of those encounters, in April and May 2013, were a Europa League semi-final tie. Chelsea, steered by former Liverpool manager Rafa Benítez, won comfortably in both legs, and progressed to the final where they beat Portuguese giants Benfica in Amsterdam.

Benítez had been a curious choice to lead Chelsea, where he was appointed as 'interim manager' in November 2012. His earlier arrival at Anfield in the summer of 2004 coincided with the rise of Chelsea, who became a prominent domestic and European rival of Liverpool following Roman Abramovich's 2003 takeover. Suddenly, Chelsea – who in 2005, won their first league title in fifty years – were able to compete with Liverpool on the pitch by outmuscling them in the transfer market.

The appointment of José Mourinho as manager by Abramovich came in the same summer as Benítez's arrival at Liverpool. Over the next three seasons, the teams faced each other sixteen times across all competitions and, though Chelsea often had the edge, it felt like only Liverpool could stop them from winning in the Champions League, a competition where Liverpool prevailed in two semi-finals between the clubs.

Nagrig: Salah was born in a village in the Nile Delta, a three-hour drive north of Cairo. He would play football on a rocky patch of ground in front of a mosque.
(Mahmoud Khaled/Stringer/Getty Images)

Egypt: Other famous Egyptians come from the Nile Delta but Salah's reach stretches further than any of them. In Nagrig and in other towns and cities across the country, his status is marked on crumbling brickwork and peeling walls. *(Khaled Desouki/Getty Images)*

Cairo: In 2011, Egyptians gathered in Tahrir Square and the revolution began. With football suspended across the country, Salah decided to play abroad and his life changed forever. *(Kim Badawi Images/Getty Images)*

Basel: Salah's goals on the Swiss club's run to the Europa League semi-final in the 2012–13 season alerted the rest of Europe to his abilities. This one helped knock Tottenham Hotspur out of the competition, an opponent he would score against many times in a Liverpool shirt. *(Julian Finney/Getty Images)*

London: Chelsea had not lost a Champions League match at home for nearly a decade but that record ended when Salah and Basel won at Stamford Bridge. Soon, he would become a Chelsea player. *(PA Images/Alamy Stock Photo)*

Premier League: After signing for Chelsea, Salah lasted just a year in London, playing a handful of games. He would leave for Italy in early 2015, initially joining Fiorentina on loan. *(Darren Walsh/Chelsea FC via Getty Images)*

Roma: Salah's relationship with Edin Džeko convinced Liverpool's scouts that he'd fit in well at Anfield due to the Bosnian striker's similarities with Roberto Firmino. In Rome, Salah relaunched his career, learning more about the defensive side of the game under the tutelage of Luciano Spalletti. *(Luciano Rossi/AS Roma via Getty Images)*

Ramy: Post Chelsea, the lawyer Ramy Abbas became a central figure in Salah's life, helping direct his career while creating his brand. As Salah won multiple individual awards after joining Liverpool, Abbas was always on his table. *(PA Images / Alamy Stock Photo)*

Anfield: Salah broke all sorts of records during his first season at Liverpool. Each time he scored a goal, he performed the Islamic act of prostration, the *sujood*. *(PA Images/Alamy Stock Photo)*

Cairo: Salah's goals against DR Congo sent Egypt to the World Cup for the first time in twenty-eight years and for only the third time in the country's history. *(NurPhoto/Getty Images)*

Kyiv: Liverpool reached the Champions League final at the end of Salah's first season at Anfield but his involvement lasted less than half an hour after being yanked to the floor by Real Madrid defender, Sergio Ramos. *(VI-Images/ Getty Images)*

Grozny: Salah found himself at the centre of a political PR exercise during the World Cup. The Egyptian squad was based in Chechnya and the state's warlord leader Ramzan Kadyrov was never far away. *(Karim JAAFAR/Getty Images)*

Russia: Three games, three defeats, the last of which came against regional rivals Saudi Arabia in a dead rubber. Though the game meant little in the context of the World Cup, history was at stake. Salah scored his team's opening goal but the campaign was an unmitigated failure. *(Catherine Ivill/Getty Images)*

Liverpool's distinctly working-class local fanbase resented the newfound appeal of the *nouveau riche* Chelsea, whose supporters were filmed waving money at Anfield on the opening day of the 2003–04 season. Though Benítez came more from the right in a political sense, at Liverpool he knew how to mobilise a largely left-wing local fanbase, and his six years at the club were pockmarked by criticisms of what Chelsea were doing financially to stay ahead of Liverpool.

By 2012, however, he had been out of work for almost two years when he replaced the popular Roberto Di Matteo, a former midfielder at Chelsea, whose spectacular goal against Middlesbrough in the 1997 FA Cup final at Wembley remains one of the fastest in the competition's history. Just six months before his dismissal, Chelsea had won the Champions League for the first time by beating Bayern Munich in their own stadium on penalties, but their position had declined by November.

Over the months that followed Benítez's appointment, he was abused by large sections of the Chelsea fanbase, partly because he'd succeeded Di Matteo, but also because of his previous rivalry with the club during his time on Merseyside. The calls for his removal continued even in victory. A win at Middlesbrough took Chelsea to an FA Cup semi-final. The team, of course, was also making good progress in the Europa League, and positioned to secure a place in the Champions League.

Yet the calls for Benítez to go were more audible than they'd ever been on Merseyside, and this prompted him into some post-match revelations, during an extraordinary press conference in which he accused his critics of failing to understand that the club was in transition after the loss of several experienced players before his arrival. He had felt undermined from the start. 'It's because someone made a mistake,' Benítez said. 'They [the club] put my title as "interim manager", which was a massive mistake. Why put "interim" in the title? Why did they need to do that? Maybe they [the board] thought that, because I was at Liverpool, they will put "interim" in.'

Benítez suggested the supporters were risking the club's future because the negative atmosphere they were creating was affecting the players. 'They are wasting their time with banners and songs,' he added. 'They don't need to waste time with me. I will leave at the end of the season. They have to concentrate on supporting the team, that's what they have to do.'

Such an outburst might have pushed the hierarchy at most clubs into sacking him. Yet Benítez remained in charge, and Chelsea swept Basel aside in the Europa League by winning 5–2 on aggregate. Chelsea's fans had become used to impressive results against bigger opponents in more famous competitions since Abramovich's buyout. Yet Basel had emerged as an increasingly problematic team for some of the most prestigious European clubs that season. En route to the semi, they had beaten Sporting Lisbon from Portugal at home, as well as Ukraine's Dnipro, and Russia's Zenit St Petersburg. Salah's first goal in the competition would come against Tottenham Hotspur, a Premier League opponent that Basel would knock out on penalties following a 4–4 draw on aggregate.

Though Benítez delivered on Abramovich's remit, his contract was not renewed later that summer. The Russian oligarch's position as owner was untouchable (at least until Russian tanks rolled into Ukraine a decade later, leading to the British government sanctions that forced him to sell up).

In 2013, he realised he needed some unity and that led to Mourinho's rehiring, six years after Abramovich had sacked him. The fans came back on side and Chelsea were in the Champions League again. Yet the campaign in that competition began badly, with a 2–1 defeat to Basel at Stamford Bridge. It was Chelsea's first Champions League group-stage defeat at Stamford Bridge since October 2003, while it was also a landmark victory for the Swiss club, as it represented their first European win of any kind in England.

Salah's performance and yield was crucial, with a rapid run and whipped finish bringing Basel's equaliser in the seventy-first minute, before Marco Streller's winner arrived ten minutes later. Though he started on the right of Basel's attack, Salah would switch flanks. Chelsea's players considered him raw, but he caused problems, exposing the vastly experienced Ashley Cole and Branislav Ivanovic for periods of the game.

Basel could not match their performances and those results against the weaker opponents in the group – German side Schalke and Steaua Bucharest from Romania. The Swiss club would achieve just two wins, but both were against Chelsea, with the second of those in Switzerland completing a famous double. Another three points were secured thanks to the speed and composure of Salah, who raced clear of Chelsea's defence to dink a shot over Petr Cech. The Czech international had been one of the best goalkeepers on the planet for nearly a decade, but Salah made everything look so easy.

Despite the result, Chelsea qualified for the next stage because Schalke could not beat Steaua. 'The only positive thing is that we go through,' Mourinho reflected. 'But we don't go through because we got the result. We go through because Schalke did not get the result they wanted. That for me is not the same. I want to praise Basel. They won because we were sleeping in the last minute. But they also won because they were the best team.'

Salah was twenty-one years old. A question to Mourinho about his abilities was asked by the Swiss press but it was not reported in England. 'Fantastic,' he said. 'In both games, he has caused us problems. I suspect there will be a lot of interest in his career.'

Two months later, Chelsea made their move to sign him. Mourinho had asked himself the question: If Salah could hurt some of the best players in the world when playing against them, what could he achieve if they were teammates?

If Benítez's reign at Chelsea had been tumultuous over a short period of time, it was nothing compared to his much longer reign at Liverpool.

By the time he left the club in 2010, just a season into a new, five-year contract, the club was accelerating towards a financial collapse, with the Royal Bank of Scotland announcing that summer it was uncertain if Liverpool could continue operating as a business for much longer.

Liverpool had reached this position barely three years after a takeover by the American businessmen Tom Hicks and George Gillett, who completed a deal to buy the club through leveraged debt. The pressure on Liverpool's former owner, the local multi-millionaire, David Moores, had increased when Abramovich bought Chelsea and accelerated spending on players to new levels overnight, altering the way fans thought about money.

By that point, Liverpool's last league title had come thirteen years earlier. The club had previously been the most successful in England, dominating the old First Division in the 1970s and 1980s, as well as the European Cup.

Yet Manchester United, who themselves had gone twenty-six years without a domestic title until 1993, were better positioned in the '90s to take advantage of the new interest and investment in the game which largely came from Sky television. While Old Trafford, United's home, was quickly modernised to a capacity that was almost twice as big as Anfield, Moores could not find a solution to the geographical problem of his own stadium. It was hemmed in on three sides by terraced houses, then on the other by a busy shopping street that was crucial to an impoverished area of the city.

Chelsea had become a fashionable club in the '90s, one which famous foreign players liked to play for due to its location in west London. Abramovich's buyout threatened to leave traditionally successful clubs like Liverpool trailing for some time longer.

Improbably, Liverpool would win the Champions League in 2005, beating AC Milan on penalties in Istanbul after a 3–3 draw which involved the Italians being three goals to the good at half-time.

The achievement made a significant section of Liverpool's fanbase believe that Benítez was a genius. Ahead of the FA Cup final in 2006, a group of supporters carried a painting of the Spaniard around the streets of Cardiff, naming it the *Rafatollah*.

After beating West Ham on penalties following another dramatic 3–3 draw, Benítez's power would grow again. Yet he was still unable to compete with Chelsea financially. Moores had known this all along and between 2003 and 2007, he had quietly been attempting to find owners that could change Liverpool's economic possibilities.

Initially, Gillett presented himself as a lone interested party but Moores and Liverpool's chief executive Rick Parry were more enthusiastic about selling to Dubai International Capital, the investment arm of the Middle Eastern state's sovereign wealth fund.

When that deal fell through, Gillett came back, this time with a new business partner. Hicks was a Texan and a card-carrying member of the Republican party, who showed up in Liverpool's city centre with a cowboy hat. Plans were laid out for a new stadium in Stanley Park, a few hundred yards away from Anfield. Meanwhile, Liverpool broke their transfer record to sign Fernando Torres from Atlético Madrid. Things were looking up, until it became public knowledge that Hicks and Gillett had not used their own money to buy the club.

Hicks would compare running Liverpool to that of a company in charge of a breakfast cereal. He would fall out with Gillett and, over the course of an eighteen-month period, Benítez would ally with whichever owner seemed most favourable to him. Parry described the ownership situation at Liverpool as 'a civil war'. Yet Liverpool nearly ended their wait for a title in 2008–09, which would have been a 'miracle' according to Parry.

Inside that eighteen months, Parry left, Benítez left, and Hicks and Gillett were ousted as owners following protests from fans and a meeting in London's high court, where New England Sports Ventures (later FSG), became Liverpool's new owners.

The Massachusetts-based venture capitalist firm had transformed the fortunes of the Boston Red Sox, a baseball institution that had gone eighty-six seasons without a World Series title until 2004, just three years after New England Sports Ventures became involved in its running.

At Liverpool, the organisation would find historical success a little harder to come by. FSG believed in paying big transfer fees for unproven talent on lower wages. The formula had worked for them in baseball, where a lot of the decisions were influenced heavily by data.

By November 2013, Liverpool was already on to the third manager of the FSG era. After purchasing the club in late 2010, they sacked Roy Hodgson, replacing him with a club legend in Kenny Dalglish. Though Dalglish delivered a trophy in the form of the League Cup, FSG were unimpressed by the team's performance in the Premier League.

This led to the appointment of Brendan Rodgers, who at thirty-nine became the youngest outside managerial appointment in the club's history. Following a transitional first campaign in charge, Liverpool's performances and results in the first months of the 2013–14 season brought hope that the good times were returning.

On the night Salah's goal for Basel against Chelsea invited comment from Mourinho, Liverpool were four points off Arsenal at the top of the Premier League table. Beside them in second place were Chelsea. Over the months that followed, the clubs were competing again, both on and off the field, and the future of Salah would become central to that story.

After beating Chelsea in Switzerland, Basel went to Schalke knowing a draw would send them into the knockout stages of the Champions League for the first time.

The early dismissal of Bulgarian defender Ivan Ivanov reduced the chances of that happening. With the extra man and additional space, Schalke were able to control the best attacking instincts of the visiting team and goals from Julian Draxler and Joel Matip – a future Liverpool defender and a teammate of Salah's – sent the hosts into the next round.

In attendance in Gelsenkirchen that night was Rodgers. Liverpool's manager was looking to add firepower to an attack spearheaded by Luis Suárez, with support coming from Daniel Sturridge and Raheem Sterling. Rodgers felt that his team needed an injection of pace, and he flew to Germany after Salah was recommended by the club's recruitment team.

Sascha Empacher, the German founder of SPOCS, the agency representing Salah, later suggested Liverpool were already speaking about money with Basel by the time Rodgers watched him in person.

By November 2013, following his goalscoring performances against Chelsea, they had seen enough to make their move. Yet Empacher suggested the initial offer from Liverpool was worth just £5 million to Basel, 'and the salary was very low', he told Ed Aarons in his book, *Made in Africa*. 'I could see that Mohamed was feeling under pressure because everyone in Egypt was talking about Liverpool,' Empacher said, 'but the problem was their bid hadn't been accepted. English teams are always very slow.'

In the same interview, Empacher described Ian Ayre, Liverpool's chief executive as 'a complete amateur'. Though the club would later embrace a sporting director model, with Michael Edwards targeting players and leading transfer negotiations and FSG president Mike Gordon signing off the finances, the structure was different in 2013–14. Publicly at least, there was confusion as to who, exactly, was in charge of what.

In the summer of 2012, the club's newly hired press officer Jen Chang became the first person to coin the term 'transfer committee' when he spoke to a selection of Merseyside-based journalists about a new era at Liverpool under Rodgers, where recruitment would involve an appreciation of data and a process called 'moneyball', which FSG had taken from the Oakland Athletics baseball team under its general manager Billy Beane. He had little cash to spend compared to the rest of the league and came to believe that the tradition of following the opinion of a coach or a scout over transfers was outdated.

Beane instead built a team that was capable of challenging for the World Series by using 'sabermetrics', following data to reach decisions, which tended to mean he sourced baseball players for very specific purposes, rather than for their overall talent. As principal owner of FSG, John Henry wanted to bring Beane to Boston when he took over the Red Sox. When Beane turned him down, he used the same methods and this contributed towards the World Series finally landing at Fenway Park. Upon buying Liverpool six years later, Henry was confident he could transform the club following the same principles. He wasn't quite sure which individual in football – a sport where most of the leading figures were still suspicious of data's benefits – was capable of leading a club that commanded the interest of Liverpool.

Initially, that responsibility fell to Damien Comolli until his sacking. The youngest of FSG's leading figures, Gordon, quietly became more influential at Liverpool, albeit from his base in Brookline, Boston. It quickly became his view that Edwards, who had arrived as an unknown to anyone without a serious interest in data analytics, could eventually become Liverpool's Beane, yet it would take time for him to build up the experience and respect that was needed to justify a senior title. Though internally Edwards was having more of a say and began to work closely with the club's senior scouts, between 2012 and 2014, Liverpool reverted to the old way of a boardroom director leading contract negotiations.

It therefore felt like Ayre, who in early 2014 held the title of managing director, had the most significant role in the 'transfer committee', an awkward term Henry especially came to regret. Any deal would rely on his ability to make the finishing touches, even though it wasn't really him setting Liverpool's boundaries. While the manager would have a say on what he thought a player was worth, it was ultimately Gordon's decision as to whether Liverpool stretched themselves financially, pulled out of a deal or let a rival get in front of them.

A cynic would say Ayre, a Merseyside native with a squat figure and a big ego, became a useful fireguard for FSG against criticism. He could not resist the opportunity to take a front-facing role at a club he'd arrived at in 2007, when he was merely a commercial director, after a life in the Royal Navy, fighting in the Falklands War. Later, Ayre served in Hong Kong, then a British territory. His duty was to ensure that illegal immigrants didn't reach land. Upon leaving the forces, he returned to Hong Kong to work for a technology company. In the late 1990s, he became Huddersfield Town's managing director where, in Ayre's own words when he spoke to the *Sports Business Journal* in 2023, 'I was CEO, sporting director, commercial director. I sold sponsorships, sourced players, did the final piece of the construction for a new stadium, ticketing, merchandise. What a great way to learn the business.'

Ayre had returned to the Far East, where he was running a marketing firm from Malaysia, when an intermediary for Hicks and Gillett asked him to come home and work for the club he'd supported as a boy. As Liverpool lurched from crisis to crisis and numerous leading executives departed, along with players and a Champions League-winning manager, Ayre somehow not only survived but his profile and power base grew. FSG's buyout did not impede his ascent and, with the organisation based in Massachusetts keen to retain some local influence at board level, Ayre essentially started to run the club on a day-to-day basis.

Internally, Ayre was highly thought of because of his capacity to get commercial contracts signed. He was more comfortable in that world. A shirt sponsorship with Standard Chartered was controversial because of later alleged connections between the South East Asian bank and terrorism, but it was the biggest of its kind in Liverpool's history when it was brokered by Ayre in 2010.

Externally, however, it was often thought that Ayre did not have the gravitas to command the respect of sporting directors at other European clubs with far more experience of brokering transfers. Like one of his predecessors, Parry, Ayre was Liverpool's chief negotiator and, like Parry, he became the target of fan criticism following the collapse of several high-profile deals.

Certainly, Empacher seemed to attach blame to Ayre for Liverpool's hesitancy when trying reach an agreement with his client. He said, 'The guys in Liverpool never understood it. Football transfers are very complex.'

Basel were developing a reputation in Europe for their production of players and their ability to turn around a profit on sales. Under president Bernhard Heusler, a former lawyer, the club would record a turnover of 100 million Swiss francs for the first time in 2015. A year earlier, in the space of two months,

Heusler had brought Ayre northwards for Salah – if the figures suggested by Empacher are to be believed – from £5 million to £12 million. By the end of January, the pair had verbally agreed the trade, only for Heusler to insist that he wanted to sleep on it overnight before signing off. Fallows, who had travelled to Switzerland with Ayre, had returned home sensing something unusual was about to happen because neither Basel's sporting director Georg Heitz, nor his colleagues, were willing to close the deal at what would have been a normal point.

Heitz promised to call Ayre the next day. Except that call did not come. The next contact between Basel and Liverpool was instead by an email, which simply said, 'The player has decided to join Chelsea.' When Ayre tried to call Empacher, the line rang out.

Liverpool were now fourth in the table, three points behind third-placed Chelsea, who had a game in hand. A dispiriting 2–2 draw at home to Aston Villa had preceded the attempt to finalise the move for Salah. Rodgers was dealing with an injury crisis and though he'd done well to get Liverpool into a position nobody expected at the start of the season, there were concerns about his over-reliance on Luis Suárez. To critics, the result against Villa was evidence that Rodgers' team were short of what was needed to end the club's wait for a league title. Arsenal, at the top of the table, were now seven points ahead.

With a derby against Everton approaching, the pressure on Merseyside was rising. Salah was at Chelsea and Liverpool were scrambling around late in the transfer window to try and find solutions to some of Rodgers' problems. The manager seemed let down by some of the people he was working for and working with.

'The club did everything they felt they possibly could to get a deal but it wasn't to be,' he suggested, before he was asked how Liverpool had decided on their valuation of the winger. 'That's for the money guys to say that,' Rodgers replied. 'It's the construction of the whole deal, not only with the player and the agent but also Basel as a football club. It was deemed in this case that we couldn't do a deal and Chelsea could. So the boy has gone there.'

Clearly, Rodgers wanted to distance himself from any blame. Though he was a part of the 'transfer committee', Liverpool's failure to sign Salah was 'out of my control'.

Rodgers' explanation partly contradicted that offered by Ayre when he spoke at the launch of a two-year commercial deal with airline Garuda Indonesia, who would sponsor Liverpool's training kit and remain the club's official airline partner for £16 million annually; more than it took Chelsea to land Salah.

Ayre said, 'We haven't been held back from concluding a deal, it would be wrong to say that. The player decided he didn't want to come to Liverpool. We know what the value of the player is and how far we were prepared to go. That is something myself, Brendan and the others involved in the process discuss openly. We won't overpay. In every transfer window you win some and lose some.'

While Liverpool's fans tended to lurch between blaming Ayre for his supposed incompetence and FSG for being too thrifty, Liverpool's owners were furious with Rodgers for breaking ranks. Gordon lived just around the corner from Henry in Brookline, while Liverpool's chairman Tom Werner was based in Los Angeles. Gordon tended to communicate with them over significant issues by email because they were often in different parts of the world. Rodgers' outburst prompted him to fire off a message in which he suggested he was 'fighting the urge to call him and tear him a new asshole', bemoaning Rodgers' thinking. If FSG paid too much for a target, he would complain that too much of his budget was being used on a player he did not think was worth it. Meanwhile, if FSG paid too little and lost the deal as they had with Salah, he would complain that Liverpool and by extension, FSG were not big enough to compete.

Gordon told Henry and Werner that when negotiations with Basel reached an advanced stage, he decided to get Rodgers' view by calling from Boston, pulling him out of a meeting and plainly explaining his own frustrations with the manager's thinking. Rodgers told Gordon that he liked Salah but he would only pay a maximum of €16 million to sign him, certainly not €20 million.

Gordon was also taking advice from Edwards and the scouts below him. The FSG president felt that they had undervalued Salah relative to the market. Liverpool's final bid was a significant increase over the first, which was, according to Gordon, the maximum both Edwards and the scouts would have paid at the time. Remember, that fee according to Empacher was just £5 million.

Liverpool had already agreed terms with the player but it was Gordon's view that Chelsea came in extremely late, having sold Juan Mata for £37 million to Manchester United. Salah was just going to be another player for their bench but they met Basel's demands of an €18 million fee to conclude the transfer immediately.

Gordon was infuriated by Rodgers because privately he'd supported FSG's approach before, during and even after Salah signed for Chelsea. He suspected his words in the pre-match press conference ahead of Everton's visit to Anfield was the result of big game tension, as he'd said precisely the opposite to him on the phone only a day earlier.

Liverpool ultimately beat Everton, and resoundingly so — by a margin of four goals to nil. This would help relations between the owners and manager over the next few days, with Rodgers and Gordon agreeing that reinforcements were still needed.

The transfer window culminated with Ayre spending several days in Ukraine with Liverpool's medical staff where he met the £16 million buyout clause in the contract of Dnipro winger Yevhen Konoplyanka. When Dnipro's president Ihor Kolomoyskyi refused to sign the paperwork after the player had agreed his own terms, Liverpool were stuck again, with Rodgers admitting a few hours before the deadline that the deal was 'complicated'.

Oliver Cabrera, owner of Konoplyanka's representatives, OML Sports and Marketing, admitted he did not want to upset Kolomoyskyi. 'We have a very good relationship with the president and he doesn't want to sell the player. Yehven and his father respect that, so a move is very unlikely.'

Konoplyanka may have respected Kolomoyskyi, the billionaire co-owner of a Ukrainian state-run bank, but he was also very upset. 'I was crying,' he revealed eight years later. 'A delegation of serious people from Liverpool came to Dnipropetrovsk. We ate dinner. "Deal done," they said. They were to pay as much as Ihor Kolomoyskyi wanted.'

Ayre got Liverpool's Slovakian defender Martin Skrtel to send Konoplyanka a message. 'We are waiting for you,' it read. The club's captain Steven Gerrard also sent his blessing. Yet Kolomoyskyi wasn't budging. Konoplyanka said, 'I had to go to him. "Please, please, please, let me go, it will make my dream come true," I begged.' According to Konoplyanka, Liverpool offered £20 million, a figure that was above his release clause but Kolomoyskyi 'turned out to be unforgiving'.

For the second time in successive weeks, Liverpool had suffered a significant disappointment in the transfer market, raising more questions about the club's strategy and the personnel involved. Yet before they failed to get Salah and Konoplyanka, there was the summer of 2013 when the club were unable to land Henrikh Mkhitaryan, Diego Costa and Willian, who also went to Chelsea.

By the winter of 2014, Rodgers was saying that he would be 'disappointed' if players were not added to his squad. He only wanted signings who could improve his first team as he had enough 'support players'. Speaking after the collapse of the Konoplyanka deal, he was more diplomatic about the role of other people in the transfer process: 'It certainly hasn't been because of a lack of work by the football club. There are lots of people who have worked tirelessly to identify and find the right types of players. A lot of those players haven't been able to become available for us.'

Externally, Ayre would take much of the heat. He was now regarded as the director who travelled thousands of miles to trigger a release clause and agree terms with a player only to fly home without signing anyone. It might be tempting to think there was little he could do if Kolomoyskyi simply refused to sign the paperwork. Yet Ayre had infuriated him by his approach: Kolomoyskyi – a businessman who was used to getting his own way – believed that Liverpool had engaged Konoplyanka before informing him. Late in the window, the Dnipro president could have sold Konoplyanka and reinvested that money had Ayre given him more notice. Instead, he was left feeling like he was cornered. He knew the story about Liverpool's owner John W. Henry refusing to sell Luis Suárez to Arsenal several months earlier even though the London club triggered his release clause. Kolomoyskyi's response was to give Liverpool a taste of their own medicine.

Liverpool's pursuit of Salah had been undermined by procrastination. It had been FSG's determination to follow a holistic approach to key decisions, taking in opinion from a range of people. This included the lead data analyst, Edwards, the scouts, Fallows and Barry Hunter, as well as Ayre, Rodgers and Gordon. Later, the balance of figures in equivalent roles would lead to better decisions but in 2014 relationships were still in their infancy and the operation was not yet as slick as it became.

Gordon's email to Henry and Werner revealed that he believed Chelsea had simply reacted to the sale of one of their players, Juan Mata, by burning some of the proceeds on a player in Salah who he believed would only end up sitting on their bench. Gordon was right, yet if he thought Liverpool's hard yards on the player reflected well on them, the opposite was the case. According to Empacher, Liverpool had spent two months trying to get a deal done, with both Basel and the player rejecting their initial offers. Had he moved to Anfield in 2014, the fee should have been more than double what Liverpool had intended. Though they were willing to go up, up and up, it made them seem indecisive and weak. It said to Salah that Liverpool valued him somewhat less than he valued himself.

Though Liverpool liked to think of themselves as a global name, they had not won the Premier League in twenty-four years, and since 2009, the club had not even featured in the Champions League. Chelsea had won that competition in 2012, and two years before that they were crowned as Premier League champions for the third time in six seasons.

Basel were minnows by comparison, but Salah had got the better of Chelsea twice. These were memories that were fresh in his mind. If he could perform as well as he did against them as an opponent, surely he would be able to get a place in a team that had more talent than Liverpool?

José Mourinho was also a major factor. During the Portuguese coach's first spell at Stamford Bridge, when he delivered two Premier League titles, Rodgers was alongside him at the club, initially a head youth coach and then a reserve team manager. Though Rodgers was regarded as one of the most exciting young coaches in British football, his name simply did not carry the same weight as Mourinho. Before returning to Chelsea he had been at Real Madrid, where he managed Cristiano Ronaldo – one of the European players that made Salah realise what he had to do with his body.

Some of the leading figures at Liverpool would come to believe that Chelsea signed Salah simply to stop an emerging title rival in Liverpool from getting him, and there might be some truth in that, given Salah's subsequent lack of impact in London. Yet there was no guarantee he would have started lots of games at Liverpool straight away. Suarez was on course to complete an extraordinary season, where he'd finish with thirty-one goals, Daniel Sturridge would score twenty-four times and Raheem Sterling, still a teenager, registered double figures for the first time.

Liverpool knew Suarez was leaving at the end of the season, after agreeing with the player to sell him the previous summer. His departure would have created space for Salah, but one of the major pulls of Liverpool was his presence. It was unlikely Salah was ever going to be reassured by the prospect of that particular space in the team because it meant the impending sale of a star player, who ultimately went to Barcelona for a British record fee of nearly £65 million.

As Liverpool would later find out when Jürgen Klopp was in charge, players would often choose managers over clubs. It was a lot easier recruiting when someone as famous as Klopp was making the calls. In 2014, Mourinho was regarded as one of the most charismatic coaches in world football.

He started Chelsea's charm offensive by sending Salah a text message, to which he did not receive a reply. When Salah spoke about the one-way exchange on Egyptian television in 2015, he explained that he had not paid his phone bill, and this meant he could not contact him back. Eventually, on WhatsApp, Salah asked Mourinho to call him. 'It had a huge effect on me,' Salah admitted. 'He told me I was a player he needed, and a player that will have an important role. He also told me that Chelsea's style of play will suit me, and . . . that's enough.'

According to Mourinho, it was Salah's view that he had helped nurture attacking players like Mesut Özil, Arjen Robben and Oscar in the past, and these, added Mourinho, were players with similar talents to Salah. 'I tried to help them,' Mourinho said, 'and he [Salah] trusts me to help him.'

In February 2014, Mourinho spoke enthusiastically about his

new signing: 'I like the way Salah has that adaptability to play right, left or behind the striker,' he said. 'He's fast in the space, fast with the ball, creative, enthusiastic and left-footed. When we analysed him, he looked the kind of humble personality on the pitch, ready to work for the team and adapt to a new life.'

Mourinho would later be cited as the manager who did not give Salah a chance, allowing another club to benefit from his talents, but he was adamant that he drove Chelsea's interest in signing him in the first place. 'People try to identify me as the coach that sold Salah,' Mourinho said in 2019, 'but I am the coach that bought Salah. I played against Basel in the Champions League. Salah was a kid at Basel. When I play against a certain team I analyse a team and players for quite a long time. And I fell in love with that kid. I bought the kid. I pushed the club to buy him and, at the time, we already had fantastic attacking players – [Eden] Hazard, Willian, we had top talent there. But I told them to buy that kid.'

The need to sign another attacking player was created, as Gordon at Liverpool had thought, by the unexpected decision to sell Juan Mata to Manchester United. Mourinho was not satisfied by his attacking options. Fernando Torres, who arrived from Liverpool for a British record fee of £50 million, was still struggling to settle three years after his transfer to London, while the career of the legendary Samuel Eto'o, who Mourinho had managed at Inter Milan, was coming to an end. This left Demba Ba, who was nearly twenty-nine and did not have the sort of profile that fitted a player who stuck around at Stamford Bridge for long.

Like Liverpool, Mourinho wanted to sign Diego Costa from Atlético Madrid but that deal was on ice until the following summer. Meanwhile, Chelsea were under pressure to comply with new financial fair play (FFP) regulations, instigated by UEFA. With Abramovich's new money and enjoying billions of pounds' worth of investment, Chelsea had objected to FFP, believing it would merely preserve the status of the clubs already at the top of English football. Once the new rules came into force, however, the club adopted the policy of selling a player if they bought one and vice versa.

This represented a cultural shift. Under Abramovich, the club would buy big and didn't need to sell for similar fees. This meant players often left on the cheap or wound down their time at Stamford Bridge before leaving at the end of their contracts. Mostly, Chelsea did well in the transfer market because their finances allowed them to sign whoever they wanted.

When Mourinho felt that Mata didn't quite fit into the structure of his team, United offered big money, allowing Chelsea to make a profit. Mata was a two-time player of the year and at twenty-five, he was still at his peak. In the same month, Mourinho had already allowed Kevin de Bruyne to join Wolfsburg. The Belgian would emerge as a legendary figure in Manchester City's midfield under Pep Guardiola, who in 2024 described him in the midst of the club's most successful era as one of the club's greatest players because of his 'numbers, presence, consistency'.

De Bruyne's departure from Chelsea following just two league starts in the 2013–14 season was a reminder that Mourinho tended to lean on players with more experience. The average age of the Inter Milan team that he coached to the Champions League title in 2010, for example, was just under thirty. If he was a developer of talent, it tended to be players who were in the middle of their careers rather than those near the start – and Salah was just twenty-one.

While the money for a twenty-two-year-old De Bruyne was reinvested in a taller, more physical midfielder in twenty-five-year-old Nemanja Matic, Chelsea directors travelled to Switzerland to try and get Salah, as Mata's sale went through.

'It was a surprise for us that Juan was leaving, so we had to work fast,' Mourinho admitted. 'When we decided to go for Salah we started from zero. There'd been no contacts with the club or player. We knew absolutely nothing. We didn't even know who his agent was. The first step was an agreement with Basel. That is done, no more discussion. Everything is signed, subject to the medical. And now we know the player wants to join us.

'I know he has in his mind to become a great player, not just in top European football, but to be a top player for Egypt and in Africa, a player who will win individual awards at this level,' Mourinho added. 'This is a different level to what he has seen so far, but he has some experience in Europe so he's not a naive boy arriving in the jungle. With the talented players we have, we can all move forward together. And, of course, he won't be able to score against Chelsea any more, which is a good thing.'

Mourinho wanted to build a team that was more adventurous than those he'd previously created, albeit 'without losing the factors that normally bring our teams to a special level – solidarity, commitment, organisation'.

Despite acknowledging Salah needed a three-month settling-in period, he saw enough in early sessions at Cobham, Chelsea's training ground, to give him his debut as a late substitute during a 3–0 win over Newcastle United, even though it had been two months since his last appearance for Basel. Salah's contribution to the victory was not the talking point. Instead, Hazard's hat-trick hoisted Chelsea to the top of the league table, above Arsenal – who were ripped apart by Liverpool at Anfield on the same day, with a 5–1 scoreline owing much to the electrifying performances of Suárez, Sturridge and Sterling.

The result for Liverpool was the first of eleven victories on the bounce, a run which earned a whopping thirty-three points, putting them in contention for the title. The prospect of that happening would only recede two and a half months later, when Mourinho fielded an apparently understrength team at Anfield that included Salah. It would transpire to be one of the most infamous afternoons in Liverpool's recent history.

Salah finished the season at Chelsea reasonably well. His first goal for the club was Chelsea's sixth against Arsenal, wrecking Arsene Wenger's thousandth game in charge. A fortnight later, Salah scored again, this time in a 3–0 victory over Stoke City.

Though Chelsea had been in the running to win the Premier League, injuries took their toll on their results. Yet when the team went to Anfield in April, with Liverpool at full steam, and now favourites to win the title, Chelsea knew that a victory for them would keep their thin hopes alive.

Mourinho, a self-announced serial winner, did his best to underplay Chelsea's chances. The game fell in between the first and second legs of a Champions League semi-final against the soon to be crowned La Liga champions, Atlético Madrid. Mourinho claimed to be furious that the Premier League and broadcasters Sky would not move the game against Liverpool to an earlier kick-off slot to accommodate Chelsea's needs.

Such rescheduling had never happened before, however, and

broadly it was felt that Mourinho, a master of misdirection, was simply creating a distraction from what was going to be Liverpool's biggest domestic fixture since they last won the league twenty-four years earlier.

Mourinho, whose needle with Liverpool went back a decade to when he was overlooked for the manager's job at Anfield, had come to be thought of as an enemy by Liverpool supporters. He had overseen the initial rise of Chelsea into a super club, threatening Liverpool's position at the top table of English and European football.

Mourinho relished the opportunity to send Liverpool's title surge onto the skids. The game against his team was framed as the fixture where Liverpool could more or less confirm their status as champions. After Chelsea, they had just two winnable games left: at Crystal Palace, then at home to Newcastle.

Mourinho felt as though Chelsea's role was to lie down as this procession passed over them. In his mind, Liverpool were the 'neutrals' favourite', a theory which may have had some truth, given the media focus on the club's quest to win its first title in so long. It didn't totally stack up, however, given the amount of hostility aimed at Liverpool fans throughout a season where the team promised to end a long period of unwanted history.

Yet the impression suited Mourinho. Normally he would dress smartly for matches, but at Anfield he turned up in a track-suit and gilet. His unshaven appearance made it seem as though he'd slept the previous night in the boot of a car. It was all a deliberate attempt to downplay the significance of the game, showing his players they should not respect the occasion because of what it meant for their opponents.

Mourinho would later claim that, as he approached Anfield,

he saw street vendors selling T-shirts with the words 'Liverpool Champions'. At Chelsea, he concluded, any such merchandising or marketing would be 'kept in a box'.

Though this may have increased his determination to spoil the party, most of the planning was already done. In a team meeting at the Malmaison hotel overlooking the River Mersey, he had told the Chelsea players they were not going to be pushovers. He had already decided by then to field a weakened team in preparation for Atlético, following a goalless draw in the first leg; a team that did not include captain John Terry, its world-class goalkeeper Petr Cech or its star, Hazard.

This afforded an opportunity for Salah, who replaced Hazard. Meanwhile, Mark Schwarzer, aged forty-one, came in for Cech, and twenty-year-old Tomas Kalas, who'd never started a senior game, replaced Terry. In an interview a fortnight earlier, Kalas had joked that he was merely 'a player for training sessions'.

Mourinho fired Chelsea's players up by suggesting they were being cast as 'clowns'. He wanted to change the entire mood of the day by frustrating a Liverpool team that had developed a reputation for its fast starts that blew opponents away. Schwarzer later told the *Independent* that, from his very first goal kick, it was Mourinho's instruction to the team's right back Branislav Ivanovic to amble over to the touchline, as far away from Schwarzer as possible, and appear to want to receive the ball from the goalkeeper, only to signal to him to instead kick it long. Mourinho wanted to waste time and subdue a hostile Anfield crowd. Schwarzer even suggested Mourinho had demanded at least two of his players return to the dressing room at half-time on bookings because of time wasting.

That did not happen but Mourinho was happy because the

pressure got to Liverpool, who fell behind after captain Steven Gerrard lost his footing near the halfway line, allowing Demba Ba to run away and score in front of the Kop. Earlier that month, following what felt like a key 3–2 victory over City at Anfield, Gerrard's rallying call on the pitch in front of the television cameras to his teammates had been, 'This does not slip.'

Now, the moment was like watching a car crash in slow motion and neither Liverpool nor Gerrard were able to recover. As Liverpool pushed in hope rather than conviction for an equaliser, gaps were left in defence. Late into the second half, Willian – another player Liverpool had tried to sign only for him to choose Chelsea instead – added a second goal on the counterattack to blow the title race open.

For Liverpool, the day could only have been worse had Salah's performance influenced the result, given how close the club had come to signing him only a few months earlier. Yet he was substituted for Willian on the hour mark, having barely affected a game defined by Chelsea's cynical defensive strategy.

While Liverpool would miss out to City in their quest for the Premier League and ultimately have to wait another six years before they could rewrite history (thanks in no small part to the influence of a certain Egyptian winger), Salah was cup-tied for the Atlético game at Stamford Bridge, which the Spanish side ended up winning 3–1.

Chelsea finished the season without a trophy and between them, Ba, Torres and Eto'o had scored just nineteen Premier League goals. Mourinho's response was to forensically close out a squad, getting exactly what he wanted in the transfer market. That involved spending nearly £85 million on new players – three of those being strikers. Atlético's Brazilian-born Spanish international Diego Costa was the most expensive, while the returning Didier Drogba was the cheapest because he arrived from Galatasaray on a free transfer.

Neither Costa, nor the Ivorian – who had been the focal point of Mourinho's attack during his first spell managing the club – necessarily threatened Salah's position in the team. For Salah, however, it might have felt different when Mourinho signed Loïc Rémy from Queens Park Rangers a few hours before the transfer window shut in August. Like Salah, the Frenchman was rapid and could play in any of the forward positions. Previously, Rémy had been close to signing for Liverpool, only on this occasion it had been Liverpool's decision to pull out of the deal. Rémy had flown to Boston during the club's pre-season tour, only to fail a medical.

Mourinho described Rémy as 'one of the players we had in our objectives, one of the players we had ready to try and get in case a space opened'. That happened when Torres secured a loan move to AC Milan. It meant that Mourinho now had three new options in attack, and publicly he was speaking enthusiastically about each of them.

'So now we have a guy like Didier, a kind of striker for whom the box is his natural habitat, the best of the three in the air,' he said. 'Diego is a player we were chasing for about a year, waiting to get him, and we think he's a player very adapted to the style of play we want to implement in the team. Rémy is very fast, he attacks spaces, he can play even from the sides like he does for France, coming in from the right or, with Alan Pardew at Newcastle, from the left.'

In fairness, Mourinho was not asked about what any of these deals meant for Salah, but he did not choose to mention him in any context either. His last words about the Egyptian came at the end of the previous campaign: 'Salah is a kid who is coming through and, next season for sure, he'll be better,' said Mourinho in early May 2014. 'His English is not bad, but I did not hear his voice for a couple of months. He was shy in training, shy in our social life. In the last months he speaks, communicates, laughs, participates in the jokes, communicates with me. It was as if he was afraid of me before.'

Salah married his wife Magi and their daughter Makka was born in London in the months after he joined Chelsea. Not only was he focused on his life at home, he was also trying to assimilate into a dressing room dominated by huge personalities; it was not easy for young players to find their place. This was illustrated in 2023, when John Terry, the club's captain for a decade by 2014, told a story about the early stages of André Villas-Boas's reign. The Portuguese manager had been a part of Mourinho's staff during his first spell in charge and returned to Stamford Bridge in 2011 fresh from leading Porto to Europa League success.

Villas-Boas brought comparisons with his fellow countryman Mourinho but lasted less than a year at Chelsea. The problems started, according to Terry, during the club's pre-season tour to the Far East. It was a thirteen-hour flight to Hong Kong and Villas-Boas decided it was a good idea to break up any dressing-room hierarchy by allowing the club's young players to fly first-class, while the senior ones sat in economy. It was Terry's view, however, that the established first-team players deserved the privilege as they had 'built the club' and, after challenging Villas-Boas as the plane waited on the tarmac, he got his own way. On day one, the new manager had attempted to make a statement, 'failing instantly'. Managers would come and go regularly at Chelsea under Abramovich, while the leaders in the dressing room remained and were becoming increasingly difficult to shift.

Salah, a twenty-one-year-old Egyptian village boy, had never experienced the sort of environment that existed at Chelsea, with French and Brazilian cliques, filled with Champions League winners and where considerable egos tended to get what they wanted if they demanded it, even if it sometimes went against the coach's wishes. Such egos would survive, even at the expense of someone as formidable as Mourinho, who described Salah in 2018 as 'a young kid' who was not ready for Chelsea on every conceivable level. 'Physically he was not ready. Mentally he was not ready. Socially and culturally he was lost and everything was tough for him.'

Mourinho later said Salah was 'just a lost kid in London, a lost kid in a new world', but that ignored the fact he had made some friends, one of them being the Brazilian defender David Luiz. The image Mourinho created, however, portrayed Salah as fragile and distanced the manager from any difficulties he experienced at Chelsea, especially in a second season where Mourinho only selected him in the matchday squad nine times across twenty-three league fixtures. This amounted to just three substitute appearances and half an hour of playing time.

On one of the rare occasions Salah did play during that period, he was targeted for open criticism following a 2–1 victory at Shrewsbury Town in the League Cup. 'I expect people that are not playing a lot to raise the level, to create me problems,' Mourinho reflected, before confirming who exactly he was referring to. Salah barely played for Chelsea again. Eddie

Newton, Chelsea's former midfielder, who was then employed as Chelsea's loan manager, suggested the struggles of both Salah and Kevin De Bruyne before him were not about ability. Instead, 'it was about a personality clash' with Mourinho. 'I think they were more than good enough, but it was the manager who didn't see eye to eye with them, so it wasn't going to work,' Newton said in 2021.

Mourinho was an abrasive character and Salah was quiet, still developing his language skills. To some of his Chelsea team-mates, he did not seem to have the social awareness to fight his corner. Eight years later, when Salah reflected on the period, he admitted, 'my personality was very different' during his spell at Chelsea. As he ran riot after finally joining Liverpool in 2017, manager Jürgen Klopp tended to agree with Mourinho's theory. 'He was a kid when he came to Chelsea and in that time they were really successful. It was quite difficult to come through,' he said. 'A little bit less muscle, a little bit less physical and you can't fly through the Premier League – not like he's flying now – but [sent flying] with one body check. He's a man now. He was a kid at Chelsea, now he's a man.'

Mourinho would win the Premier League in his second season, when goals from Rémy and Costa especially were pivotal at the end of the campaign. Chelsea finished eight points above reigning champions City and twenty-five above Liverpool, who failed to qualify for the Champions League. When asked about why Salah and De Bruyne had not flourished under his guidance, Mourinho suggested the players in front of them were 'not easy to replace'. Aside from Costa, Rémy and Drogba, Salah was also competing with Hazard, Oscar and Willian, as well as World Cup winners André Schürrle and Cesc Fàbregas, who was pushed into a number 10 role by Mourinho having arrived from Barcelona in the summer of 2014.

'It's hard for these guys to come from clubs where they are the first faces in the team and have to fight for a position in our side,' Mourinho reasoned. 'If you have a player knocking on your door and crying every day because he wants to leave, you have to make a decision.'

For Mourinho, there was also an economic reality at play. Decisions at Chelsea were increasingly being made more quickly because the club did not want to lose value on talented players. 'If he had stayed here, not happy and not motivated, and we'd sold him after a year, we'd have got 50 per cent of what we sold him for,' Mourinho reasoned when talking about De Bruyne. 'So, at that moment, it was very good business. He had hit a wall here, a block. He was not ready to compete. He was an upset kid, training very badly. He needed motivation to train well by playing every game. But if you think these are my mistakes, then it's also my "mistake" that Eden Hazard is now worth more than £100 million. If I didn't play Hazard and instead played De Bruyne or Schürrle, Salah or Cuadrado [who replaced Salah at Chelsea in 2015], for sure they would still be playing for Chelsea. But Hazard wouldn't . . .'

Hazard was one of the Chelsea teammates who suggested that Salah did not get a chance at Chelsea, 'maybe because of the manager, because of the players, I don't know'. Yet the hypnotically skilled Belgian viewed him as a 'top player for sure', someone who 'in training, did everything'. Hazard's view was supported by Ivanovic, the hulking Serbian defender, who had struggled to contain Salah when he was playing for Basel. 'With the ball he is very quick, very smart with his movement, and the kind of player we need in the squad,' he said. 'He reminds me of Robben, the way he plays off the right wing but always looking to go inside, to shoot left-footed. He is a great player. He is young and has time.'

Filipe Luís, the Brazilian left back that Mourinho signed from Atlético in the summer of 2014, came up against Salah in training sessions and described him as being 'like Messi'. His teammates at Chelsea saw his performances on a matchday somewhat differently. Mourinho demanded structure and the only way he was going to get that was through organisation and discipline. Salah was dedicated but he sometimes played off the cuff, following his instincts whenever he saw space. In an effort to impress Mourinho, Chelsea's players wondered whether he curbed those instincts, a decision that led to him becoming risk-averse.

Mourinho would conclude Salah was 'just a kid with a huge desire to play every week, every minute, and we couldn't give him that'. A loan deal with Fiorentina, agreed in January 2015, was evidence that Mourinho was, to some degree, keen at some point on bringing him back to Chelsea, though that would never happen. After returning to London briefly following a successful time in Florence, Salah asked not to be included in Chelsea's pre-season tour of the USA. In Italy, he'd had a taste of first-team football in a top European league. And he wanted more.

Chapter 6

Pyramid schemes

Chelsea was not a wasted experience for Mohamed Salah, not least because his exit from the club would bring engagement for the first time with the person who would help design not just the rest of his career but his whole life.

Ramy Abbas Issa is a Colombian-born, Dubai-based lawyer with a Lebanese father. In 2015, he was approaching his thirty-first birthday, having graduated from the University of Leicester a decade earlier with average marks. It had not been the classic English education he expected. Leicester was multi-ethnic and, despite his own stewed cultural background, he struggled to find his own place.

On campus, Abbas was remembered as a quiet, studious, but occasionally prickly character: someone who did not impose his views in a conversation without an invitation, but if the opportunity was there, he would tell you exactly what he thought, even if it was unpopular. Abbas seemed to enjoy watching the reactions of others. Law, ultimately, was not a matter of opinion but it was open to interpretation and Abbas was noted for his ability to spot gaps in arguments, particularly if they were small.

He did not possess the casual left-wing spirit of some of the other students. Having grown up in Colombia at the height of the country's drugs war, he had seen a succession of governments fail to deal with kingpins like Pablo Escobar. The most unsuccessful of them, according to Abbas in his conversations with other students, were the leftists, under whom the violence in Colombia got worse.

It was not a secure time for anyone with a reasonable amount of money in Colombia, especially in the city of Cali where the Abbas family lived and one of Escobar's rival cartels operated. By Colombian standards, the family was upper-middle class. They ran two independent shoe shops. They were not millionaires but they were comfortable, living in a gated house, with cars.

Abbas would develop a paranoia about his safety because of the drugs war. As a young boy, he was always taught not to talk to strangers. There were no mobile phones and if a family member turned up somewhere late, concerns were raised. He could see his parents panicking. There was a risk of kidnapping. This meant he was only ever permitted to play inside the gates of his home.

Despite the security, a family property was raided by gunmen who pinned his mother to the floor and pressed a revolver against her head, telling her she only had sixty seconds to give them the code to a safe owned by Abbas's grandmother. She did not know the combination but, fortunately, the gunmen gave up.

These experiences informed Abbas politically from an early age. Even if he was liberal when it came to LGBTQ+ issues and women's rights, he was a self-confessed right-winger in most senses. Though he saw the flaws of the economic and cultural West, he identified more with the region than other parts of the world.

All of this meant his relationship with Colombia was complicated. He rarely cried but he could not help himself when Colombia were knocked out of the 2018 World Cup in Russia on penalties by England. The time he cried before that followed their elimination from the 2014 World Cup in Brazil. His passion for the national team was heightened because he lived so far away. His first language was Spanish, he got goose bumps when hearing Colombian music, and he felt very connected to the country. Yet he had no plans to return to Colombia to live because he worried for his safety. Safety was something he valued above anything else, and it explained why he continued to live in Dubai. Abbas might not be able to walk down the street holding hands with his wife, but he can ignore some of its prohibitive laws because it is one of the safest cities in the world.

When he was six, he moved with his family to the UAE, initially settling in Abu Dhabi when the city was a relatively modest fishing port. This was just before the 1990 World Cup in Italy, where Colombia made it through the group stages and into the first knockout round, losing to Cameroon after the country's eccentric goalkeeper René Higuita tried to dribble past the veteran striker Roger Milla, only to get dispossessed, allowing Milla to score. Colombia went out but Abbas was hooked, fascinated by the perm of star midfielder Carlos Valderrama. When Valderrama got injured during the tournament, Abbas, sitting in front of the television thousands of miles away, started to cry about his country for the first time in his life. Colombia would qualify for the next two World Cups, in 1994 (when they were eliminated at the group stages despite being one of the favourites), and 1998 (out at the group stages again, losing to England), but they missed out on 2002 altogether – this being the year Abbas started to get closer to the game he was now fascinated with.

Before Sheikh Mansour bought Manchester City in 2008 and changed the face of football by ploughing billions of pounds into an underachieving club, he had invested in Al Jazira, a team based in Abu Dhabi. One of its earliest foreign signings was the Colombian Elson Becerra, a forward from America de Cali, who in 2001 helped his country, as host, to win the Copa América for the first time in its history. For many Colombians, it felt like the country had finally achieved something positive on the international stage and Becerra was one of its heroes. For him to be moving to the United Arab Emirates was a big deal, especially for an eighteen-year-old Abbas. So he went to the training ground, hoping to meet him. His studies in Leicester did not stop him from getting involved in the player's affairs. Initially, Abbas worked as his translator, and this sometimes involved travelling back from England. Steadily, Becerra began to trust Abbas, whose understanding of contract law improved and he was asked to work as a bridge between the player and the directors of the clubs he represented.

In 2003, Becerra had been the closest player on the pitch to Cameroonian midfielder Marc-Vivien Foé when he dropped dead during a game at the Confederations Cup in France. Becerra could not save his life and his own world was as fragile. Three years later, Becerra was due to fly back to the UAE following his Christmas break in Colombia when a gunman shot him and a friend four times on the dancefloor of a Cartagena nightclub, supposedly in response to a fight that had happened a few nights earlier. His murder has never been solved.

Abbas's contact with Becerra had provided a way into football and in 2005, aged twenty, he registered as a football agent in Colombia. When he found out from another agent working in the Middle East that Al-Ittihad, the Jeddah-based Saudi Arabian club, was looking to sign a centre forward, he was able to get involved in a deal. He contacted the president of the club himself, but only after his father had bought him a SIM card on his phone that allowed him to make international calls, as it was impossible on landlines from the UAE. The experience taught him that being bold could result in lucrative business because the player moved for millions of dollars without him ever meeting anyone from Saudi Arabia face to face.

Though Abbas was able to put deals together, he enjoyed it less than the legal work, where he specialised in litigation. Fortunately for him, the UAE was just starting to ramp up its investment in football and he was ideally placed, working mainly with Al Jazira to bring several high-profile signings to the club, most notably the Brazilian international forward Ricardo Oliveira from the Spanish side, Real Betis.

The business made him a rich young man. Before he started representing Salah, he estimates he was wealthier than the footballer. Abbas was already living in a luxurious apartment, having bought two Maseratis and an Aston Martin. Together, however, their economic possibilities would become even greater, and Abbas would be able to pay a driver to steer him around the hot streets of Dubai.

Abbas was waiting with Juan Cuadrado in the lobby of the Chelsea Harbour Hotel for a taxi to take them to dinner when Salah, sitting alone, suddenly signalled him over in January 2015.

The pair had met for the first time earlier that day. Salah had not known who Abbas was, but Abbas was familiar with Salah because he'd seen him play for Basel a few years earlier, albeit by accident. As a Colombian, Abbas was always interested in South American footballers, and Basel had a few of them. He was surprised to see an Arab in the team and was immediately drawn to Salah's speed. It was his conclusion that Salah had a Latin style about him because of his daring: he would always go for goal.

Cuadrado, a Colombian, had been that type of player. Abbas had travelled to London to primarily work on his image rights in the deal that would take him from Fiorentina to Chelsea. This opportunity had come about because of Abbas's working relationship with Breno Tannuri, a Brazilian lawyer based in São Paulo. Tannuri's client was Cuadrado's agent, and he had enlisted Abbas's help to check over the documents in a contract worth £26.8 million.

Abbas had started working with Tannuri several years earlier. In the UAE, Abbas had been asked by Al Jazira to litigate on behalf of the club against Alejandro Sabella, an Argentine who backed out of a contract before taking a coaching role with his country instead. It was suggested to Abbas that he would be wise to bring in someone with more experience, so he called Tannuri, who he'd met when Al Jazira started signing Brazilian footballers.

When Cuadrado's transfer was finalised, Tannuri was photographed with the player wearing a finely cut suit, while an unshaven Abbas was casually dressed in blue jeans. It would prove to be a busy day for the pair because Tannuri was invited to other meetings relating to the movement of footballers.

One of them was instigated by Cristina Marice, who had recently started representing Salah when he tried to leave

Chelsea, having taken on the responsibility from SPOCS. Abbas was told that Salah was being sued on different fronts. Marice and Tannuri discussed the best course of action while Salah became frustrated because everyone in the room was communicating in English. Abbas translated for him – despite his legal background, he wasn't to act as his representative, but simply helped him with the language.

Gradually, Salah started to relax in the company of his new acquaintance and by the end of the day, it seemed as though he was getting the exit he wanted from Chelsea by replacing Cuadrado at Fiorentina, who did not have any representatives in London. Instead, everything was done by email.

After Abbas got showered, however, he would find Salah in the lobby of the hotel with concern etched across his face. In beckoning Abbas over, he said, 'Can I show you something?' In his possession was the contract from Fiorentina, which he thought was heavily weighted in favour of the club. It seemed as though they had an option to exercise a five-year deal on him if he performed well. This was a problem for Salah because he wanted to keep his options open: if he did well in Florence, a better opportunity might come along.

What did Abbas think? The lawyer was in a rush because the taxi was arriving shortly and Cuadrado was looking over at him in confusion. Yet he could see that Salah was desperate for help. While standing up, Abbas quickly drafted a paragraph on his Blackberry phone, a new loan contract lasting only six months, superseding anything else Salah had signed. Abbas realised it would shatter his legal reputation in football had he got anything wrong working at such speed, but he was confident the contract was watertight.

★   ★   ★

If anyone had got Salah out of Chelsea, it had been Marice when she convinced Mourinho shortly after the Portuguese manager had insisted publicly, 'He can't leave.'

Mourinho had suggested that even if Salah left on loan, the club would have to spend money to bring someone else in. That player ended up being Cuadrado but, in the meantime, Marice had stressed to Mourinho that Salah was so desperate to get out, he would take a significant pay cut to go.

Marice had studied at the University of Bologna before moving to Vienna in Austria, where she worked for her country's chamber of commerce. Her specialism was resolving disputes and this helped when she met Mourinho on Salah's behalf, five years after she registered both as a player agent with FIFA and a match agent with UEFA.

Her second role involved attending fixtures, ensuring the event ran smoothly. It also brought her into closer contact with players, managers and their representatives. Sometimes she was pitch-side, while the job brought tunnel access. In the meantime, she'd also set up her own marketing agency, which was registered in the tax-free haven of Monaco.

She would meet Salah for the first time in Switzerland, where he was playing Champions League football with Basel. Before the start of that relationship, she had got to know Ulisse Savini, the agent of Xherdan Shaqiri, the Kosovan-born winger who Salah had essentially replaced in the Basel team six years before they became teammates at Liverpool.

Shaqiri would initially join Bayern Munich but only after Savini had discussed the possibility of moving the winger to Italy. In 2011, Savini spoke publicly about Roma's interest, having held conversations with the club's sporting director, Walter Sabatini.

Savini took care of several African footballers at Serie A clubs. One of them was Keita Balde, a winger born in Spain who represented Senegal and whose performances for Lazio had supposedly encouraged interest from Liverpool, according to Savini in 2014.

Having spent time in Basel watching Shaqiri, Savini also knew all about Salah, and he would get to know more about his frustrations at Chelsea through Marice. She promised to get him out of the club before enlisting the help of the intermediary she'd met while studying in Bologna.

According to Savini, Roma, Fiorentina and Inter Milan were interested in taking Salah from Chelsea, and this was relayed to the player. He became excited, especially about Roma, who pushed the hardest, but when the club moved instead to sign the Ivorian striker Seydou Doumbia from CSKA Moscow, after a delay of three weeks, he began to lose faith.

Marice and Savini had to act quickly. The pair knew that Fiorentina were negotiating to sell Cuadrado to Chelsea and this knowledge allowed them to encourage Fiorentina. On the same day Marice was photographed by Tuscan paparazzi wearing dark sunglasses at Peretola airport on the outskirts of Florence, Abbas turned to Instagram: 'I consider the last three days to be the most important of my career.'

The responses to this would suggest he was writing about Cuadrado and the scale of a deal involving one of the most exciting footballers to come out of the country he was born in.

Yet looking back, especially knowing what happened next, it would be understandable if Marice or Savini believed Abbas was instead referring to the start of his relationship with Salah.

★　　★　　★

Salah's exit from Stamford Bridge was made more complicated because of wider uncertainty about who really represented him. This became a public issue just a few weeks before he joined Fiorentina, initially on loan.

He would clarify his position on social media towards the end of January 2015: 'Please don't take any news from my ex-agent Oliver Kronenberg,' Salah wrote emphatically. 'He no longer represents me, and for all negotiations, there are people I have appointed who are taking care of them.'

This statement came after Kronenberg, a Swiss lawyer who had headed FIFA's legal department after a career mainly working with pharmaceutical companies, suggested he was likely to leave Chelsea. 'I spoke to Roma, but the cost of the operation is very high,' Kronenberg told *La Gazzetta dello Sport*. 'He is on big wages at the moment and would like to maintain them. We'll wait and see what happens.'

Kronenberg was a partner at SPOCS. He had helped broker Salah's transfer to England from Basel, working with Sascha Empacher, the German who had previously been employed as a football journalist and a television host. SPOCS believed it retained a binding agreement to negotiate Salah's move until the end of the transfer window in the winter of 2015. The organisation threatened to appeal to the English Football Association to air its grievance, suggesting three other agents were illegally operating on Salah's behalf to engineer the move to Italy. The famous Israeli super-intermediary, Pini Zahavi, would deny any involvement, along with Juan Figer, a Uruguayan who was familiar with Breno Tannuri, the Brazilian lawyer Marice had met in London.

Kronenberg made the headlines but in truth, Salah's

association with SPOCS had more to do with Empacher, who discovered the player after being invited to Egypt in 2007 to watch the country's international friendly with Argentina in Cairo. He had been a guest of two local students who had started their own agency by recruiting younger players. Yahia Ali and Ibrahim Azab had very different backgrounds to most agents: Ali was a qualified engineer and Azab was an accountant. Empacher's presence in Cairo became a focus of national discussion. He would appear on Egyptian television because it was so rare to see a European paying an interest in the country's footballers. 'At the time nobody was going to Egypt,' Empacher said when he spoke to the journalist Ed Aarons for his book *Made in Africa*. 'It's a complicated market with a different mentality that is difficult for western European clubs to handle.'

Empacher came to an agreement with Ali and Azab, who joined the SPOCS umbrella, which by 2024 had bureaus in nearly every continent. Empacher insisted the alignment with Ali and Azab created a pathway for Egyptian footballers that did not exist before, because inside a year, he was heavily involved in the deal that took Amr Zaki from Zamalek to Wigan Athletic. Zaki announced himself as a centre forward of Premier League standing by scoring with a scissor-kick in front of the Kop at Anfield, a strike that briefly took him top of the competition's goalscoring charts in October 2008.

Zaki's rise to prominence was rapid and so was his fall. He would leave Wigan with manager Steve Bruce calling him, 'the most unprofessional player I have ever worked with', after he returned to the north-west of England several days late following an international fixture with Egypt. Empacher noted that this claim did not help the perception of Egyptians.

In 2011, Empacher took a call from Azab about a winger he'd seen come off the bench for El Mokawloon, one of Cairo's less-supported clubs. Empacher spent time with Salah, getting to know his family. He could see his determination to do well. Other Egyptian players dreamed of representing Zamalek or Al Ahly but Salah was fascinated by the thought of a career in Europe. Empacher arranged for him to go on trial at clubs in Germany and Belgium but no one wanted to take the risk. Basel felt differently.

Ali would fly to Switzerland every couple of weeks, while Empacher travelled from Germany to try and help Salah settle in. Though he later hit out at Kronenberg as he tried to get out of Chelsea, Salah's falling-out with SPOCS began with a dispute with Ali over money, though neither party has ever given precise details.

When Empacher spoke to Aarons for his book, he suggested that during his attempt to leave Chelsea, Salah was 'badly influenced by other people, and didn't understand the way of professional football'. He was also supportive of Ali. 'What I can say is that without me, Yahia or Ibrahim, there would be no Mohamed Salah.'

Marice and Savini had brokered the deal with Fiorentina for a modest initial fee of £550,000. It was widely reported at the time in England that the club had agreed to pay another £11 million to make the move permanent the following summer, though in Italy it was believed he could remain at the Serie A club for as little as £1 million, albeit in another loan deal.

Fiorentina certainly wanted to keep him in Florence, where he scored on his debut against Sassuolo before ending the campaign with six goals in sixteen appearances. Two of those were against old rivals Juventus in the Coppa Italia, ending their

forty-seven-game unbeaten home run. An electrifying performance against at Tottenham Hotspur in the Europa League then
showed that Salah was capable of impacting games against
Premier League opponents, even if he hadn't been able to do
that in a Chelsea shirt.

Tottenham were reported as being interested in taking him back
to London. Yet Fiorentina were determined to exercise the option
they believed they had on Salah, who had worn the number 74
shirt during his time in Tuscany in honour of the fans who'd
perished in Port Said three years earlier. In June 2015, however,
Savini suggested instead that it was Salah's decision whether he
stayed in Tuscany or not. This prompted the club's director
Vincenzo Guerini to reveal that Fiorentina had made Salah an
'insane' offer to remain amidst additional interest from Roma.

'If any player, not just Salah, turned down a proposal like that,
then it's best he doesn't stay at Fiorentina,' Guerini bristled.
'However, I think Salah will accept. He made a huge impact
with us, so it's normal that he should receive calls from elsewhere. He wants to earn more, but Fiorentina made a truly
important proposal.'

Later on the same day, Salah's position became clearer. On
Twitter, Abbas appeared to claim the player was instead joining
Roma by simply releasing a picture of the club's badge on his
page. Savini and Marice were aware of Abbas's growing influence on their client after Abbas posted photographs of their
meetings on his Instagram page.

With Egypt keen to find out what was happening with their
star player, Abbas granted an interview to one of the country's
football journalists, Ahmad Yousef. Abbas revealed that Fiorentina
were threatening legal action, but called it 'completely baseless,

and without any grounds'. The lawyer suggested many teams were interested in Salah and he would only join a club on loan if there was an obligation to buy him. Savini was furious, taking to Italian radio a week later to confirm his relationship with Salah was over.

'I won't mingle my professionalism with the scant professional behaviour shown by the player's representative,' said Savini, in reference to Abbas. Savini's interview came after Salah took to Twitter to reveal he was leaving Fiorentina.

'Salah was supposed to have provided an answer by yesterday and he did that in the least professional manner possible,' Savini continued. 'I think it's clear that there's another club backing him, and I wonder who they are because they're going against Fiorentina too. The player's way of saying farewell to Florence is not transparent, he could simply have stated earlier that he didn't plan on staying. He should have shown greater respect to the supporters and to those who earn much less than he does.'

This was all getting very messy. Salah had left a trail of frustration and bitterness behind him since his departure from Chelsea six months earlier. SPOCS were still reeling from his decision to work instead with Marice and Savini, who in turn felt outmanoeuvred by Abbas, who was the one ultimately standing beside Salah when he was unveiled as a Roma player at the club's Trigoria training ground. This time Abbas wore a suit rather than jeans and a T-shirt.

'Finally,' Abbas concluded on Instagram.

Marice especially felt that she had helped engineer this move, though her name never appeared on the paperwork. It was her view that Abbas convinced Salah they should work together because of shared frustrations. Salah, the most recognisable footballer in Egypt, had developed the feeling that everyone wanted something out of him and Abbas believed in the spirit of independence and the rise of the individual, sensing too many people in this world wanted something for nothing.

Ultimately, it helped the relationship more that Salah wanted to move on from Fiorentina and the club was threatening legal action against both him and Chelsea. Abbas was in the centre of this because he had hurriedly drafted the contentious document six months earlier on his Blackberry. Abbas was also a litigator, having worked with a string of high-profile clients who have taken contractual cases to the Court of Arbitration for Sport (CAS) in Lausanne, Switzerland. One of those was Rivaldo, the Brazilian former World Player of the Year, who was connected to Tannuri. Abbas described this in an interview with *GQ Middle East* as 'a pretty big deal. This guy is a World Cup winner and one of the greatest players in history. I have represented him in court and that, for me, was huge.'

After FIFA rejected Fiorentina's claim against Salah, the club took the case to the same CAS courthouse in Lausanne, where they tried to argue that they were owed €32 million in compensation because the contract drafted by Abbas did not have any legal weight. Abbas, sitting beside Salah, was able to argue otherwise and the two cases ended up with Fiorentina paying legal costs of 60,000 Swiss francs. Abbas used Twitter to express his feelings: 'How do you say clowns in Italian?'

With Abbas's guidance and reassurance, Salah was able to get out of Fiorentina believing that the legal wrangling was not going to have an impact on his career or finances. In June 2017, shortly before Abbas brokered the deal that took him from

Roma to Liverpool, the case in front of CAS finally concluded, and Abbas congratulated his client on Twitter: 'You deserve to embark upon your new adventure clear-headed, and without any frivolous suits against you,' he wrote.

During his six months in Florence, Salah asked Abbas lots of legal questions. They would meet a couple of times in Italy, where Abbas reassured him the document he'd drafted in London was legally sound.

It is Abbas's version of events that Salah approached him to act as his representative, telling him he was now free of agents, including Marice, who had opened discussions with Roma. Abbas was in a position to continue and he advised Salah that the deal on offer was a good one. Abbas also respected Roma's enthusiasm to make it happen. Roma were taking a risk because the player had an outstanding lawsuit against him. Had Salah lost and subsequently received a ban, the club would have been stuck with him. It was clear to Abbas that Roma believed in Salah and were willing to support him. The club's CEO, Mauro Baldissoni, was a lawyer. He understood the case and thought Salah would win.

Abbas was waiting when Salah landed in Rome in the summer of 2015. He would live in a villa in the area of Casal Palocco, close to the seaside resort of Ostia. There, he built a private training pitch in the grounds of the property, where he worked on his shooting with a coach. It was in Rome he also started meditation and visualisation training every day after reading about how it had improved the performances of the Olympic Gold-medal swimmer Michael Phelps. Salah woke up every morning imagining himself about to score. He would sit up on the edge of his bed or a chair, with his back straight and his eyes closed, attempting to see into the future. Ahead of games, he also would research the goalkeepers he was coming up against, understanding better their tendencies. With time, he would find that all of this made him calmer in front of goal – if it seemed to him that he'd been in a certain situation before, it was because he'd pictured himself there. 'I just say if you really want to improve on something, just do it every day – five, ten minutes,' he later reflected. 'It sounds easy but trust me, it's not going to be easy if you do it every day. Do it every day and you will see the result at the end.'

The new process coincided with the best form of his career. The precision of his shooting improved dramatically. At Chelsea, only 35.5 per cent of his shots were on target but that figure rose to 40 per cent in his first year with Roma, then 44.7 per cent in his second, before it hit nearly 50 per cent at Liverpool, where only one other player – Lazio's Ciro Immobile – in Europe's top leagues was more accurate.

In his second season at Roma, indeed, Salah scored fifteen times and provided eleven assists, as the team qualified for the Champions League by finishing second in the Serie A table. Meanwhile, Abbas would experience for the first time some of the complications of having the best Egyptian footballer on the planet as a client. Salah had fronted a campaign for the Egyptian tourist board but this brought some unwanted attention following the death of Italian national Giulio Regeni near Cairo in February 2016.

The victim's body had shown signs of torture and Amnesty International later asked Serie A clubs to display a banner 'Verità Per Giulio Regeni' ('Truth for Giulio Regeni') before matches.

Roma did not want to embarrass Salah and instead ballboys carried the message before the players appeared.

Abbas has never pretended to know much about Egypt, a country he would visit only twice over the next seven years, as the player and the lawyer came to think of each other as business partners. By 2022, Abbas had stopped taking on new clients, partly because he didn't really need to financially, but also because he realised football was increasingly becoming an individualised sport in every sense. The alignment between the pair meant Salah got the attention and support he craved. It also allowed Abbas to focus on making them as much money as possible.

Except, Abbas did not see himself as an agent. He remained, emphatically, Salah's lawyer. In Italy, he would be thought of as a *consigliere*, a councillor. 'When you represent thirty or forty players, you can't really look out for them with the same specialty at the same level,' Abbas told GQ. There was also the potential for legal and moral conflict. What happens if a player fell out with the club but the agent had other players at the same club? At which point does the agent risk what might be a lucrative relationship for just one player?

Abbas later outlined some of the pitfalls for clubs, players and agents working together when he spoke to lecturers at Harvard University. 'Imagine an agent representing four players at the same football club, and their contracts are up for renewal,' he proposed. 'Is the agent going to fight equally hard for each one? The day after you've negotiated one player's contract, are you going to come in with a clean slate, smiling and shaking hands with everyone and trying to get the best possible deal for another? That is not how it works. Someone is going to be used to get a better deal for someone else – you see it all the time with the larger agencies, where a single agent may represent thirty or forty players.'

Salah agreed with him, suggesting, 'They often do what benefits them – not what benefits the player.'

Abbas was also dismissive of the trend for players turning to family members for advice. One such arrangement existed at Liverpool, where Trent Alexander-Arnold was represented by his older brother, Tyler. 'There are too many emotions,' Abbas said, 'and they always end up following the money.'

It helped Abbas's own relationship with Salah that his family members were not involved in his affairs. Salah's father Ghaly had never tried to insert himself into the small details of his son's career, unlike the parents of other players. Abbas believed he did not have the patience or diplomatic skills to deal with that sort of interference, which ultimately just wastes a lot of time.

They saw each other as a partnership yet it was not a typical player–agent relationship but rather one that was more of a throwback to a bygone era when players tended to use lawyers or accountants to run over their contracts. The surrounding land-scape was very different for Salah and Abbas, of course, because of the number of brands and organisations that wanted to work with them and, potentially, the amount of money at stake. Abbas would enlist a dozen or so external advisors, including on a retainer one of the biggest law firms in the Middle East, Al Tamimi & Company, as well as lawyers and tax advisors in Egypt, and two legal firms in the UK. Al Tamimi, for example, would represent Salah during an infringement dispute with the Egyptian FA in the buildup to the 2018 World Cup when a large-scale image of the player appeared on the side of the team's plane. The image had been provided by the country's sponsor, Presentation Sports, who executed marketing deals based on the image rights with Egypt Air and many others, which the EFA approved, without any prior consultation with Abbas or Salah.

Abbas appreciated businesses like Al Tamimi knew their markets best, but they were not ultimately in-house: he liked to keep a distance, thus maintaining his own influence and control.

'I think high-profile players are much better off with someone who is dedicated to them,' Abbas told Harvard.

'At the end of the day, we have one goal – not two goals,' said Salah. 'I have never had the feeling that he is doing things for himself – he is doing everything for me.'

Abbas was willing to go to war for his partner but, by his own admission, he was not the most elegant fighter. This was illustrated several times in his battles with the EFA, who Abbas became accustomed to threatening. Abbas would tell Salah more than once that the more powerful the opponent, the harder you have to hit them – and then hope for the best. It was Abbas's view that the first blow usually defined any outcome. The approach sometimes came at a cost but he believed no one deserved respect by default.

The pair would come to talk to one another more than they did the other members of their own families. Abbas would learn things about Salah that no one else knew, and the level of confidence was reciprocated. Abbas compared the relationship to that of LeBron James and Maverick Carter, the manager and businessman who in 2021 brokered a deal with Liverpool's owners Fenway Sports Group to purchase a stake in the Boston Red Sox.

Yet Abbas steered clear of giving Salah advice about his

football career. When there was uncertainty about his direction, he did not speculate where he might fit in better, as some agents might. It was Abbas's view that Salah understood his own industry.

'We know there is a line,' Salah told Harvard 'and we don't try to cross it.'

Chapter 7

Pride of the Arabs

In 2018, as Egypt prepared for its first World Cup appearance in twenty-eight years, a host of columns from writers specialising in Islamic affairs appeared in British newspapers. One of the most far-sighted was published in the *Independent* by Nabila Ramdani, a French journalist of Algerian descent, who suggested that for anyone who wanted to trace the recent history of the most populous country in Africa, 'then the life story of the Egyptian footballer Mohamed Salah would be a good starting point'.

A few weeks earlier, Salah had become the first Egyptian to win English football's prestigious Player of the Year Award, issued by the Professional Footballers' Association (PFA) and, separately, the same accolade by the Football Writers' Association (FWA). At the PFA ceremony, he encouraged Egyptians to 'chase their dreams' as he had done, having signed for Basel on his twentieth birthday, leaving Egypt – fresh from a revolution, had its domestic league suspended and no one knew for certain when it would return.

Egypt had been in desperate need of hope and, after 2012, Salah's rise gave that to millions of people. He had always dreamed of playing in Europe but in truth it was difficult to imagine a future at home after what happened in Port Said, which at first appeared to be a case of violence between sets of rival fans that culminated in chaos and death.

As Bob Bradley suggested, however, things were not always what they seemed in Egypt. It was later established that many of the Al Ahly supporters were instead running for their lives, pursued by men from Al Masry carrying weapons that ranged from stones to swords. Despite the obvious threat, the police inside the stadium did nothing and refused to open the gates that might have saved many of those who perished. Instead, with the lights inside the stadium cut, more than five hundred were injured in the darkness and seventy-two people died, the majority crushed to death in an exit tunnel as they tried to escape.

The theories that quickly spawned as to why this was allowed to happen were inseparable from the political background of Egypt. The Mubarak regime had survived for decades because state and society was held together through an extensive coercive apparatus; elements of that apparatus remained in place thirteen months after a revolution that was inspired to a significant degree by the organisation of Al Ahly's ultras.

With this in mind, people asked, Was this revenge? Was it an attempt by the post-Mubarak powers to justify the introduction of more stringent security measures?

What was absolutely clear was Mohamed Aboutrika's role during and in the aftermath of Port Said. The already legendary midfielder cradled a child in his arms as he died. Aboutrika decided to retire from football but then reversed his decision, saying, 'I need to play for the people who died that night.'

In an earlier part of his life, Aboutrika had studied philosophy to degree level. It was his view that 'every athlete has a humanitarian role in society'. Aboutrika was already painted as a selfless figure because at his first club, Tersana, he rejected a pay rise, insisting each of his teammates should earn the same money for helping him flourish. He would become a symbol of the revolution due to his public support and, beside Tahrir Square, a giant mural of his face was daubed on the wall of a building, including a beard, showing what he meant to this part of the Islamic world.

In Egypt's first democratic elections since 1952, Aboutrika endorsed the Muslim Brotherhood candidate, Mohamed Morsi. This would not be forgotten by Field Marshal Abdel Fattah al-Sisi when he seized power from Morsi and put him in jail without a fair trial along with other Brotherhood leaders, having suspended the country's constitution, a moment that inspired more jail sentences for political opponents, and more beatings and executions.

The move included the decision to place all members and associates of the Brotherhood on a terrorist watchlist, and Aboutrika was the co-owner of a holiday company accused of 'committing hostile acts against the state'. Having moved on from Al Ahly to Qatari's Baniyas, where he wore the number 74 shirt in honour of the supporters who lost their lives in Port Said, Aboutrika's assets in Egypt were frozen and he was warned that he faced arrest if he ever returned to the country.

Salah's Twitter handle until April 2018 was @MoSalah22 as a mark of respect to Aboutrika, because twenty-two had been the number on the back of Aboutrika's shirt at Al Ahly. His fame and exile would stand as a warning to every Egyptian that nobody was immune from the country's politics. The tools of the state were sharpening again.

By 2018, Salah was well on his way to becoming an internationally renowned footballer, having filled the cavernous space of interest and adoration left at home by Aboutrika's absence. The rise and perceived fall of Salah's hero meant he would know all about the potential consequences of aligning with the forces whose interests ran against the controlling powers.

It would be Salah's goal from the penalty spot in 2017 that sent Egypt to the World Cup for only the third time in the country's history, a feat Aboutrika never achieved. Yet by this point, the role of the national team for the post-Mubarak authoritarian regime had changed significantly since the golden era of 2006 to 2010, when Aboutrika contributed towards two of Egypt's three Africa Cup of Nations (AFCON) titles.

The last of those fell almost a year to the day before the start of the 2011 revolution, when suddenly many in Egypt became politically engaged for the first time in nearly sixty years of army rule. Amidst free speech, the formation of new parties, a constitution and an election, the importance of a national football team disappeared into the background, especially amongst Mubarak's fiercest critics who believed Egypt's football success had helped him distract the population from the real problems in the country.

When Egypt failed to qualify for the 2012 edition of AFCON for the first time since 1978, nobody seemed to care that much because other, more important things were happening. The conversations in cafés of Cairo and Alexandria were instead focused on the politics of the future and the civil society Egypt was promising to create.

After fourteen successive AFCON qualifications, an Egypt team now involving Salah failed to reach three in a row, between 2012 and 2015. Perhaps such disappointments can be explained by a lack of suitable preparation by the country's domestic play-ers, who were dealing with multiple suspensions of the calendar during and just after this period. Following the aftermath of Port Said, the Egyptian Premier League was again suspended in 2013 amidst Sisi's coup d'etat, and again two years later when police fired tear gas into a Cairo stadium, leading to the deaths of twenty-eight Zamalek fans who were crushed as they tried to escape.

By now, the ultras' popularity had waned and they too were designated a terrorist group. Amidst political turmoil, the fail-ures of the national team, the suppression of fan groups and those episodes when the domestic game disappeared altogether, it would be understandable if Egyptians were beginning to lose interest in a sport that was increasingly marginalised.

If the final years of Mubarak and the early years of Sisi had shown one thing, it was that it was potentially problematic to care too much about the game. Under Mubarak, football had been used politically, and for many Egyptians, it epitomised a feeling of being 'fooled into a craze that was exaggerated and went too far', according to the social anthropologist, Carl Rommel.

Under Sisi, football remained dangerous.

Salah was not connected to Al Ahly or Zamalek, the two biggest clubs in the country, which had previously had the largest ultra groups. Salah was, therefore, someone everyone in the country could love. Yet simultaneously, he did not stimulate as strong emotions as someone like Aboutrika. Salah had a broad appeal because, like Aboutrika, he was visibly proud to be Islamic. He performed the prostration after each goal, he fasted in Ramadan, he regularly read the Qur'an, and he named his daughter, Makka, after Islam's holiest city, Mecca. Whenever he spoke, he appeared shy, like the average Egyptian vendor on the street.

Though Egyptians felt connected to him, they were not as wholeheartedly devoted to the forces around him, including a national team which by now was inspiring ambivalence and hesitation, not least because it was not as homegrown as it had been during the Aboutrika era. The stadium bans also meant fans were not experiencing close relationships with any of the players. Football became more of a sport that Egyptians consumed through television. Watching Salah perform in England, Italy and England again while huddled around a screen became more of a natural thing to do, as football became less of a match-going experience in Egypt. The implementation of an ID card system in the stadiums that were partially open for some games meant only certain people were allowed in. It increased the sense that football was becoming exclusive rather than inclusive.

Briefly, the mood would change in 2017 when Salah's goals sent Egypt to the World Cup. The way this happened secured a hero's status for him. Egypt might still have qualified had they drawn with Congo in Cairo, as they seemed poised to do following an equaliser from the visiting team with just three minutes of the game remaining. Having already scored Egypt's opening goal, Salah would step forward in the fifth minute of injury time when the hosts were awarded a penalty. He used the opportunity to write his name into history.

What followed was Salah-mania. The following year, just two months before the start of the World Cup, the runner-up in Egypt's election was not Moussa Mostafa Moussa, the sole opponent to president Sisi, but the country's most popular foot-baller. Five candidates had been sidelined or jailed in the lead-up to the vote and Moussa, a politician who was barely known before entering the race, had endorsed Sisi just days before registering himself. His involvement ultimately allowed the regime to claim it had not been a single-candidate race.

More than one million Egyptians struck out the names of Sisi and Moussa when casting their vote, and instead applied Salah's name on the ballot. Sisi would win 97 per cent of the vote, prompting a coalition of eight Egyptian opposition parties and some 150 pro-democracy public figures to call the result an 'absurdity' befitting 'old and crude dictatorships'.

Yet Salah's unexpected inclusion in the whole charade reminded the government of his increasing popularity, and by extension, his potential power. The new dynamic meant both Sisi and Salah would have to tread carefully around one another.

The first public sign of conflict between Salah and the compet-ing forces around him came six weeks before the World Cup, when the EFA announced an agreement with Egypt Air to fly the squad around Russia.

Salah's face featured prominently on the plane's fuselage beside branding from the team's sponsor, a telecommunications company called WE. For Salah, this was a problem. He already had a sponsorship deal with rival firm Vodafone, and the terms of his contract prevented him from any public association with competitors. Salah was compromised and he took to social media, describing the move as a 'major insult'.

'I was hoping the handling would be classier than this,' Salah wrote.

Ramy Abbas followed this up by using his feed to remind the EFA that it had no right to use his client's image without written consent from his image rights company registered in the Cayman Islands, MS Commercial. Abbas revealed that, despite attempts to engage the EFA, the organisation had not even acknowledged his queries.

The posts would trigger waves of online support for Salah, and swiftly the matter was being dealt with by Khaled Abdel-Aziz, a minister in Egypt's department for youth and sports. At a meeting with the EFA, committee members were told to meet Salah's requests.

'I assure everyone that we will stand by him to honour all the contracts he entered in England,' Abdel-Aziz said, a few hours before he appeared on a popular television show in Egypt where he suggested that the EFA were to blame for the dispute, claiming the organisation might not have the expertise or experience to deal with the commercial aspects of an emerging global superstar. 'Consider that all the demands made by them [Salah and Abbas] are met,' he announced. His superior, Farag Amer, then stated on television later that week that Sisi, the Egyptian president, was behind the order to resolve the feud.

The episode made the EFA nervous. Chairman Hany Abou Rida revealed that he'd spoken to Salah on the phone, telling him, 'Anything that annoyed you will stop. What is more important to me is that you and your teammates are relaxed so that you hold your heads high in the World Cup.'

It was the first time Salah's power and sense of otherness had played out so publicly. While huge sections of Egypt's youth population were behind him and nearly everyone in Egypt tended to identify the EFA with incompetence after so many changes of administration, some with longer memories questioned why money should be the focus of any discussion ahead of the most important sporting event for Egypt in generations. For Salah and his lawyer the point was that allowing the authorities in Egypt to step on his toes on this occasion would mean they would inevitably try again. For those Egyptians with an understanding of how sport and politics in the country overlapped, Salah's reaction was understandable, but for the regular Egyptian with no appreciation of such a dynamic, Salah might have come across as arrogant.

It promised to be a momentous summer for Salah, with appearances in the Champions League final for the first time as well as the World Cup. If the possibility of winning the former was wrecked by Sergio Ramos, he would come to think the latter was undermined by forces beyond his control.

For Russian president Vladimir Putin, hosting the World Cup presented the opportunity for Russia to play a subtle geopolitical game; tying the country closer together with regimes in the Middle East and Africa at the expense of the West.

Salah and the Egypt squad would stay at a luxury hotel called the Local in the Chechen capital of Grozny. It was the first hotel in the Muslim region of the North Caucasus to be founded by a foreign funder – namely, the Fabulous Abu Dhabi Hotel Management company – and crown prince Mohammed bin Zayed attended its launch party.

Moscow's political, economic and military relationship with Cairo was getting closer before 2018. Three years earlier, Russia signed a $30 billion deal to build a nuclear power plant, with

Russia later extending a loan to cover the cost of its construction. 'The cooperation between our two countries continues and is developing,' Putin said in 2024. 'Egypt is a close friend of ours and a strategic partner.'

A significant figure in the Kremlin's relationship with Cairo was the head of the Chechen republic, Ramzan Kadyrov, whose father Akhmad had fought against Putin's administration in the second Chechen war of independence before switching sides. After Akhmad was assassinated in 2004, Putin installed Ramzan in 2007 and two years later, his horses began racing in the Dubai World Cup. Over the years that followed, Kadyrov was able to lead Putin's courtship in the Middle East, sporting his hallmark beard of the ultra-conservative Muslims known as the Salafis.

Kadyrov was repeatedly accused of human rights abuses, including torture and the killing of political opponents. He denied allegations about a crackdown on homosexuality in Chechnya by insisting there were no gay people living in the region.

Salah's presence in Grozny was an opportunity to reinforce credibility. Within hours of landing, Salah, still recovering from the shoulder injury sustained in a challenge by Ramos in Kyiv, was resting in his room at the Local, when he received a call from the hotel's reception, asking him to meet an important guest in the lobby. There, Kadyrov insisted on escorting him to the stadium named after his assassinated father, where the Egyptian team were training. Amidst a flurry of photographs and loud cheers, both figures were given a standing ovation as they walked onto the pitch.

'Mohamed Salah thanked us for our surprisingly warm and good hospitality, great affection for the team and excellent conditions for their stay and training,' Kadyrov wrote on Russian social network VK. 'I'm sure our Akhmat club and the Egypt team will at some point hold a friendly match in Grozny.'

The stunt led to criticism from human rights groups, who accused Kadyrov of using Salah as a tool to boost his own profile. Kadyrov angrily denounced that he was using Salah's presence in the city he rebuilt to generate positive publicity. 'I didn't invite Mo Salah or the Egyptian team,' he insisted. 'They chose us themselves.'

Yet Kadyrov was just getting started. After Eihab Leheita, one of the EFA's many directors, said he had 'no regrets whatsoever' about the choice of Grozny as a base for Egypt's all-Muslim squad, Kadyrov held an honorary banquet at his palace, which coincided with Salah's birthday on 15 June. Sitting at the top table beside Kadyrov were Hany Abu Rida, the chairman of the EFA and Salah, who was given a special birthday present, which Kadryov announced on social media: 'Mohamed Salah is an honorary citizen of the Chechen Republic! That's right!' he wrote, revealing he had signed the official directive, marking the decision by pinning a badge bearing the Chechen flag to Salah's shirt, before awarding him a silver plate and a signed jersey from Akhmat Grozny, the football club that Kadyrov had renamed in honour of his late father.

Initially, it was unclear what Salah thought of all this. Though he appeared to play the role of unassuming guest, he did not give a speech or make any public comments about his reception. Quietly, however, reports in Egypt were emerging that he was frustrated with the management of the camp, which included too much focus on staged publicity events rather than training and match preparation. His feelings would become clearer later in the summer. For the time being, Egypt had matches to play.

Ahead of their third group fixture, Egypt already knew they were going home. A narrow defeat to Uruguay came without an injured Salah, who would score against the hosts Russia in the second game, but the goal was only a consolation because Egypt were already 3–0 down. Outside of Egypt, the third game – against an also eliminated Saudi Arabia – appeared to be a dead rubber but for two Muslim countries separated by the Red Sea, there was an enormous amount of historical rivalry.

Saudi Arabia had oil and was now a much richer state, but Egypt felt superior because of its movie culture, its literature and its intellectual scene. In Egypt, more recently stained by poverty, there was a desperation for this perceived advantage to be translated into football.

Relatively fresh in the memories of many was the final group match in the 1999 Confederations Cup, where Egypt needed only to draw to qualify for the knockout stages but lost 5–1. Controversially, three Egyptian players were sent off and an unfounded conspiracy spread across the country that the match officials had been bought off by Saudi Arabia. Nineteen years later, there remained a feeling that the embarrassment needed avenging.

In Volgograd, Salah scored but Egypt lost again, this time 2–1. Salah's goal had a historical context because it was Egypt's first from open play since their first World Cup appearance in 1934. It had also given Egypt the lead, yet Salah did not really celebrate. Instead, he trotted back to restart the match, like it was a routine moment in a friendly match.

After succumbing to another defeat, Salah started to feel the heat from the Egyptian public for the first time. They had wanted to see that he understood the feelings of his fellow Egyptians, especially those with longer memories. Instead, it was clear that attitudes did not align. He was not sharing some of these concerns, and it was realised he had a different way of thinking.

Salah was brooding. When Egypt had travelled to St Petersburg for their second group game with Russia, the players sat at the back of the plane while the EFA members had first-class seats. Then, in the hotel, preparations were disrupted, this time by celebrities, musicians and other notables appearing in the early hours of the morning.

'When you have a player or players who get to sleep at six a.m., there is a problem,' Salah later said. In his case, people were still arriving at the door of his room at 4 a.m. for introductions and photographs. He wanted all of this to stop so that he and the players could prepare properly for a huge game that Egypt could not afford to lose. When it became a public matter that he'd asked the EFA to review its security operation, he felt as though it was 'painted to make me appear like I am acting arrogant, but I am not'.

More and more details were leaking to the Egyptian media about Salah's frustrations. After Ramy Abbas prompted speculation that the player was considering his international future on 28 June, Salah returned to pre-season training with Liverpool, where his club manager insisted he was committed to playing for his country. 'It's 100 per cent clear, his heart is there,' Klopp said. 'When was the last time Egypt had a player like him? They need to get used to it. So far, maybe it was not perfect. Make it perfect, and everything is fine at the end.'

He would not feature for Egypt again until the following September, in a 6–0 victory over Niger in an Africa Cup of Nations qualifier. At Liverpool, he started a season that ended in Champions League glory by scoring twice and contributing one assist in three successive wins during which time the team did not concede a goal. After Salah hit Liverpool's match winner at Anfield against Brighton, however, his difficult relationship with the national team would flare up again when the EFA once more refused to engage with Abbas, who asked twice in August for guarantees to be made in relation to his client's 'wellbeing'.

Abbas took to social media: 'I cannot think of any other national association which would treat any player in the disgraceful and abhorrent manner you have treated Mohamed,' he wrote. He would ask that his client be picked up from the airport in Cairo and taken to the team hotel, 'in the most discreet manner possible'. He also wanted security guards to accompany Salah to training sessions and that calls to his hotel room be blocked. There were to be no promotional appearances or impromptu opportunities for pictures or autographs.

Abbas was acting on the instruction of his client, who used his social media pages to make his position clearer. 'It's normal that a football federation seeks to solve the problems of its players so they can feel comfortable. But in fact, what I see is exactly the opposite,' Salah wrote. 'It is not normal that my messages and my lawyer's messages are ignored. I do not know why all this [is happening]? Do you not have time to respond to us?!'

Eventually, the EFA responded, initially insisting it would not meet any of his requests, branding some as 'illogical' and that it would not 'favour one player over another', intimating that Salah was being selfish. Separately, Magdy Abdelghani, an EFA official, told an Egyptian television channel he had not been able to contact Salah since the World Cup because his 'WhatsApp number changes all the time'.

The organisation would soon insert a different face in the discussions when Ahmed Megahed, another one of the EFA's many board members, suggested Abbas had initially tried to contact the organisation during the Eid holiday, 'but its language was inappropriate and difficult to accept. It included a request by Salah's agent [Ramy always referred to himself as the player's lawyer] for the association to resign if it doesn't accept the player's demands.'

It suited the EFA to present Abbas as an aggressive influence, giving Salah some distance from the diplomatic impasse between player and authority, while also subtly inferring that he was increasingly becoming a remote type of figure. Yet Megahed added that Abbas had sent further correspondence after Salah went public over the matter, this time only without 'threats or resignation requests', and the organisation was now considering his requests. 'Some of these demands will be accepted but others not,' Megahed added. 'We fully care about Salah and his performance as he is one of our sons.'

Salah, however, was furious, urging the officials to focus on 'solving the problem, not the language of Ramy Abbas', before stating clearly that he was not only looking out for himself, but those around him as well. 'The problem is not a personal one. What I call for is for all the players. They are carried out very easily,' he said in a one of two videos published on Facebook, where he made it clear he did not wish to be disturbed again by visitors wanting to meet him in the middle of the night, as he had been in the chaos of St Petersburg. 'I'm the person that these things happen to. I'm the person who gets harmed by these things,' he said. 'These requests are very small but make things easier, they make the player focused in the match.'

The posts prompted Egyptian business tycoon Naguib Sawiris to call for the resignation of the football association's board members. 'Treating an Egyptian figure like Mohamed Salah who raised his country's name in an unprecedented way should not have been like that,' Sawiris said. 'Resign and relieve us after the abject failure.'

Then, the inevitable happened: an electronic invasion of the EFA's platforms, as the federation was told to give Salah whatever he wanted. Egypt had never had a player of this ability or fame. Inside twelve hours the hashtag #SupportSalah was trending in Egypt, the president of the football association intervened, and Salah thanked his young fans for their support.

Yet not all Egyptians were impressed by the positions Salah was taking. It had never been the custom in Egypt to complain about any type of national service, and here was Salah – at a time of tremendous economic hardship – asking for first-class plane tickets back to the country for international duty because it helped him prepare for games.

It was possible, of course, that two or even three positions could all be right at the same time: Salah *was* attempting to drive new standards rather than acting like a pampered footballer returning from the West. Meanwhile, it was understandable if sections of a mainly impoverished public did not really understand that Salah was only trying to bring the country in line with global trends. Everyone in Egypt was treading new ground. None of this had ever happened before.

★   ★   ★

In the end, the EFA gave Salah more or less everything he wanted. Ahead of the game with Niger in Cairo, Salah had two bodyguards beside him so often that Egyptian journalists wondered whether they'd join him on the pitch. Instead, they would stand on the touchline and when a training session was over, everyone was kept away, including autograph hunters and reporters. Some of the country's media would become more cynical and resentful towards Salah. Suddenly, most of the Egyptian players on national duty were less accessible and the EFA were not as helpful to journalists.

'The atmosphere was totally different after 2018,' says one of them. 'It felt like only the players' jobs mattered. None were as famous as Salah and the distance seemed to make some think they were more important than they really were.'

Egypt was hosting AFCON and the country sailed through qualification. Though Cameroon had initially been due to run the tournament, the country's new stadiums were behind schedule and with CAF, Africa's governing football body based in Cairo, the authority knew which country to turn to as host.

The tournament would start in the summer of 2019 and by then Salah was a Champions League winner with Liverpool. This was his third opportunity to achieve what the golden generation of Egyptian footballers had delivered – not once, but three times between 2006 and 2010.

Mexican Javier Aguirre was now Egypt's manager and suggested before the competition that a victory for Egypt would place Salah in pole position to win the Ballon d'Or. While the comments did nothing to reduce the focus or pressure on Salah, Aguirre was surely right. Since George Weah in 1995, no African had won the award. And not only was he the last player from the continent to take the trophy, he remained the only one. Yet Salah would still be breaking new ground: by winning it, he would become the first Arab.

Egyptian commentators had already started calling him the 'Pride of the Arabs', a title which Algerians had also given to Riyad Mahrez, the Manchester City winger who was born in France and did not speak particularly fluent Arabic. During the periods where he was often named as a substitute by Pep Guardiola, Egyptians liked to call him the 'Pride of the bench'.

The chances of Salah claiming each of these official and unofficial titles were ultimately reduced because of Egypt's performance at home in a competition that was instead remembered for a scandal. Part of the way through a group also containing Uganda, DR Congo and Zimbabwe, Salah's teammate Amr Warda was accused of sexual harassment by Merhan Keller, a British–Egyptian model, who shared screenshots sent over WhatsApp showing a string of lewd messages from the midfielder. Keller also shared images allegedly sent by Warda to other women allegedly subjected to similar forms of harassment.

The EFA acted straight away, dismissing Warda from the team's camp 'in order to maintain the state of discipline, commitment and concentration', following discussions with technical and administrative staff. Yet Egypt's players were not consulted and after the team beat DR Congo to reach the last sixteen, Salah suggested his colleague 'should not be sent to the guillotine' for his alleged offences. 'No means no,' Salah wrote on Twitter, adding, 'Many who make mistakes can change for the better. We need to believe in second chances . . . we need to guide and educate. Shunning is not the answer.'

Salah had not defended Warda's actions but his comments would split Egyptian society, with many women claiming Salah's words allowed other men across the country to condone sexual harassment. An angry reaction online followed and within a few days, his post had received five thousand comments.

Salah was joined in his support for the player by other teammates. He was not the team's captain – that responsibility fell to Ahmed Elmohamady, the Aston Villa right back, who scored against Congo before using his two fingers to mark Warda's number 22 shirt. Meanwhile, Ahmed Hegazi asked Egyptians to 'forgive' Warda and Walid Soliman tweeted a Qur'anic verse that suggested, 'Allah forgives all sins.'

Most of the focus fell on Salah, however. He was by far the team's most famous player and a few months earlier, he had granted an interview to *TIME* magazine, where he spoke about the importance of women's equality, especially 'in my culture and in the Middle East.

'I support the woman more than I did before, because I feel like she deserves more than what they give her now, at the moment,' he said. 'It's not optional.'

Salah was unaware of previous allegations against Warda when he defended him. In 2017, during a short-lived loan to the Portuguese team CD Feirense, he was accused of harassing the wives of two teammates. This led to Salah being reminded that Warda had already had his second chance. Between him and his lawyer, Ramy Abbas, it was one of the occasions where the pair realised they'd got it wrong.

Though Warda was initially in denial, when he released an eighteen-second video clip promising no repeat of such incidents, the EFA reversed its decision and he returned to the squad, appearing as a substitute in Egypt's defeat to South Africa, a result that sent them out of the tournament early.

Amidst claims from Keller that Salah's defence of the player, 'as one of the most recognised figures in the world', had 'pushed people to harass me even more', the model, who had been living in Dubai for seven years, said she was afraid to return to Egypt because she thought 'people might attack me in the streets'.

After Salah and his teammates were booed off the field in Cairo, he would take to social media again to thank the country's 'loyal fans' for their support, promising, 'We will learn from the mistakes we made.'

In a sporting sense, it was an anti-climactic end to a campaign that with a different outcome – the tournament was in the event won by Algeria – could have resulted in Salah being closer to the Ballon d'Or. Scoring the opening goal in a Champions League final victory before lifting one of the world's major international tournaments in his own country would surely have been enough to push him up the rankings. Instead, he was not the first- or second-highest Liverpool player on the list of nominees, which included Virgil van Dijk and Sadio Mané ahead of him.

Even so, in finishing fifth, after coming sixth the year before, Salah now was officially in the same league as some of the best players in the world. Though Egyptians were proud, they would increasingly ask why with such talent at their disposal, a team led by Salah was not getting close to the form of the side that dominated African football a decade earlier.

Though Aboutrika was that team's best player by far, the players around him had proven in 2010 that success could be achieved when he was not there. It therefore became the new narrative around Salah: that his sense of individuality had come at the expense of a collectivism and spirit.

As in other parts of the world, fans were now becoming obsessed by the cult of the individual. Football was becoming more like tennis. Salah's army of online supporters were as strident and noisy as those who followed Lionel Messi and Cristiano Ronaldo wherever they went in their careers, rather than the clubs or countries they represented.

Traditionalists in Egypt bemoaned this cultural change, and for some Salah came to represent everything that was wrong about it: they believed every bit of negative information about him, especially when it showed him to be overbearing. One such rumour involved team selection: a post online by an anonymous account suggested he was pushing Egypt's coaches to pick his friends. There was no evidence of this happening. Yet neither were the claims pushed by his supporters that he'd paid for the marriages of couples in Nagrig, or that he'd purchased the land in the village for a water purification factory. Such saintly offerings became the new truth and showed how keen so many were to believe in the greatness of the country's new national hero.

The focus on his influence over the national team sharpened after Egypt tumbled out of their own AFCON early, an outcome that earned Aguirre the sack. Three of the country's previous four coaches had been foreign and amidst the clamour to rediscover a sense of national identity came the appointment of Al Ahly stalwart Hossam El Badry.

According to state news channels in Egypt, President Sisi himself had ratified the decision, a report that in any other country would surely have been enough for FIFA to launch an investigation into whether the country's football association was suffering from state interference.

There was no reporting, however, that linked Sisi to El Badary's first big call – appointing a captain. The Egyptian team had tended to lean on experience when it came to selection but many players were now considered by the public to be too old. This created speculation over who would be the next player to lead the team.

Egypt had joined FIFA in 1922 but a football team had gone to the Olympics in Belgium two years earlier. For nearly a hundred years, it had been tradition for the veteran player in the squad, regardless of ability or position, to be named as captain: basically, it was the player who'd made his international debut before everyone else. In 2019, this figure had been the solid-but-unspectacular, soon-to-be thirty-five-year-old right back Ahmed Fathy, who had a place in the squad but was no longer guaranteed a place in the team because of the presence of Elmohamady. Fathy, a strong personality, was deeply respected, having won ten Egyptian Premier League titles during his career, as well as those three AFCONs between 2006 and 2010.

Fathy remained the sole survivor of that side but fans were creating pressure on social media for change. It was argued that Egypt had never seen a player even competing for the Ballon d'Or and that the armband should go to Salah as a reflection of the country's appreciation. It was also argued that Egypt, which felt the least African of all the African nations because of its proximity to the Middle East and because the Sahara Desert separated it from the rest of the continent, had suffered from unfavourable decisions from officials in key moments. It might be different if a referee had to communicate with someone of Salah's status.

When it was finally decided that Egypt should move on from Fathy, he did not go quietly and this led to him being left out of the squad altogether. Ahmed Hegazi was the next player in line, a defender with West Bromwich Albion who was widely considered as captain material because he was a charismatic figure with an emboldened personality. He was loud on the pitch, direct with the media, and, as well as Arabic, he spoke English and Italian. To many Egyptians, Hegazy had the DNA of the golden generation because of his fighting spirit. In a friendly game against Brazil in Doha, he would try and prevent a goal by colliding with the post, injuring his knee.

This was all in contrast to Salah, who did not seem to relish speaking publicly and was increasingly thought of as selfish and somewhat dispassionate about the team due to reports about him turning up late for international duty. Hegazi had made his debut for Egypt in the same game as Salah but in theory, he was ahead of him in the reckoning because of a previous call-up. As the campaign to replace Fathy ramped up, Salah returned home to Nagrig because he wanted to show his London-born six-year-old daughter his roots.

Almost as soon as this development leaked online, along with his address, a crowd of three to four hundred people started gathering outside his parents' apartment. He was planning to go for a walk and to Nagrig's mosque to pray but he became concerned about the safety of his family. After he expressed his unhappiness the following day at the lack of privacy he was being afforded, a new debate raged, with the critics reminding him that restraint was not a part of Egyptian culture, especially in rural areas. This was not Cairo, where he could escape to a compound. Parts of the public were offended, suggesting he should express his gratitude for the interest in him – it was not as though he was going to be in Nagrig for long. It might have been unfair, but it seemed another sign that the traditional and shy version of Salah was disappearing.

The incident had a profound effect on Salah's thinking and he was more careful about sharing his personal details. Yet just as inaccurate rumours started circulating that he had stopped giving his mobile number to new teammates on international duty, another story broke about the EFA and the country's existing captain, Ahmed Elmohamady, deciding not to vote for Salah in the FIFA World Player of the Year awards. The EFA intervened at the growing speculation, admitting it had made an 'unintentional mistake' by voting for Salah but writing his name in capital letters, which rendered the ballot invalid. With that, 'Egypt' disappeared from Salah's Twitter bio.

Just as it seemed as though Salah was on collision course with the EFA, however, he was suddenly announced as the team's new captain. If other players were unhappy with the decision, they did not speak about it.

Ultimately, they would have known that Sisi was listening.

Chapter 8

Temple

In pre-season training at Liverpool, Jürgen Klopp was an omnipresent force, acting like a hawk, circling the pitches, and swooping down on anyone who did not follow his orders. His control was absolute. Whenever he saw something he didn't like, he'd intervene quickly, moving the pieces around until he was satisfied.

Those pieces were, in fact, the players under his command. During these camps, usually held in France or Austria, he would push them to their physical limits. If Liverpool were going to be as successful as Klopp wanted them to be, he knew they would have to play lots of minutes. This meant being both physically and mentally prepared for seasons that were long, sometimes involving more than sixty games.

Klopp liked to have access to a running track. On the first day of camp, the players would be asked to sprint as fast as they could at one-kilometre intervals. This was torture, and these sessions usually ended with at least a few of them throwing up.

Klopp had developed a reputation for being a forward-thinking manager. He was open to new ideas. His door at Liverpool's training ground was also always ajar for players who knew they could speak to him. Yet his training methods, especially in pre-season, leaned on old-school thinking. While some members of his staff questioned the wisdom of pushing the players so hard, and pointed out he was actually risking injury with some of the things he was ordering, they could see a residual benefit.

These 'meat grinders', as some of the people involved called them, offered little physical value. Yet the players began to believe that once July was over, everything else became easier and they could take anything on. 'Mentally, it made them stronger,' admitted one of the cynics on Klopp's staff.

In the summer of 2018, eight weeks after the Champions League final in Kyiv, Klopp took the squad to Evian, southern France, where they stayed at a five-star hotel overlooking Lake Geneva. 'There's nothing else to do apart from football – this is my week,' Klopp said, enthusiastically.

Klopp had an appreciation of the interest in Liverpool when he was Borussia Dortmund's manager but he only began to realise the club's appeal and what it would take to manage this when he embarked on a pre-season tour of the USA two years earlier.

The tour was a commercial enterprise, one which he had little to no control over. Fenway Sports Group's determination to run its sports clubs in a real financial world of profit and loss meant Klopp and his players had a huge number of commitments to sponsors during the fortnight. It began in San Francisco, where there was a tour of Alcatraz prison on arrival because it was decided the travelling party needed to stay awake to beat the jet lag. The US tour schedule – in terms of the games Liverpool had to play, when they had to play them and the surfaces they had to play on – was decided before Klopp's appointment in October 2015.

Under Brendan Rodgers the club had toured the USA twice in four summers and on both occasions, the staff and the players returned to the UK drained of energy. Training sessions were not prioritised over the gruelling programme and it worried staff that the players' bodies were not being given enough rest time before they headed out into whatever city they were visiting for a commercial activity. The days were long and staff also had to make themselves available from early in the morning until late at night. Some would finish their work at 2 a.m. and be awake four hours later. It frustrated some of the staff that Rodgers did not seem to be willing to fight their corner in relation to their concerns. 'The only benefit of these tours was financial,' concluded one of the players. 'The boys were knackered, the staff were knackered and the manager barely got any prep work for the season done.'

By contrast, Klopp would tell Mike Gordon that a tour of the USA or the Far East was fine, so long as he got at least a week during the summer to run his own camp without any distractions. It was the sort of forceful diplomacy that Rodgers lacked in his management of the club and, under Klopp, it led to the post-tour periods being ringfenced for intense training schedules.

In 2018, Premier League rivals Southampton, Leicester City and Fulham had all used Evian as a base earlier in pre-season. Unlike in the USA – where Liverpool had impressively beaten Manchester United in one friendly match – there were no player appearances to satisfy sponsors, no open training sessions in front of fans and no press conferences.

The players were on the track at 7.30 a.m. for a running session and after a short break they were back on the training field by 11 a.m. A third session followed in the afternoon. Klopp was following roughly the same routine as he had the previous summer, when Adam Lallana broke down. His injury meant he only appeared in fifteen of Liverpool's fifty-six games across all competitions in the campaign that followed. By comparison, Salah, back in the Premier League after an eighteen-month absence, played fifty-two times. 'Mo's body could withstand the pressure Jürgen was placing on the players,' says one staffer, who recalls Evian as being just as testing as the USA on the physios and medics because of the difficulty of the training.

Staff needed to be on hand to deal with any of the issues or concerns the players were facing. These were often aches or pains, but Salah never seemed to complain. His demands were instead around preparation, ensuring his body was ready for the next day of gruelling challenges, which he appeared to relish. 'Mo was only focused on maintenance,' said someone who had worked with him on his recovery. 'You'd get players needing work on pulls and strains and this took up a lot of time but Mo's focus was always on being ready for the next session. He was a machine. A freak.'

Only James Milner really compared to Salah. The midfielder, thirty-two in 2018, was the oldest outfield player in the squad, but he was always at the front of the pack in those exhausting running sessions. The Yorkshireman's steadfast commitment to fitness was notorious and he emerged as one of the most influential players in the Liverpool squad, a player who others tended to follow because of his dedication to training.

Throughout Klopp's time as Liverpool's manager, Milner would win the lactic acid test on the first day of Liverpool's pre-season schedule, which started on Merseyside. This involved a prick of blood being taken from each player's ear to measure how their bodies were responding to physical strain, which helped measure their level of fitness. Players were then grouped according to the data. Salah was always in Milner's group and usually, he was only marginally behind him.

Even though camps like Evian stretched the players to their limits, Salah wanted more. He seemed to crave it. Three training sessions in the day were often preceded and followed by gym work. Each of these individualised sessions involved assistance from the physios and rehab team.

He was an early riser but he also went to bed late. It was not uncommon for Salah to order room service way past midnight, as he refuelled his body in preparation for the next morning. It was sometimes dark when he finished in the gym, but Liverpool allocated a team of helpers to assist the players at all hours of the day. When Salah was hungry, a call would go in. His standard order was porridge and walnuts with honey and raisins.

In 2017 it was decided that mobile phones would be banned in the treatment room in an attempt to get players interacting more with staff. Previously, players would often sit there receiving a rub, ignoring the person who was helping them. Without distractions, newcomers like Salah were able to get to know people who worked for the club a lot quicker, promoting professional trust and helping him settle.

Staff enjoyed working with him. Some of the players could be rude and demanding but he was neither, though it was clear he was serious about his health. In those early months at the club, he seemed to gravitate to those teammates who felt similarly about their upkeep. He would speak a lot to Georginio Wijnaldum, the Dutch midfielder, who seemed to be friends with everyone, as well as Sadio Mané – another Muslim footballer from Africa.

Over the years that followed, as the team grew, and both Mané and Salah became established parts of one of the most feared forward lines in Europe, the pair's relationship would shift significantly and an internal rivalry would end up blowing up in public. In 2017, however, Salah and Mané would often sit next to each other in the physio room, receiving rubdowns after games, as part of the screening that tested how their bodies had responded to the strain of ninety minutes in a Liverpool shirt.

Each of the players completed a form using an app, measuring how tired they were, through the quality of their sleep or muscle soreness. Other tests would follow, measuring hamstring tenderness or abductor stiffness, maybe other aches or pains.

Salah did not have regular problems with any part of his body. A variety of reports showed staff that he had a well-balanced structure. There was quite a lot of soft tissue work after matches but he devoted a lot of time to the gym from his earliest days at the club, focusing especially on his abdominal area, and this reduced his needs.

In subsequent years, after scoring goals, he would sometimes earn a yellow card from a referee by throwing his shirt into the air after scoring a goal. Comments would follow about his six-pack. Yet Salah did not develop this necessarily to impress people. He realised the connection between core, availability and performance. One member of staff said, 'His injury history is not extensive. That's because he keeps himself in excellent condition. He listens to advice and he listens to his body. He was really good to work with.'

Salah's focus was on his rotational strength. In laymen's terms, this meant being able to twist his body as he moved. Footballers are different to track sprinters because they need to be able to turn quickly. If a footballer's legs move, it doesn't always mean that the upper body will travel at the same speed. He therefore needs to ensure the connection between the body and the legs is as strong as it possibly can be. Salah understood this. Though people would talk about that impressive six-pack, this was more a reflection of his lifestyle and his diet than anything he did in the gym.

Melwood, Liverpool's training ground until 2020, was roughly a fifty-minute drive from Salah's home in Cheshire, where several of his teammates also lived. Though he was one of the furthest away, he would often be one of the first to arrive at the facility. Some of the staff joked whether he was simply trying to beat the motorway traffic, but it quickly became clear he was there for a purpose because he never wasted his time.

While other early starters arriving from Cheshire would play pool, Salah was nearly always working, trying to maximise his abdominal strength. This would allow him to turn faster and decelerate quicker. He could jump higher, land safely and set off on a run, twisting and turning. Quickly, he became more agile. 'His commitment to himself was unwavering and he became unstoppable,' said one member of the club's fitness team.

Salah had been a gym-user as a teenager on the fringes of the Al-Mokawloon team. It was not until he joined Chelsea, however, that he really began to understand the importance of weight training.

In London, he was usually on the bench or not involved at all in the matchday squad. He would look at the other players in the dressing room and they all seemed to be bigger than him. Though Eden Hazard, the team's most exciting player, was smaller, he was also tougher. Salah recognised his speed would only get him so far in the game. He had to be able to survive.

This led to him focusing on his upper-body strength. At Liverpool, he became a 'gym addict', according to one of the fitness team. Yet in many ways, it was his experiences at Chelsea that had the most profound effect on him: being out of the team also brought a sense of despondency about the direction of his career. The gym exercise made him feel alive. He could see himself getting bigger. Ultimately, though, he went to fill the time he had on his hands in a foreign country he barely understood, one where nobody particularly rated him that highly. 'I used to go every day because I knew I would not play,' he told GQ magazine in 2022.

Throughout his time at Liverpool, he also worked on himself away from the training ground. While weightlifting brought muscle growth through repetition, his definition and tone were aided by Pilates, which controlled each of his movements in a slower fashion, stimulating endurance, increased core strength, stability and posture alignment.

'Mo had a fully sculpted physique because of all of the additional work he did away from Melwood,' said one rehab worker, who suggested that Salah could be trusted to manage his own body because he tended to take advice from the right sources, while other players sometimes had too many advisors and the conflicting guidance led to bad decisions.

'These players became more difficult to manage from the club's perspective because we weren't always able to monitor exactly what they were doing all of the time. Some of them arrived at training with injuries because of the work they were doing with specialists. It was very frustrating. But that never happened with Mo.' Salah's dedication, even by the standards of any supremely fit Premier League footballer, was 'extreme' and his faith would not get in the way of his desire to 'create a machine' out of his body.

During Ramadan, some of Salah's workouts and refuelling at home would begin at 2.40 a.m. His nutritionist would tell him that he did not have any body fat and he could eat whatever he wanted but he still managed his consumption carefully. 'Nutrition is so important, it's part of the game,' Salah said, somewhat mundanely, in 2018. 'It has helped with my recovery, allowed me to sleep better and helped my body adapt quickly.'

While his house was filled with fitness and medical equipment, he also practised meditation and yoga, which introduced him into a realm of alternative thought. Yoga had its physical benefits, reducing the risk of injury, lengthening his stride and increasing core strength. Salah would follow a slower-paced programme that focused on deeper stretches and involved one-legged squats to improve his balance. After a thunderous goal in front of the Kop secured a late victory against his old club Chelsea in 2019, he celebrated with a tree pose. Yoga lowered his heart rate, making him calmer. He came to believe that the discipline also aided his focus, concentration and sleep patterns. He practised breathing from his stomach rather than his chest and this helped reduce stress.

Salah would continue to begin days sitting on the side of his bed, with fifteen minutes of the visualisation training that had worked so well for him in Rome. His interest in self-improvement was an 'obsession' according to a Liverpool teammate, who would often see him retreat into his hotel room on away trips with a self-help book in his hand.

In July 2018, after Egypt's exit from the World Cup at the group stages, Salah published a photograph of himself on social media reading Mark Manson's *Fan el La Mobalah*, the Arabic translation of the hit book *The Subtle Art of Not Giving a F★ck*. Egyptians wondered whether this was his way of giving two fingers to his critics but it nevertheless became a bestseller in the country. Salah would also use scripture as a reminder to anyone who doubted him that he was a proud Egyptian. Another piece of writing he liked was *Fagr el Damir*, the Arabic version of *Dawn of Conscience* by James Henry Breasted, a book which explored the greatness of the ancient Egyptian civilisation.

His favourite author was Napoleon Hill, who in 1937 published *Think and Grow Rich*. Salah would conclude that in difficult periods, the only thing to do was to 'have a serious conversation with yourself'. He told *GQ* in 2022 that sometimes he would sit at a table over a coffee and ask himself questions. 'Some people can't face themselves properly,' he said. 'But I have no problem with that. If I'm struggling, I just face myself and feel where I am.'

Perhaps it was difficult for Salah to understand what he was going through because no other Egyptian footballer or sportsperson had ever reached his level of fame. He could only learn about his new world by leaning on the experience of others.

Liverpool won the Champions League under Klopp as a suffocating counterattacking team, but a year later, having become Premier League champions with Salah the top scorer for a third season in a row, they had started to become more efficient in possession, often grinding opponents down.

The data supported this evolution. During the 2017–18 Premier League season, Klopp's team averaged 60.3 per cent possession (fourth in the possession table). A year later, the team became better, competing for both the Champions League (which they won) and the Premier League title (which they narrowly missed out on). Domestically, Liverpool averaged 61.8 per cent in the possession table, where they came third.

Liverpool emerged as champions in 2019–20 but the manner of the team's approach was different. Rather than try and blow teams away in the opening twenty-five minutes as they often had done previously under Klopp, they were now more patient, churning out result after result.

Though it felt as though Liverpool were becoming more mature, Klopp and his staff realised that winning the Champions League brought increased respect. Other managers were happy to defend deep and try to steal a point, even some of the best ones. It meant Liverpool had to become better at waiting, and cleverer with their passes. They were second in the possession table that year, but in terms of percentages, Liverpool averaged 62.9, the highest measurement in that metric during the Klopp era so far.

Having secured the Premier League crown for the first time in the club's history, it wasn't going to get any easier for Liverpool. Goalkeepers would waste more time, defences would sit even deeper, midfields would become more compact. Having been given control of the planning and execution of first-team training sessions, assistant coach Pep Lijnders became a significant figure in Liverpool's response in terms of the team's tactical strategy.

Klopp was the manager who had delivered Liverpool's first league title in thirty years. He was up there with some of the greatest in the club's history. Players who represented Liverpool under the great Bill Shankly (who took the club from the old second division into the first, before becoming champions and then FA Cup winners for the first time), suggested only Klopp rivalled the Scot for charisma and impact.

Klopp was wanting more of a say on the club's transfer policy. This came after the decision in the summer of 2020 not to meet Georginio Wijnaldum's demands on a new contract. Though Liverpool would not scrape back any of the £25 million on a midfielder they had signed from Newcastle in 2016, sporting director Michael Edwards did not think the wages Wijnaldum was looking for made financial sense for Liverpool when the player was approaching thirty.

Wijnaldum had emerged as one of the dressing-room leaders at Liverpool. He was well respected by his teammates and his manager. Klopp described him as 'the perfect midfielder. He has all the things you need: both directions, small spaces, big spaces, hard challenges; a fine footballer.'

Though Klopp felt he was worth a new deal, owners FSG backed Edwards' decision to cut him loose when his contract was up in 2021. Both Klopp and Edwards knew about this possibility a year out, and with Liverpool's midfield evolving from one that could run, challenge and fill spaces, into one that could see gaps and pass through them, Klopp wanted to sign Bayern Munich's Thiago Alcântara, effectively as Wijnaldum's replacement.

Earlier that summer, the Spaniard was nominated as player of the match when Bayern beat Paris Saint-Germain in the final of the Champions League at an empty stadium in Lisbon, delayed because of the Covid-19 pandemic. There was no doubting Thiago's talent. At Bayern, Pep Guardiola had made him his first signing during his tenure as manager. Yet seven years later, Liverpool's recruitment team were concerned about the player's age profile (he was just five months younger than Wijnaldum), as well as his injury record. Though Thiago was considered a quick healer, he had managed thirty Bundesliga games only once in any season across his time in Munich, where the medical department was considered one of the best in the world.

Amongst Liverpool's fanbase, Thiago became arguably the most eye-catching signing of the Klopp era because of his proven quality and his background, having been nurtured at Barcelona under Guardiola before he broke into one of the greatest teams that has ever been. He played the game like a matador and his arrival for £20 million plus add-ons seemed proof that Liverpool under Klopp had become one of the most attractive clubs in the world.

Klopp's relationship with Edwards was constructive but it involved debate. They did not agree on everything, but that didn't mean they would always fall out over a difference of opinion. Yet several contacts within the club have suggested it was this deal that led to Edwards considering his position at Liverpool. They say that Klopp got what he wanted but only after speaking to Mike Gordon, FSG's president, the man who many years earlier had identified Edwards as a potential sporting director because of his understanding of analytics and his ruthlessness in decision making.

The balance of control was shifting. Though Edwards got his way over Wijnaldum (a decision that in the fullness of time would appear to be the right one given the player's struggles in Paris and then Roma, where he was seriously injured), these felt like the first steps on the way to Liverpool becoming more of a manager-led operation. Evidence of Klopp's increasing power came in August 2021, when there was a feeling within Liverpool's analytics department that it might be time to move Jordan Henderson on, but Klopp pursued a new contract for his captain and got his way.

Separately, Klopp also managed to keep hold of Ray Haughan, who had switched from being the club's long-serving players' liaison officer to another role leading the first-team operations. Haughan was tight with many of Liverpool's players and, given Klopp valued his relationship with the playing staff above any other department, Haughan was a key ally. His status was reflected by the freedom he had in 2019 when Liverpool won the Champions League in Madrid. As Tottenham defender Danny Rose lay slumped on the floor at the final whistle, Haughan was one of the first members of Liverpool's staff onto the pitch, even though he was not a player or even a coach.

Others were wary of the influence Haughan commanded. His background was in the travel industry, but at Bolton Wanderers he had briefly worked for Sammy Lee, the former Liverpool midfielder, as a scout. Lee's director of football at Bolton was Frank McParland, and later, during his time as a senior Liverpool scout, Haughan came with him to Anfield. Haughan's power base grew. 'Eventually, he controlled the training ground,' said one source.

Before Klopp, Haughan got extremely close to his predecessor, Brendan Rodgers, who underwent a fitness regime to lose weight. Haughan often went running with Rodgers around the streets of West Derby, close to the training ground. Two days after Rodgers was sacked, however, a report appeared in the *Daily Mail* under the headline: LIVERPOOL'S HEAD OF TECHNICAL PERFORMANCE MICHAEL EDWARDS IS THE LAPTOP GURU WHO DID A NUMBER ON BRENDAN RODGERS.

What followed was detail on how Edwards had allegedly built a 'cosy' relationship with FSG by dropping emails to Boston throughout the day, leading to a 'strained relationship' with the now departed manager.

'Edwards encourages staff to use his nickname "Eddie", giving a matey feel to the working environment,' the report read. 'It is understood Rodgers has another name for him.' Edwards would supposedly send emails to the States after each game, using data to try and explain where it was either won or lost. This helped him become "a trusted source of information to a group of people who are obsessed with statistical analysis".'

For Edwards, who was then in the infancy of his career, the publication of this report was damaging. Inside Liverpool, it was believed that a disgruntled former scout was responsible for the briefing, yet anyone with strong connections to Rodgers was now potentially a threat.

Haughan fell into that category. When another Premier League club offered him the chance to leave Liverpool on a better salary, it was ultimately Edwards' decision, as he was in charge of staffing. When it was suggested to Klopp that the club could not afford to match the salary he was being offered elsewhere, Klopp went to Mike Gordon to press upon the importance of keeping Haughan. This led to Haughan staying at Liverpool, where he instead worked under Klopp's direction rather than under Edwards.

Edwards would officially leave Liverpool in 2022, suggesting it was the right time to move on following a decade of service. Yet upon Klopp's departure two years later, Edwards came back to the FSG fold, albeit to lead its football operation rather than the club itself. One of the figures to depart with Klopp was Haughan at the end of his own contract, whose name and influence had largely gone under the radar for his entire time at the club.

As Liverpool's sporting director, Edwards had supported the FSG programme of buying smaller and selling bigger and this was combined with a strong belief that handing out significant contracts to players coming towards the end of their careers made little economic sense. Klopp, meanwhile, could see better the impact on the dressing room of experienced figures such as an everyman like Wijnaldum and firmly believed he could squeeze every last ounce of energy out of them.

Thiago fell into the same category. As at Bayern, however, Thiago would struggle for games due to injury, playing just ninety-eight times for Liverpool over the next four seasons before leaving on a free transfer at the same time as Klopp. Liverpool would end up spending £23.2 million on Thiago's wages while he was out injured, more money than any other player during the Klopp era.

In total, across his eight and a half years in charge of Liverpool, the club spent more than £212 million on the wages of injured players according to data collated by the Fatigue Index. Inside Liverpool, the injury record irritated the medics, the physios and the fitness coaches who wanted to bring change but were unable to because of a lack of communication between departments. It was probably true that Liverpool would have won more trophies during this period had it not been for the presence of Manchester City, a club which was found guilty on two occasions of breaking Financial Fair Play rules, and later had 115 further charges brought against them.

Yet internally at Liverpool, it was also felt that Klopp's team would have been more successful without seasons blighted by injuries. This was not always down to bad luck. Klopp was a brilliant leader of players but staff often felt he did not really know what it took to keep them on the pitch or how to maintain his working relationships with people who influenced this process. Instead, it often seemed as though he thought they were to blame for the injuries Liverpool were suffering, rather than being the source of any potential solution.

Yet staff did not really blame the manager for this: it was in theory the role of the sporting director and the owners to ensure world-class standards were met across all departments. To the staff at Liverpool, Edwards seemed to have more control of appointments in the early years of Klopp but as time passed, and Liverpool progressed on the pitch, Klopp began to have more of a say, not necessarily on who came in and who left, but who he listened to, and how staff were subsequently treated.

It was felt that, despite much upheaval, nobody ever got to grips with the issue of injury management and prevention. A study into the estimated cost during the 2016–17 season suggested a Premier League team would lose a point for every 136 days out due to injury and, approximately, every 271 days of injury would cost a team one place in the table. It was also calculated that Premier League teams were hit in the pocket, with an average team losing £45 million a year due to injury-related decrement.

The same Premier League study revealed that, on average, 345 days per season were lost to hamstring injuries, accounting for 83 per cent of injuries overall. This was compared to the calf (44 days and 10.6 per cent of injuries) and the abductor (1.7 percent and just seven days).

It would frustrate staff, desperate to improve Liverpool's injury record and give the club a better chance of winning trophies, that hires did not seem to focus on combatting specific problems that regularly cropped up, such as the hamstring. Had it been different, Liverpool might have had the edge over a rival like Manchester City, who pipped them to two titles on the final day of the season during Salah's time at the club.

Rather than bringing in experts to implement a new system and train existing staff, new people were instead brought in from other clubs, where the same problems existed. At Liverpool these hires continued to work the way they had elsewhere.

It was felt by staff in some departments that the analysis of players breaking down could have been better. For a number of staff, it seemed like full trust did not exist between the coaches and the heads of each department, and this filtered down to the staff below.

The reality of heading up medical and rehabilitation departments is that those higher up have the additional distraction of club politics and can't just focus on the more pressing issue of injury management.

Salah did not have problems with injuries, but his teammates' issues impacted his success at Liverpool. While the availability of players may have made a difference to the seasons when Liverpool went head to head with Manchester City for titles, injuries undoubtedly undermined at least two other campaigns, remembered mainly because of Liverpool's struggles and underachievements.

If the musician Neil Young was right about it being 'better to burn out than to fade away' then Klopp arguably did both. Two or maybe three of Klopp's last four seasons in charge were either disappointing or finished disappointingly. In 2020–21, as defending champions, Liverpool just about made it into the Champions League, a feat so unlikely at one point that Klopp was able to reframe the qualification as being one of his greatest achievements. Two years later, they did not, however, and this meant Klopp's final season at the club was instead spent trying to make progress in the Europa League, the only competition the manager failed to win during his eight and a half years at Anfield.

Even the good times involved 'collateral', as one member of staff called it when reflecting on the period between 2017 and 2020, when Klopp and Salah helped Liverpool emerge as a global force. It tends to be agreed that Liverpool's success probably wouldn't have been possible had Klopp not demanded so much physically from his players, though his methods also invited the possibility of burnout. But the structure below Klopp was not in place to support him season after season.

It was estimated that a Klopp pre-season, when he got all the time he wanted with the squad, would involve nearly seventy kilometres of running a week per player, with the addition of a couple of friendly matches, which were not always played at high speed. The expected mileage from his players during any successful season would subsequently drop to around fifty-five kilometres. Basic maths would support Klopp's view that the tougher the preparation, the easier the real thing became.

Yet he was also a manager who tended to operate with a small squad and a settled team. He was not a wheeler-dealer in the transfer market, and he found it difficult to say goodbye to players, especially those who had served him well. This all contributed towards him encountering serious problems relating to availability post-2020, following three seasons where largely the same group of players had run further than any other club in the Premier League across 166 games in all competitions.

The problems intensified for Klopp when two or three players became injured at the same time. The backup players, used to getting just thirty kilometres into their legs, were suddenly expected to deliver an increased capacity of almost 25 per cent. This led to many of them breaking down and Liverpool suffering from an acute injury crisis. Accordingly, results suffered.

Klopp had a huge staff at Liverpool but only his inner circle would get to see the best and very worst of his moods. A few of them insisted he wasn't naive about the potential pitfalls of his strategy. This was the way he'd always worked and, though there was a risk of a boom being followed by a bust, the booms tended to last and live longer in the memory than the busts. They also acknowledged, however, that while Klopp was probably the best manager in terms of making everyone feel great about themselves when results were going his way, he found it harder raising himself from the floor when the opposite was happening, and this affected those around him.

For those staff members outside Klopp's circle, working for Liverpool was more of a regular job, and a professional distance existed with the manager. Many were not paid particularly well. In their post-Liverpool careers, they would still have to find employment elsewhere. This contributed towards some operating very carefully indeed. It was beneficial, for example, to get close to a star player and gain his confidence. Salah fell into that category. While any such attention made the player feel good about himself, it increased the chances of one of the club's leading figures identifying that staff member's value and in turn the likelihood of them staying longer at Liverpool. The dynamic sometimes led to staff appealing to the moods of the player, rather than looking after the interests of the team.

Players influenced staffing levels at Liverpool. When Salah got injured ahead of the Champions League final in 2022, Edwards' successor Julian Ward had, inside forty-eight hours, brought the physiotherapist Chris Rohrbeck back from Mainz on a short-term contract. Given that Salah's own contract negotiations had reached an impasse at the time, the hiring of Rohrbeck made him feel better about his place at Liverpool; the German had been close to him during a three-year spell working for the club.

Klopp's relationship with most of the players was especially tight, but so was Edwards'. Lee Nobes, another physiotherapist, arrived from Manchester City following a recommendation from Milner, the midfielder who players and staff tended to agree set the standards in training, even though he wasn't a guaranteed starter in the team. Milner was Liverpool's vice captain and Klopp's enforcer. Edwards would listen to him. When unavailable, Milner would still travel to away games and have an input in dressing-room discussions. When some players in Klopp's leadership group saw mobile phones being used around Melwood, they'd sometimes let it slide even though it was against rules. Not on Milner's watch. He was difficult to please but his devotion helped create the sort of culture Klopp wanted, where attitudes towards training were total.

It became difficult for staff to convince players they should rest. If this was put to Klopp, he tended to follow the instinct of the player. Though he could be forceful, he also trusted them. Klopp would live and die by their performances, so perhaps it was understandable that he put more effort in developing his relationships with the players than with anyone else. While he could play the sensitive angle with them, the extended team especially saw less of that. It meant that some felt less valuable. This all made it harder for those who came to Klopp with warnings about player burnout.

Inside this dynamic, there was the also the issue of inter-departmental relationships. One of the defining backroom figures of the Klopp era was his countryman and lookalike, Andreas Kornmayer. The head of fitness and conditioning was one of Klopp's first hires in the summer of 2016, and he was essentially brought in to whip the players into the sort of shape that could withstand Klopp's physical expectations.

Kornmayer, who would encourage Salah to do core stability exercises upon his own arrival at the club a year later, was hired after the team suffered a spate of hamstring injuries during Klopp's first six months in charge, as the players struggled to adjust to the demands of the new regime. Kornmayer had not been a leading figure at his previous club, Bayern Munich. Yet his power at Liverpool grew quickly. He would inherit a work-space that was already divided between English- and Spanish-speaking staff but over the years that followed, new splits appeared. Several former employees agree that a culture clash was allowed to develop, this time between the English staff and those coming in from Germany. Throughout his tenure, neither Klopp nor the sporting directors he worked with were able to bring the situation under control.

Responsibilities often seemed blurred. While Klopp had worked in the Bundesliga, where the physios rarely set foot on the training pitch by comparison with the fitness coaches, in England, the role of the physio was often all-encompassing, especially around injuries. They would monitor a player's progress once he was back on the grass rather than leaving it to the fitness team or the sports scientists.

The model at Liverpool was, at best, a hybrid, but this left some staff believing there was a lack of accountability. In the midst of this, Kornmayer proved to be the sort of sergeant-major figure Klopp wanted on the training field, pushing the players to their limits, but the process-driven staff said he did not have the interpersonal skills to bring everyone together.

Over the years that followed, Liverpool improved on the pitch. Klopp's Dutch assistant Pep Lijnders led most of the training sessions, with Klopp observing from the sidelines, interfering only when he felt it was necessary. As matches got closer, he would become more involved. He also trusted Vitor Matos, the Portuguese coach, who was very close to Ljinders. Klopp believed different voices helped the players, adding energy to the working week. If Klopp was quiet earlier in the week, his words, he thought, would have a greater impact as match day approached.

Liverpool were getting better and better, and the arrival of Salah gave the team a sense of superstar status. Yet this did not mean everyone behind the scenes was working harmoniously. Kornmayer would get more miles out of the players' legs than anyone thought was possible, yet this also brought more wear and tear. When, further down the line, some of these players got older and developed muscular problems, Liverpool was not capable of dealing with them.

Not that they did not try. Edwards brought the physios and sports scientists closer together by hiring Philipp Jacobsen as head of performance. This role, in theory, meant Liverpool now had someone above each of the heads of department, with a direct link to the football operation led by Klopp. Jacobsen later described his job as being a 'sounding board' and recognised it was 'challenging'. From the outside, Jacobsen had appeared to be a Klopp hire because he was German. Yet like a few of Edwards' appointments, Jacobsen had worked with him before.

Their relationship had started at Portsmouth in 2005. Jacobsen then went to the Aspetar hospital in Qatar, where he worked for a decade.

At Liverpool, he would last two years, leaving amidst a raft of departures in the months after Klopp secured the club its first Premier League title in thirty years. Despite the splits at Liverpool, staff tended to agree that Jacobsen was on thin ice from day one after he made it clear to Kornmayer that he wanted to know more about the science behind certain decisions. This was perceived as a challenge to Kornmayer's authority.

It was basically Jacobsen's job to inspire a single but supple way of working throughout the club: this never happened, even when Liverpool were successful on the pitch. Despite his time at Portsmouth, Jacobsen had been largely an unknown in England, following so many years in Qatar, and he did not inspire the respect to make the change that was needed. 'A nice bloke,' said one staff member, 'but you had to be a bastard to get things done at Liverpool at that time.'

Jacobsen's exit coincided with the pandemic and a season as defending champions in which the squad suffered from injuries like never before. Some of these were caused by impact on the pitch and pure bad luck, but many were muscular. By the end of the campaign, twenty-three Liverpool players had missed at least one game through injury or illness. Liverpool's players missed a total of 308 matches, a figure which equated to six players being out for the entire campaign and still further injuries on top.

Of Liverpool's thirty-eight league matches, there were only eleven where they had fewer than six players unavailable and for exactly half of the fixtures, Liverpool were without seven players. While fans would curse Liverpool's luck, a lot of this was down to the lack of structure. Staff were leaving because they were unhappy with the working environment as well as pay, Edwards announced his own departure and Klopp took more of a role in off-field appointments. These included Andreas Schlumberger – as Jacobsen's replacement – whose relationship with the Liverpool manager went back decades to university. Klopp had also worked with Schlumberger at Dortmund.

In the summer of 2021, Klopp got the sort of pre-season he loved when, due to travelling restrictions in the pandemic, Liverpool did not embark on a commercial tour. Instead, Klopp took the players to Austria for a month. Schlumberger introduced the use of artificial intelligence from a Californian company called Zone7, which allowed him to pull lots of information together via an algorithm to show whether or not a player was close to getting injured. Much was made of this technology but staff remained sceptical, possibly fearing for their own jobs. It would have been much more beneficial to the players had a better harmony existed between departments, bringing about smarter decisions.

The subsequent campaign involved sixty-three games, and Liverpool came close to an unprecedented quadruple. But the effort and energy expended by an ageing team with years of Klopp's physical testing took their toll and, inside a year, Liverpool went from appearing in a Champions League final to the point where they were not capable of even qualifying for the competition.

This prompted Salah to take to social media: 'I'm totally devastated. There's absolutely no excuse for this. We had everything we needed to make it to next year's Champions League and we failed. We are Liverpool and qualifying to the competition is the bare minimum. I am sorry but it's too soon for an uplifting or optimistic post. We let you and ourselves down.'

Some of his teammates would approach him about his message, thinking he'd gone too far. He was not, after all, the team's captain. It was not his place to mention anyone else's performance in public with the mention of 'we'.

Salah, however, was unrepentant. Quite how aware he was of Liverpool's problems behind the scenes remains unclear. He had always been able to manage himself amidst the club's culture. Arguably, it had helped him flourish because he was nearly always available. He remained one of the best players in the world. Yet by 2023, he wasn't even playing for a team that was capable of making it onto a platform he'd thrived on across the previous six years.

Klopp reacted by enlisting the help of a leadership consultant with vast experience at the advertising agency Saatchi & Saatchi. Kevin Roberts had once been the company's CEO and he'd since worked with New Zealand's All Blacks rugby union side. It was his aim to 'inspire everyone I meet to be the best they can'. The PR around this move suggested Klopp and Liverpool were trying everything they could to get the club back on track. In truth, it reflected the disconnection between various departments at the club. Everyone involved was encouraged to speak openly and Klopp was taken aback by just how frustrated some people were. When the process was reported, Liverpool's manager was unhappy. Only a select few knew about it and it was meant to be top secret.

Chapter 9

Champion of Africa

Ruben Pons, from the Spanish festival town of Benicassim, was a shaven-headed physiotherapist who spent the first five years of his professional career in football working in the country's nearby ceramic capital of Villarreal. This preceded a period as a personal trainer, securing retainers to look after the physical welfare of players from clubs in the Premier League and La Liga. In 2014, he arrived at Liverpool, where he became a part of Brendan Rodgers' staff. After surviving a cull following Jürgen Klopp's appointment, he developed a bond with Mohamed Salah during his first season at the club.

Pons had seen football drift towards an individualised sport. Players had agents and not always only one agent; they were working with their own coaches, they were hiring their own nutritionists and chefs. Inside clubs, the biggest names tended to have their muscles as well as their egos massaged by snagging additional attention from permanent staff like Pons, who were otherwise trying to balance their time between several players.

Twenty-nine players represented Liverpool's first team during 2017–18, not including the numerous youth players called up for training sessions who also required assessment. Quite often, in fact, it was these players who took the focus, as staff familiarised themselves with their medical histories.

Some of the senior players at Liverpool believed the squad needed more support. Someone even thought it was necessary to have one physio per player. The budget did not stretch that far and, ultimately, this sort of dynamic did not exist at other clubs. The season started with five first-team physios, two full-time masseurs, one part-time masseur and two full-time doctors.

The most recent arrival was Chris Rohrbeck, hired from Mainz on Klopp's recommendation, with the manager telling other physios at Liverpool that he was the best he'd ever worked with. Over the following year, as the team progressed on the pitch, there were significant changes off it, with Philipp Jacobsen the new 'medical rehabilitation and performance manager', leading to the hire of Spaniard José Luis Rodriguez, who joined him at Melwood after nearly a decade at Qatar's Aspire Academy.

Rodriguez would effectively replace Pons, who was at that point close to Salah. To other staff, it sometimes seemed as though Pons's dedication to the player was total and the player had become dependent. With Salah breaking records and his status in the dressing room rising, Pons became more powerful and senior figures in other departments began to question the health of this dynamic.

After Salah was dragged to the floor by Sergio Ramos in Kyiv, damaging Liverpool's hopes of winning the Champions League final, and potentially ruling him out of the 2018 World Cup, Pons gave an interview to Spanish radio. This surprised other members of staff, as ordinarily employees at Liverpool needed permission to speak to reporters and no one at the club seemed to be aware of any request made by Pons.

'We knew that it was something serious as soon as [Salah] fell on the ground because he never complains, we were afraid of the worst,' said Pons, who was assisted by Rohrbeck on the pitch in Kyiv as Salah lay on the floor crying. 'I was devastated but I tried to transmit calmness. I told him that nothing could be done and that he did not worry too much, it was time to look for solutions and not to regret because things did not work.'

Pons and Salah followed the rest of the game by scrolling their social media pages and hoping for the best. The security personnel in their company were also able to help. Salah was in so much pain that he could not change from the kit that he was wearing into the tracksuit supplied by the club without assistance. Pons thought it would take between three and four weeks for him to recover. 'But we are going to try and reduce those deadlines, that's the big goal,' he added.

Pons travelled to Russia with Salah to oversee his rehabilitation, working closely with the Egyptian FA, but by the end of July, he was out of a job. There was some surprise that Salah did not step in and try and prevent his departure, yet the club was proactive in its attempts to reassure him. Though Jordan Henderson was the captain and James Milner was the dominant personality in the dressing room, it was clear to anyone who spent time inside the same working space that Salah liked concessions being made for him. 'He was now the main player and he wanted to feel like he was the main player,' said one staff member.

The appointment of Rodriguez was a part of this strategy. Born in Andalusia, he spoke four languages, including French and Arabic. He was an extremely well-qualified physiotherapist, with experience working with the Iraqi national team, and his appointment protected Jacobsen in his early months at the club as Salah continued to feel as though he was the most important player in the squad.

All of this was unsaid and unwritten but those familiar with the environment at Liverpool understood what made Salah tick. He seemed to respond well to attention. 'It was VIP treatment,' says one staff member.

Rodriguez was treading on slightly perilous ground as he tried to adjust to the culture of the club, where he barely knew anyone. Though it was important that Salah felt that his needs were being considered, it could not appear that way to the rest of the squad, especially the senior figures who were not receiving such specialist treatment. Footballers tend to be aware and sensitive to such imbalances. Salah was never explicitly told that Rodriguez's hire was for him, and it wasn't necessarily, though it suited the club for him to think that he was. As soon as Salah realised Rodriguez spoke Arabic, he was curious. To others, it seemed as though Rodriguez wanted Salah to create the interest himself rather than Rodriguez simply jumping straight in with him.

The pair were getting along. Yet Rodriguez had to remember that Pons had met his end at Liverpool partly by getting too close. It was also becoming clear that another Liverpool player was pushing to have the same attention. As Rodriguez and Salah gravitated towards one another, other staff suddenly noticed that Rodriguez was spending more time with Sadio Mané. One staff member said, 'It was almost, like, Boom! Sadio claimed José for himself . . .'

Salah was not the only Liverpool footballer raised as a Muslim in the African countryside: Mané was born in a remote settlement on the other side of the continent on 10 April, 1992 – two months and five days before Salah.

Bambali, Sédhiou, is seven hours by car from Dakar, Senegal's capital; a journey that involves two border crossings, in and out of The Gambia, which dissects Senegal almost in two. When Mané made a documentary about his life in 2019, which ended up being broadcast a year later by the Japanese streaming service Rakuten, with less fanfare than it might have had due to the Covid-19 pandemic, he suggested there was only one option for the villagers of Bambali. 'You could only become a farmer,' Mané said. 'There was no other work.'

In 2012, the World Bank estimated that 68.3 per cent of families in the Sédhiou province lived below the poverty line, with nearly 60 per cent of thirty-year-olds unemployed. The wider Casamance region had been at the centre of an independence struggle that began in 1982 and flared from time to time in the decades that followed.

One such period was in 1999 when the Senegalese military shelled Casamance's de-facto capital Ziguinchor, an offensive that led to more than 20,000 people fleeing towards the border with Guinea-Bissau. During this period of considerable upheaval, Mané's father died in another village where he was having medical treatment. It was impossible for the family to return his body home. This meant he was buried without anyone present. Mané, aged seven, was told of this crushing development by a cousin, just as he was about to play football. His father had been an imam at Bambali's mosque and on the anniversary of his death, the family would gather each year to recite the Qur'an. Mané grew up reading the text every evening due to the influence of the men that remained in his family, several of whom were also imams.

A big part of Mané's day was spent cultivating the fields. It was this experience that had the greatest impact on him, as he told one of his uncles that it was his dream to find a job that ensured nobody in his family had to get up as early as he did. When the uncle heard this, he told the boy that such a prospect was impossible – they were farmers to the bone and destined to live in this collection of huts made out of mud, sticks and pieces of corrugated iron.

The same uncle ran a football team that trained on a patch of dry soil just outside Mané's home. On his way to the farm, Mané would kick whatever was lying around in front of him, usually stones or pots. There were so few footballs around that when Mané started playing competitively, albeit informally, with other villagers, they sometimes used grapefruits.

These rough-and-ready encounters contributed to the fearlessness that Mané later demonstrated on the professional pitches of Europe. He would turn ten in 2002, the year Senegal qualified for the World Cup for the first time. They caused a shock in their opening group game by beating the holders France, who two years previously had also become European champions. Senegal, a country that had a significant amount of its natural resources stripped by French colonists centuries earlier, made it all the way to the quarter finals of a tournament that was watched in Bambali, where there was hardly any electricity, through a couple of black-and-white televisions.

Mané told his friends, who sometimes called him '*Ballonbuwa*' ('Ball Wizard'), that one day he'd reach the same level as his heroes. Such ambition was not a feature of the villagers. Bambali's elders thought he was just a child dreaming but Mané demonstrated his seriousness by persuading his family to allow him to make the twenty-kilometre journey to Sédhiou to play in the *navetanes* – a sports festival that was held during the rainy season.

The focus in Bambali was faith rather than football. When it was suggested that teaching might be a better option, he replied, 'This is the only job that will enable me to help you. And I think I have the chance to become a footballer.'

His early experiences taught him that sometimes he had to think for himself and act on instinct. Aged fifteen, this led to him persuading a friend to loan him some money so that he could travel to Dakar, where he thought there would be more opportunity to become a footballer.

Nobody in his family knew about the plan. He practised being alone, hiding in the tall grass at sunset with his sports bag. One morning he set off before everyone else was awake, travelling in the direction of The Gambia without any form of identification, resourcefully convincing immigration guards to let him pass through two borders. He arrived in Dakar, which seemed like another world.

It took his family a week to figure out where he was and two uncles escorted him back to Bambali. Mané was furious. He finished his education and – following several family arguments – he was back in Dakar within a year, this time on trial at the recreation pitches of the city's police academy, where scouts were watching.

Since 2000, Génération Foot had been recruiting aspirants from all over Senegal and neighbouring nations, with the objective of getting as many players as possible prepared for and into Europe. Given that 46.7 per cent of Senegal's fifteen-million-strong population lived below the poverty line, the guarantee of accommodation and three meals a day put Mané and his fellow players at an advantage.

Mané could not escape where he came from. When a coach commented on his old boots, he told him, 'But that's all I have . . .' Though he scored four goals in his first game, some of the selectors had doubts about his personality. A long way from home and surrounded by boys he did not know, he was initially shy – painfully so.

Though the coaches could see his speed and dribbling ability and it was clear after a couple of sessions that he was a talented footballer, they remained concerned about his reluctance to socialise. Mané was told that he risked being sent back to Bambali if he did not attempt to mix. In fairness to him, he was a country kid and the majority of other players had grown up in or around Dakar. While he was cautious off the pitch, he was a different character altogether on it.

Six months later, a scout from Metz, France, saw Mané retrieve the ball in his own penalty area before running the entire length of the pitch to supply a teammate with the pass that allowed him to score. The scout later described this moment as watching a 'video game'.

Metz were in attendance because of an official partnership with Génération Foot, which received financial and technical aid, supplies and equipment and, eventually, a new facility on the edge of Dakar.

Though the cost was very high, so was the return. All of the players might have been officially under registration at Génération Foot, but Metz, in exchange, had first pick of the talent. Mané was one of seventeen players to join the reserve team of Metz since 2003, while eight have been promoted directly into Metz's senior setup. Ultimately, the relationship proved beneficial for both parties.

Génération Foot emerged from the lower leagues of the Senegalese football pyramid to feature in Africa's version of the

Champions League, having won two domestic championships and the same number of cups, and four of Metz's biggest sales involved former Génération Foot players. These include the top two, Ismaïla Sarr and Pape Matar Sarr (the two are not related), who have jointly fetched almost €34 million.

Mané, who was later sold to Red Bull Salzburg for €4 million, did not appear on the same list because he came when Metz had money problems after suffering relegation to the third tier of French football at the end of his first full season at the club.

His introduction to Europe was tough. Having arrived in the winter with a small case filled only with T-shirts, he was mocked by other players at his first training session. For several weeks, Mané did not reveal to coaches a pain he was suffering because he feared being sent back to Senegal. It turned out he had a hernia that required operating.

In recovery, he suffered from loneliness and the club's psychologist was crucial in keeping him on track. Other boys with the same injury would have the support of their family but Mané was alone, thousands of miles away from home. It toughened him up and as a nineteen-year-old, he made his professional debut for the first team. Though Metz lost 5–2 in Corsica to Bastia, the club's president, Bernard Serin, described him as a 'meteorite'.

This was in the difficult relegation period for Metz, which Joel Muller, a former player, described as the 'worst in the club's existence'. The team had gone down even with future stars like Kalidou Koulibaly, who would eventually become a legend in Serie A with Napoli.

Despite the gloom, Metz's general manager Philippe Gaillot saw significant talent in Mané with his 'exceptional relationship with the ball'. He could easily switch between feet, allowing him to slalom past opponents. The team's manager, Dominique Bijotat, a former Monaco midfielder capped eight times by France, tended to agree, albeit in fairly formal language.

'He has some gaps to fill, such as his positioning and his relationship on the pitch with teammates, knowing when to pass. But he is already able to string together technical acts of a very high level.'

At the start of Salah's first season at Liverpool, he and Mané would chat quietly on neighbouring tables in the treatment room, enjoying each other's company. By the start of Salah's second season (and Mané's third, having arrived from Southampton in summer of 2016), however, the dynamic had changed.

Mané was an extremely popular player with Liverpool's fanbase but Salah's extraordinary goalscoring achievements in 2017–18 had placed him higher. There were obvious reasons why Mané would measure himself against his teammate, which prompted him to ask himself whether he should be getting some of the same staff attention, therefore increasing the chance of him making even more of an impact on the pitch.

Mané had been the club's record African buy before Salah's arrival. They were both attacking players from the same continent and followed the same faith. Mané believed Salah had benefited from his own selflessness and asked club staff to establish precisely how many of Salah's debut season goals had involved him. The figure was north of 30 per cent. It frustrated Mané that Salah had been chosen to take on penalty-kick responsibilities from Milner, who was allocated but not always selected in the starting XI.

As Rodriguez started speaking in Arabic in 2018, Mané could see that the physio's arrival at the club was another intended Salah perk. Except it did not quite work out that way. With Pons gone, Chris Rohrbeck was suddenly working more closely with Salah, and this meant Rodriguez didn't have to make himself as available. Staff believe that Salah had concluded that Rohrbeck was Klopp's appointment and what was good enough for Liverpool's manager was ultimately good enough for him.

Rodriguez's personality was closer to Salah's than Mané's. He was a lively character when he felt comfortable and Jacobsen believed he had the social skills to complement Salah, who had a tendency to emerge from his shell when accompanied by people he trusted. Yet Rohrbeck's relationship with Salah grew more quickly than anyone expected, partly because of their mutual interest in basketball. 'Chris gave Mo the love he wanted,' according to one member of staff.

Rohrbeck was a workaholic who would stay at the training ground with players long after general sessions were finished. Such was his commitment, a member of staff remembered him nearly falling asleep once as he treated a player on a medical table. He and Salah had also joined Liverpool in the same summer. It tended to be that foreign players gravitated towards staff from other countries: British staff pushed collective gym sessions, while foreign staff were happier working one-to-one, discussing their shared experiences living away from home.

This left Rodriguez in an unexpected position. Rather than looking after Salah he was instead working a lot more with Mané. Observers of the dynamic described Mané as a fisherman, hooking Rodriguez out of the water, just as he was about to nibble elsewhere. Some staff believed Mané saved Rodriguez because Mané's need gave him an obvious purpose.

It was generally OK for members of staff to get close to a player but it was crucial that information concerning that player was shared with the heads of each department. Mané could explode on the pitch, but he was otherwise introverted, a quiet guy whose girlfriend was in Senegal, while he lived alone in Formby, not far away from Klopp. Staff had found it challenging communicating with him before Rodriguez's arrival. Sometimes he did not appear to listen to advice. But as the pair got closer, it was felt that Mané's connection with the medical department became stronger and the management of the player improved.

Across the same period, the awkwardness between Mané and Salah increased. Staff said Salah could see Mané was trying to compete with him. Some noticed how Salah would only speak about Mané when his teammate was not there, enquiring about the exercises Mané was doing away from the training ground. Sometimes, when Salah would be talking to staff in the treatment rooms, Mané would walk in and Salah would stop speaking. If Mané saw someone talking to Salah, he would pull him to one side, asking him what he'd been discussing with his teammate. 'Sadio increasingly saw Mo as a rival,' said another staff member.

Some of the players, particularly the British ones – who tended to say whatever was on their minds – became somewhat curious of Rodriguez, as he tried to balance two worlds, and held secrets. Other members of staff, meanwhile, were impressed at how he managed the contrasting personalities of two of Liverpool's best players without ever seemingly losing the trust of either of them.

Mané would grumble quietly about his grievances but only amongst an inner circle of people. He never made demands, certainly not of Klopp. It was important to him (as well as Salah), that he was humble – one of the central ideas of the Islamic faith.

Meanwhile, Salah knew that he had a preferential position ahead of Mané. This meant he had less of an issue, even though he could tell that his status annoyed his teammate. Across the staff, it was broadly felt that Salah was more mature than Mané and had the social skills to deal with the pressure being created by his teammate. Though he was curious about Mané's motivations, he rarely appeared stressed by them.

The rest of the squad were acutely aware of what was happening and it was not uncommon for one of the British players to try and wind the pair up. If Salah was reminded, for example, that Mané was on a better run of goalscoring form than him, Salah would smile but barely react. If Mané was told that Salah was leading him, he would mutter something to himself, retreating into his own world.

Back in 2012, the wider world did not know much about Mané but that began to change when, like Salah, he appeared at the London Olympics, where he represented Senegal for the first time, wearing the number 10 shirt in a team that played against Great Britain, drawing 1–1, and reached the quarter finals.

In the same summer, Metz were preparing for a season in the third division and the club were keen to balance the books by selling their assets. Though Mané had played just nineteen games in Ligue 2, scoring only once, interest in him was growing across France, with Marseille, arguably the biggest club in the country, speaking to the player's agent about his availability.

Only Red Bull Salzburg, however, were willing to meet Metz's financial expectations. A £3.5 million deal on the final day of the summer transfer window would make Mané the third most expensive signing in the history of Salzburg, a club that had been transformed by a controversial takeover by the drinks manufacturer only seven years earlier.

Moving from France to Austria might have seemed like a backward step for Mané but his lack of international experience was putting most clubs outside France off because of challenges obtaining a work permit. Salzburg, meanwhile, were now able to sign players previously beyond the club's financial reach when, over seventy-two years as SV Austria Salzburg, it won just three league titles.

Another four titles quickly followed after the takeover. Mané was almost guaranteed to play regularly on a platform that would at some point involve Champions League football, even though Salzburg had been knocked out of the competition for the 2012–13 season by the time Mané signed, following a defeat to Dundelange from Luxembourg on away goals in the second qualifying round.

The press in Senegal could not believe Mané's decision to join the Red Bull revolution, which involved clubs in other parts of the world, including Leipzig, who would overtake Salzburg in terms of pre-eminence due to their rise into the German Bundesliga in 2016. Four years earlier, however, Leipzig were positioned in the regional divisions while Salzburg potentially offered a quicker route to the top.

It had nevertheless seemed like a significant sum of money for Salzburg to pay considering Mané had played so few games for a side relegated out of Ligue 2. Yet Red Bull's global director,

Gérard Houllier, insisted the organisation did everything to bring him in. Like Mané, Houllier had a connection with north-eastern France, where he was born in the mining village of Therouanne. After a spell as a teacher in Liverpool's Alsop high school, he had a modest playing career before turning coach, inspiring village side Nœux-les-Mine to reach the old French second division. This led to opportunities with Paris Saint-Germain and the French national side, though his most successful job at an elite level was with Liverpool, where, amongst collecting other trophies, he completed a cup treble in 2000–01.

Houllier was credited with modernising the club, but at his own cost. In 2001, he suffered a heart attack during a game against Leeds United at Anfield and doctors believed it was only the lack of traffic around the stadium – as the match continued without him – that allowed ambulances to act quickly and save his life. There were other jobs after Liverpool, most notably at Olympique Lyon, but after returning to the Premier League with Aston Villa in 2010, he was advised to step away from management on health grounds.

Two years later, Houllier was missing management. He remained friends with Liverpool's former chief executive Rick Parry, who was close to David Dein, holder of the same position at Arsenal. Dein's son Darren was Thierry Henry's agent and his connections stretched into Austria, where he'd spoken to Dietrich Mateschitz, the billionaire owner of Red Bull.

Mateschitz wanted someone with elite-level experience to help him oversee the running of the seven clubs under his control, including those in the USA and Brazil. As it was not possible for Houllier to return to coaching, a role a couple of steps removed – without the stresses of immediate results – suited him.

Houllier flew to Salzburg to meet Mateschitz and, arriving early, sat down to wait. He soon heard a motorbike pull up and a man entered the building, wearing jeans and a checked shirt. When he removed his helmet, he acknowledged everyone. Houllier thought it was the postman but fifteen minutes later, he was being interviewed by the same person, the sixty-eight-year-old Mateschitz. Though the meeting was supposed to last half an hour, Houllier and Mateschitz chatted away for nearly four hours and Houllier left realising he wanted the job immediately.

Houllier told this story to the *Daily Telegraph* in 2019, the year Mané returned to Salzburg with Liverpool. Strangely, Houllier's own record at Liverpool when signing players from the French market was poor, especially in his final years in charge, and these were decisions that prompted critics to question his judgement following his health scare. Two of Mané's heroes from the 2002 World Cup team moved to Merseyside after the tournament and both El-Hadji Diouf and Salif Diao were considered failures. Houllier later concluded that Diouf, despite his talent, did not have the intelligence to become an elite footballer in Europe but he saw Mané very differently following his showing at the Olympics.

After his hiring by Red Bull, Houllier was keen to re-establish his reputation as a spotter of talent. There were other considerable forces at work in Salzburg and in 2012 one of them was the director of football, Ralf Rangnick, whose remits in both Leipzig and Salzburg were broad, officially including the 'recruitment of hidden talent, the development of a youth stream, and the implementation of an attacking playing philosophy across all levels'.

It would transpire that he too had a significant role in Mané's arrival in Salzburg having watched a cup game between Metz and Tours the previous season. Mané's performance in that game seemed to reduce the chances of signing him because Metz were asking for a fee that Rangnick felt might have been too big for Salzburg.

By the end of that summer, both Houllier and Rangnick were in agreement, however. 'What I liked straight away was his speed and ability on the ball,' Houllier later said. 'It was fantastic for a boy of his age. I had also seen him on French television. I quickly discovered that Metz would be willing to sell for financial reasons. Salzburg agreed to buy him and we paid less than £4 million. The potential was there and we just had to make sure he was well looked after.'

This involved setting up a player liaison scheme at Salzburg similar to the one he left behind at Liverpool, when it was run by a man called Norman Gard. Houllier saw Mané as shy. Initially, he lived with a French-speaking family before he moved into a modest one-bedroom flat and learned to speak German. Meanwhile, Salzburg's integration manager, Mustapha Mesloub, was selected by Rangnick to be Mané's chaperone and looked after the player around the clock – to the point where Mané became so close to his own family that he came to think of him as an adopted son.

Mesloub, a French-Algerian, encouraged Mané to eat a lot of pasta as there was no African restaurant in Salzburg and it was the closest thing he could find to rice. On an old leather couch, Mesloub spent much of his time with Mané watching football on television, though Mané could not sit still for long. This led to him bringing weights home with him from the club's training ground.

In the living room of his apartment, he became obsessed by the same core stability exercises that Salah came to realise were central to his own body's durability. Mané's physique was wirier and naturally leaner. Though he was not tall, at 5ft 9in, he could resist the challenges of much sturdier defenders, who – especially in Austria – were determined to knock him off his stride. In an overwhelmingly white society, this also included racist taunts in one game against Sturm Graz, when Mané was so angry that on returning to the dressing room, he beat his hands against a wall.

A father figure in Roger Schmidt emerged, the team's coach, a trained engineer from northern Germany with a modest playing career behind him. Schmidt's appointment was made by Rangnick after just a season with Paderborn, where he implemented the high-energy pressing style that Rangnick was famous for in his previous management roles. He was another manager who tended to get good results in unlikely places.

'Sadio had some troubles with the physical style of play from his opponents and was sometimes accused of falling too easy – sometimes rightly so,' Houllier reflected. 'But he was just special, you could see that immediately.'

His ambition was also enormous. Even though he was living in a modest apartment on the edge of Salzburg, it seemed as though he wanted to take on the world, telling friends that he wanted to win the Ballon d'Or. When friends told him how unlikely that was, Mané readjusted his boundaries: instead, he was determined to take the award for the best player in Africa first.

Positioned between Salah and Mané on the pitch at Liverpool was Roberto Firmino. The Brazilian had been at Liverpool a year longer than Mané. Klopp had turned him from a skilful attacking player of no fixed position to being the club's undisputed number 9, and the leader of the press. If Firmino played well, so did Liverpool; his hard work helped the rest of the team get up the pitch. For the opposition, that regularly meant suffocation.

Across five seasons, Firmino, Salah and Mané would score 338 goals combined: 156 from Salah, 107 from Mané and 75 from Firmino. In most teams, it would be the primary responsibility of the number 9 to put the ball in the back of the net, but at Liverpool that fell to the players either side of him. Firmino had hypnotic skills but he was also a grafter. His movement unsettled defences, creating space for others. Though Salah and Mané were wide players, they often ended up in the channels, bringing them closer to a point of opportunity.

Liverpool's players recognised that Salah's goals placed him on a higher pedestal than anyone else. Yet it also annoyed some of them, including Firmino, that he could sometimes be greedy. Firmino knew how to manage his frustrations, while Mané did not. Firmino describes Mané as 'more intense in both the good and bad moments' in his autobiography.

Despite his peroxide teeth and propensity to celebrate goals with dance, Firmino, by his own admission, was shy and found it difficult to relate to Mané, who tried to talk to him in German after joining Liverpool from Southampton in 2016. While Mané had been making a name for himself in Austria, Firmino was doing the same in Germany with Hoffenheim. Eventually, however, Firmino was closer to Mané than to Salah. 'I was always talking to him, giving advice, trying to calm him down,' Firmino wrote. 'I would tell him to find peace, play for the team, and stay relaxed.'

In Mané, Firmino saw a more explosive footballer who had the physical strength to withstand considerable challenges inside the box. Salah was 'more of a dribbler and an opportunist'. It would amaze Firmino how often Salah seemed to be in the right place at the right time.

Firmino conceded that tensions between his teammates began to emerge during the 2018–19 season. It was his view that both wanted to be the team's top scorer. Sometimes, the determination of each player led to distractions and missed opportunities for others. In Firmino's mind, it became easier for Klopp to substitute him rather than Salah or Mané because the Liverpool manager knew that he would react calmly while the other two might get upset and end up throwing a water bottle on the floor.

On the pitch, Firmino found himself in the centre of a cold front, separating the teammates and rivals. There were 'accusing glances' whenever the ball wasn't passed properly, or if a move ended badly. Klopp did not intervene directly but addressed the issue in front of the whole squad by insisting that whenever a teammate was in a better position, the ball had to be passed. According to Firmino, this was a 'clear hint' to Salah.

Salah and Mané finished the 2018–19 season tied as top scorers in the Premier League for Liverpool with twenty-two goals each. Despite the shared experience of winning the Champions League title at the end of that campaign, the achievement did not bring them closer together.

Four games into the following season, Liverpool were closing in on their fourth victory in a row at Burnley when Klopp substituted Mané. Moments earlier, Salah had tried to create an opportunity for himself rather than pass to Mané, who was in a much better position. Klopp's decision to then substitute Mané prompted a series of angry gestures caught on camera as he left the pitch, with Mané continuing his complaints as he simmered on the bench.

Inside the dressing room, Klopp chose to say nothing about the incident. By then, everything had calmed down following Liverpool's 3–0 win. He could not avoid questions about what had happened, in Turf Moor's press room, just a few yards away, however. 'He was upset but everything is fine,' Klopp reasoned. 'We are individuals. We are emotional. It was a situation in the game he was not happy about. Would he do it in the same manner again? Probably not. Nothing really happened. He didn't say any wrong words, he just looked a little bit different to how he does usually.'

Klopp would call both of the players into a meeting at Melwood the following week, where he insisted whatever was going on simply had to stop. Though the players nodded in agreement, by the start of October Liverpool had played in five more league fixtures (nine in total) and Salah had still not created a single goalscoring chance for Mané, having played just twelve passes to him. The feeling was mutual: Mané had passed just fourteen times to Salah, compared to records of 112 (Salah to Mané) and 105 (Mané to Salah) the year before.

Publicly, the spat might have been considered over but there was another Mané outburst in the course of 2019–20, only this time it did not directly involve Salah. Internally, it was thought that the friction between the pair had the potential to create confrontation with other players. Generally, Mané did not want to show he was in any way jealous or annoyed by Salah but this took effort and sometimes, he'd take it out on others.

In one game, Mané was shouted at by a player for supposedly not releasing the ball quickly enough. Earlier in the same game, Mané had been visibly irritated when Salah had chosen not to release to him. At half-time, Mané entered the dressing room and blew his top – not at Salah but at the player who had confronted him. 'Fuck you!' Mané shouted more than once, before throwing a bottle of water at the floor. This prompted Klopp to try and intervene before he was given the same treatment.

The players and staff had never seen Mané act like this. It was very out of character. Klopp reacted by stepping back, allowing Mané to let off steam. 'Everybody relax,' Klopp insisted. By the end of the day, it did not seem to matter as Liverpool secured another victory, taking the team closer to their first title in thirty years.

Mané's anger and frustration with Salah had accumulated, manifesting in a stand-off with teammates. Klopp, however, never spoke to any of the players about the incident, including Mané. Nor did he try to engage any of the staff that were close to him, including, supposedly, Rodriguez. Other staff thought the time might have come to take the Spaniard's advice but Klopp rarely spoke about serious matters with anyone outside his inner circle. Rodriguez was a 'club' appointment.

★   ★   ★

Though Mané was often quiet, he would react if he sensed an injustice – or any sort of impediment that might stop him from becoming the player he wanted to be.

This was evident when he tried to force a move away from Salzburg after deciding not to train. When he subsequently failed to turn up for a team meeting citing a headache, he was banished from the squad for what turned out to be a defeat to Malmö, which ended his club's chances of qualifying for the group stages of the Champions League for the first time.

Despite later reconciling with some of the teammates who were unhappy with him, as well as some influential members of the club's fanbase, he would leave under a cloud when, a few days later, he ultimately got what he wanted by moving to the Premier League with Southampton in a deal worth £11.8 million.

Though Salzburg had been a platform for his development, Mané had felt that the club was pushing him around in the summer of 2014, trying to force lucrative moves to countries like China and Russia.

Tempting as it might have been to cash in, or alternatively sign for a bigger European club, where he was likely to earn more money – albeit while also sitting on the bench – Mané agreed with his agent Björn Bezemer that he wanted to continue on the path that served him well by bringing him to Salzburg in the first place. That meant finding a home at a higher level where there was an increased chance of playing time.

'We said, "No, now is not the time to make just big money or sitting on a bench in a top club, we want to take a career step,"' Bezemer revealed in 2017. 'So he accepted the offer for less money from Southampton because we felt this was the right move at that stage. Our plan for Sadio has always been to make him Africa's best player.'

Earlier that year, Mané indicated he could cope with playing against some of the best players in the world, by scoring and assisting in a 3–0 victory over Pep Guardiola's Bayern Munich during a winter friendly match in the middle of a campaign where he ended up registering twenty-three goals across all competitions.

Liverpool were aware of Mané's development at this point but Michael Edwards told Ralf Rangnick that the club wasn't confident enough about making decisions relating to the Austrian market because it had not established a scouting model capable of evaluating one player's ability against another.

Perhaps moving to Liverpool at that time would have proven too much anyway. Certainly, the timing would have proven to be bad, given what followed in the 2014–15 season, when Brendan Rodgers' team fell down the league table and respect for his management drained away. The slide would lead to Klopp taking over in October 2015 and then Mané's arrival at Anfield nine months later.

He had made a huge impact at Southampton during his two seasons: ending the first by breaking a Premier League record on the final day against Aston Villa – held previously by Liverpool's Robbie Fowler – for completing the fastest hat-trick in the competition's history, inside just 176 seconds. His second season was then marked by his performances against Liverpool. After an equalising goal and a red card at Anfield in October denied Klopp, on his home debut, a first victory since taking charge, Southampton were 2–0 down at St Mary's in March 2016 when Ronald Koeman introduced Mané as a half-time substitute. Though he proceeded to score twice in a 3–2 win, Klopp was impressed more by the way Mané tired his defenders out.

He knew who to call. Dortmund had approached Bezemer when Klopp was in charge but when Mané arrived in the German city for talks, Klopp began to think twice because of his appearance. Klopp recalled in 2020, 'There was a really young guy sitting there. His baseball cap was askew, the blond streak he has today. He looked like a rapper just starting out . . . I did not have time for this.'

It did not help that during the half-hour meeting, a dozen or so other people were buzzing around the room. Klopp later realised it would have been easier to get a better understanding of Mané's personality if they were left alone for just ten minutes. Yet then, in Dortmund, Klopp concluded his team was already strong and he was looking for a player who he could develop while handling the fact he might not initially feature in his start-ing XI every week. He tended to work better with outward personalities and, despite Mané's style, he decided the player wasn't what he needed. He would later find that Mané was a serious person but was trying to appear cool, presenting a rather blasé attitude. Was he acting? Did this show that he was a bit insecure? These were questions nagging at Klopp, who admit-ted to misjudging his character: Mané was, in reality, thoughtful and sensitive – the sort of qualities Klopp, like Roger Schmidt at Salzburg, liked.

In the summer of 2016, Mané was given a tour of Tottenham Hotspur's new, state-of-the-art training ground but he was closer to joining Manchester United, having agreed a contract. Klopp called while he was watching a movie and started telling

Anfield: The site of many Salah goals, one of the most spectacular coming against Chelsea in 2019 when he celebrated with a tree pose after embracing yoga. *(Paul Ellis/Getty Images)*

Madrid: Liverpool reached the Champions League final for a second time after beating Barcelona at Anfield 4–0, having been three goals down from the first leg. Would Madrid end differently to Kyiv twelve months earlier? *(Paul Ellis/Getty Images; SOPA Images/Getty Images)*

Madrid: Liverpool are awarded a penalty in the opening minutes and Salah converts in front of the Tottenham supporters. *(Richard Heathcote/Getty Images; Alex Caparros-UEFA/Getty Images)*

Madrid: Victory is secured by Divock Origi's late goal. While Liverpool emerge as European champions for a sixth time, Salah becomes the first Egyptian to lift the Champions League trophy. *(SOPA/Getty Images; Antonin Thuillier/Getty Images)*

Champions: Without a league title in thirty years, Liverpool set about changing that record by opening up a huge lead over their rivals at the top of the Premier League table. After Salah's late goal confirms a 2–0 victory over Manchester United in January, Anfield is rocking. *(Nick Taylor/ Liverpool FC/Getty Images)*

Six pack: Salah celebrates by removing his shirt, revealing his stomach. Much of his success is down to his body maintenance, though his six pack is a result of nutrition rather than any gym work. *(Michael Regan/Getty Images)*

Merseyside: Liverpool prepares to celebrate, though the club's league title win would be like no other. The pandemic and Covid-19 restrictions mean fans are shut out of stadiums. *(Anthony Devlin/Offside/Getty Images)*

Speed: Much of Salah's threat in his early years at Anfield was because of his searing acceleration but as his career developed, he became a much more rounded player. In either phase of his life, one thing did not change: his capacity to score goals. For seven seasons in a row, he registered twenty-three or more goals for Liverpool. *(Laurence Griffiths/Getty Images)*

Gym: Salah took to the punchbags in the pre-season tour of the United States in the summer of 2024. He was very much at home in the gym. His Cheshire mansion included the latest equipment and he would often work late into the night, preparing his body for the next day of gruelling training sessions under Jürgen Klopp. *(Andrew Powell/ Liverpool FC via Getty Images)*

Mané: Between them, Salah, Sadio Mané and Roberto Firmino would score hundreds of goals for Liverpool, becoming one of the most feared forward lines in Europe. Yet the relationship between Salah and Mané was a fiercely competitive one, with each player attempting to become the best in Africa. *(Andrew Powell/Getty images)*

Another European final: A semi-final victory over Villarreal in 2022 puts Salah into his third Champions League final. Salah was confident of victory but Real Madrid's 1–0 victory in Paris left him in no mood to join a parade on Merseyside, organised to celebrate the team's two domestic cup triumphs earlier in the season. *(David Aliaga/NurPhoto via Getty Images)*

Mykonos: Salah is on holiday in the Greek Island when he finally agrees a new three-year contract at Liverpool. The process had rambled on for the best part of two seasons. *(Nick Taylor/ Liverpool /FC/Getty Images)*

Abidjan: The one medal missing from Salah's collection remains the Africa Cup of Nations. He is judged against the previous era of players' success in the competition. In the 2023 edition, held in Ivory Coast at the start of 2024, he gets injured and Egypt are eliminated in the first knock-out round without him. *(MB Media/Getty Images)*

Klopp: Salah never worshipped at the altar of the messiah and just a few weeks ahead of the German manager's departure from Liverpool, the reality of their relationship is exposed on the touchline during a 2–2 draw with West Ham United; a result that all but ends Liverpool's slim title hopes. *(Justin Setterfield/Getty Images)*

Old Trafford: the scene of some of Salah's most important goals for Liverpool against their greatest rivals, Manchester United. With Klopp gone, the 2024–25 season starts promisingly under his successor Arne Slot and Salah scores again at United in a resounding 3–0 victory. *(Michael Regan/Getty Images)*

him, 'Sadio, listen, I want to explain to you what happened at Dortmund. We have a big project at Liverpool and I want you to be a part of it.'

Mané was keen to know about what position Klopp wanted him to play. At Southampton he had featured on the right of the attack, but he felt more comfortable on the left. At Liverpool, the only space was on the right because Philippe Coutinho, more often than not, took up the role on the other side of the pitch.

Yet Mané was so taken by the idea of joining Liverpool, attempting to succeed where his hero El-Hadji Diouf had failed, that playing off the right wasn't such a problem for him. Within a year, anyway, the signing of Salah would allow him to move to his favoured position, as Klopp prepared for Coutinho's exit to Barcelona by selecting him in a more central role for the first half of the 2017–18 season.

Mané took confidence from the money Liverpool were willing to spend on him – a lot was made of him becoming the most expensive signing in the club's history. At £36 million, he was also not only the most expensive Senegalese footballer of all time but the most expensive African as well.

In Mané's mind, the continental dimensions of the deal were further proof he was getting closer to becoming the player he wanted to be. He would hold the record, however, for only one year – Salah's arrival at Anfield came in at £500,000 above his own fee, knocking him back into second place. Though Mané did not show any reaction to this development in the company of his Liverpool teammates, some believed it ate away at him, contributing towards the way he came to feel about Salah, whose goal record at Liverpool was greater than his own, leading to increased admiration amongst the fanbase as well as global attention.

In those early years, another divide between the pair emanated from the realities that Mané was firmly Klopp's signing, while the arrival of Salah had more to do with the club's scouting network. Throughout his first six months at the club, Klopp would tell other staff regularly about how highly he regarded Mané, openly suggesting he was a player who would do well for Liverpool.

While Mané always felt as though Klopp had his back, Salah was aware that Klopp's preference in his case had been instead to sign Julian Brandt from Bayer Leverkusen. Klopp stressed to Salah that this was not because he did not rate the Egyptian, and rather a consequence of his knowledge of German football being greater. Yet Klopp rarely praised him publicly in his early months at the club despite his astonishing goalscoring achievements. There were no answers for this necessarily. It might have just been Klopp's way of ensuring his feet remained on the ground, but was it also because he wanted to appease the other egos in the dressing room, namely Mané?

There was enough noise about Salah; it scarcely needed Klopp to add to it. In return, Salah spoke respectfully enough about Klopp, but Mané was willing to travel further. After Liverpool won the Champions League in 2019 by beating Tottenham, with Mané's cross earning Salah an early opportunity to score from the penalty spot, Mané suggested Klopp made him 'want to go to war'.

The achievement in Madrid meant Mané was on a career high but evidence of his forceful personality was again present after the 2–0 victory as the players embraced in the dressing room. Amidst the singing of '*Campeones*', and the popping of champagne corks, Roberto Firmino shook up a bottle of lager before opening it up, spraying the alcohol all over his teammates, including Mané.

Though it was an act of celebration, not targeting anyone in particular, Mané remembered his faith – the Qur'an forbids drinking and any indirect association with alcohol. He let Firmino know that he was not happy and his teammate reacted by briefly removing himself from the singing and the drinking as they continued around him, instead cleaning up his possessions.

Staff at Liverpool considered Mané cocky and aggressive on the pitch but while occasionally playful off it, he was quiet and nevertheless hugely determined. Salah was more secure about himself but he liked to see evidence of others feeling the same way.

To other players, Klopp didn't seem to mind the friction. Mané was popular, and ahead of every game, Klopp's assistant Pep Lijnders would oversee a ritual where teammates, often Virgil van Dijk, would compete with him in the dressing room to see who could jump the highest. Neither player was embedded in any social group and this meant their frustrations did not impact on other parts of the dressing room. Some teammates found the rivalry amusing.

Though Salah sometimes frustrated others on the pitch because of his single-mindedness, many understood that he was the Liverpool player opponents really feared if he followed his instincts. The players tended to agree that more was expected of Mané, who had a greater involvement in the team's structure and buildup because of his ability to press at the right time. There was more of a window for Mané to get criticism, to some degree protecting Salah from similar treatment.

It was perhaps difficult for Mané to step back and see the bigger picture because he was so consumed by his own ambition. Meanwhile, Klopp did little to address these issues because they did not impact negatively on the team's results – most of the time, it felt as though the competition was helping drive the Liverpool team on to bigger things.

Yet all of this, over many years, carried on eating away at Mané, who felt undervalued. Eventually, it would contribute towards him leaving Liverpool.

Mané realised he could never become the best player in the world if he was not regarded as the best player in Africa. Though he'd finished third in 2016, he moved up to second in 2017 and 2018, but Salah jumped ahead of him in both years. In 2019 and 2022, however, Mané came above Salah, winning the crown in successive years (taking into account the pandemic hiatus).

While Mané would join Salah in the Senegalese capital of Dakar when the Egyptian beat him into second place in 2018, Salah did not reciprocate the gesture when Mané finished above him at a ceremony held in Cairo a year later. This was after what happened at Burnley and according to staff, Mané saw this as an amusing slight. On this occasion, he'd beaten Salah, so he could afford to laugh. Salah, however, told other people at Liverpool that he decided not to attend because of a dispute with the owner of the hotel where the award was being handed out. If he really felt like he was being taken advantage of again, he did not deem it necessary to inform Mané. When in Cairo, Mané was heard correcting someone calling him a 'King' with Salah nowhere to be seen: it was thought he did not want to be associated with 'Egyptian king', the term used to describe his Liverpool teammate.

Across the four seasons where they fought to become the best player in Africa, neither Salah or Mané received enough votes to feature in the top three of the Ballon d'Or award, given to the best player in the world. Liverpool had featured in two Champions League finals during that time and each player had scored in one of them. Though Mané featured on the losing team against Real Madrid, Salah's penalty against Tottenham helped Liverpool to a sixth European crown at the end of a campaign where he shone but not quite as radiantly as his first at Liverpool.

Since its inception in 1956, only three African players with African heritage had won the award. Mozambique-born Eusébio was the first in 1965, though he represented Portugal. Thirty years after that there was Liberia's George Weah, then in 1998, Zinedine Zidane was nominated after his two goals in the World Cup final inspired France to its first success in the tournament. Zidane's parents were born in Algeria before moving to Paris at the start of the Algerian War. Zidane, however, was raised in Marseille. 'I have an affinity with the Arab world,' Zidane later said. 'I have it in my blood. I'm very proud of being French, but also very proud of having these roots and this diversity.'

It tends to be much harder for players like Salah and Mané, those who were born and brought up in Africa and have to make enormous sacrifices by leaving their families behind just to begin the process of realising their dreams, never mind getting anywhere near some of the game's most prestigious individual prizes. Both players still had a lot to prove within the continent of Africa as well. Though they were now at an elite level in Europe, and had taken individual awards in Africa, neither had been involved in winning the most illustrious team prize, the Africa Cup of Nations.

At home, Salah and Mané were regularly accused of being more focused on their clubs, where they seemed to perform better. Such criticism was often unfair, as it is arguably easier for any player to establish a rhythm at club level when he is training and playing with the same teammates each week.

Great players can often lift the confidence and disguise the abilities of those around them, but changing attitudes and cultures is often more challenging due to time limitations. Inside Africa, the Senegalese federation has long been considered to be a better-run organisation than Egypt's but until 2022, the nation had never won an AFCON, while Egypt had won seven.

This meant that both Mané and Salah were considered to be underachievers: Mané, because he could not inspire Senegal when it felt like it was finally their time and Salah, because he could not match the achievements of the country's past.

During their time together at Liverpool, Mané especially had experienced some bad moments in the national squad. In 2017, he missed the team's last penalty in a quarter-final tie with Cameroon, which led to fans destroying his car back in Senegal. When Senegal missed out on qualification for the World Cup the following year, Mané cried on the pitch as he beat the ground. Salah, meanwhile, fired in the penalty that took Egypt to their first finals in twenty-eight years – though the team struggled badly in Russia, and that was when Salah's reputation in Egypt really began to turn.

After Egypt, as hosts of the 2019 AFCON, tumbled out in the round of sixteen to South Africa and Senegal made it to the final, losing narrowly to Algeria, both players went to Cameroon for the 2021 edition (held in 2022 due to the pandemic). They were hoping to get their hands on a prize that had so far eluded them, and on the pursuit of which they were both being judged.

Mané's determination to inspire his country was evidenced by his reaction to getting injured in Senegal's round of sixteen tie when he collided with the Cape Verde goalkeeper. While Vozinha stumbled as he got to his feet and was sent off, Mané was also visibly shaken but continued – scoring soon after, at which point he was substituted after going down again, seemingly dizzy, just before play restarted.

Mané went to hospital with concussion and Liverpool wrote a letter to the Confederation of African Nations (CAF) insisting that he needed at least five days' rest. That would have meant him missing the quarter finals against Equatorial Guinea. Senegal's doctor was willing to follow the ruling but Mané called the coach, Aliou Cissé, as well as the president of the Senegalese federation, telling them he would give up his life to play.

Mané was willing to sign a disclaimer to show he was risking his health but on the morning of the game, a scan cleared him to play the whole match against Equatorial Guinea, which Senegal won 3–1. After beating Burkina Faso by the same scoreline in the semi, Senegal met Egypt in the final and, when the game went to penalties, Mané and Salah were allocated their team's fifth, and possibly decisive, kick. Salah, though, did not get to take his because Mané scored Senegal's winner to claim the title for the first time in the country's history.

It cannot be overstated how important this moment was to Senegal and to Mané, as well as to Egypt and to Salah. Yet after he described it as 'the most important trophy of my career', eclipsing both the Champions League and Premier League medals with Liverpool, Mané did not receive the reception he was hoping for back on Merseyside, like other returning Senegalese players when they went back to their clubs.

As Mané spent a few days celebrating in Dakar, Salah flew straight to Liverpool. This left the club facing an awkward situation because any serenading of Mané following his unprecedented achievement had the potential to upset Salah. Staff at Liverpool remember being told to recognise what Mané had done but to otherwise keep it low-key. Mané saw this as another example of pandering to Salah.

'I think Mané left Liverpool precisely because he didn't feel as valued as Salah within the club,' Firmino later reflected. 'He felt he was being treated as less important.'

Mané had done six seasons at Liverpool and it was this moment that made him realise that he should take on a new challenge. There was a strong interest from Chelsea led by Thomas Tuchel, who thought Newcastle United were ahead of them in the queue to sign him. Yet Bayern Munich were willing to spend the most money on a player who was now thirty years old, almost allowing Liverpool to recoup their investment in him when he was just twenty-four.

A deal suited all parties but in Munich, Mané did not settle. This was a different dressing room altogether, and even though he was recognised as one of the biggest signings in the club's long, successful history, he struggled to find a sense of place and rhythm. When Tuchel replaced Julian Nagelsmann as manager partway through his first season, the coaching staff thought they would be able to fire him up again. At Chelsea, Tuchel had recognised that Mané was the only opponent to consistently get the better of emerging right back Reece James, but still he could not establish a happy place.

After losing 3–0 at Manchester City in the Champions League in 2023, reports in Germany suggested Mané punched Leroy Sané in the dressing room, leaving him with a bloodied lip. Mané later confirmed the story, but only after he'd moved on again, to the riches of Al Nassr in the Saudi Arabian Pro League, where he trebled his wages. He would not be the only famous African footballer to have such a move presented to him. At the end of the same summer, Salah too had a decision to make.

Chapter 10

Fight for independence

While Sadio Mané worked with an agent and was supported from Senegal by several advisors, Mohamed Salah came to be guided by just one person, and this brought a sharpness to his off-field strategies.

Ramy Abbas realised Salah's brand potential towards the end of 2017, when his goals for Liverpool led to calls from magazines that were not focused on football. Soon, he was invited to feature on the cover of *Sports Illustrated*. Over the next five years, Salah's income away from the pitch would come to be as lucrative as on it. It was the view of both the player and the lawyer that this was only possible because of their focus: Salah knew he had the total attention of Abbas, and such attention meant Abbas was never thinking about making money for other clients.

In 2019, *GQ Middle East* described the Abbas–Salah relationship in a headline as a 'curious case' as the lawyer proceeded to explain he was able to build trust with Salah because he did not try to take advantage of him. 'By not ripping them off,' he said. 'That's always a very good start. I think that there's no substitute for time when it comes to getting someone to trust what you're doing, the advice you give and that you will put their interests before your own. That doesn't happen very often in this industry, unfortunately.'

According to a 2023 study with Harvard Business School that analysed the process behind Salah's most recent Liverpool contract, the player admitted to Abbas when they first met that he did not know how much he should be paying him. Salah was Egypt's most recognisable footballer but he was only six months out of his miserable time at Chelsea. Many Egyptians would stare at his face on the billboards of Cairo and wonder whether he'd give up on Europe, as many Egyptian footballers tended to do, and end up returning to the country, playing for Al Ahly or Zamalek. In Rome, however, Salah was clearly more confident about the direction of his career than many of his countrymen. When Abbas suggested a figure, Salah replied, 'No, I will pay you double that.'

This meant that Abbas was paid a fixed fee from Salah's salary but did not receive earnings from the bonuses he received for achievements on the pitch, like goals or trophies. Abbas's firm, Magic Circle, instead worked on the basis of a consultancy agreement with Salah's foreign image company, which Abbas managed and controlled. Upon moving to England a year later, Salah was listed as the only director for an operation called 'Salah UK Commercial Limited', which focused exclusively on the market in the UK, though again it was heavily influenced by Abbas.

The arrangement was not out of the ordinary. Increasingly, elite sports people were setting up companies to which payments from image rights would go rather than the individual. Though Salah paid corporation tax (which amounted to £2.3 million in 2023), he would benefit from lower taxes than the 45 per cent taken on standard earnings.

Figures from the UK only offered one glimpse into the economic world Salah had created. In 2023, Abbas suggested the foreign rights were 'far more lucrative' than those sold in the UK, where Salah was still playing. Abbas would take a percentage of these earnings. In other markets, he would hire agents to bring in endorsements, and Magic Circle would pay them for every contract brokered. Abbas did the negotiations and his responsibilities extended into logistics and attending shoots and events with his client. Ideally, he'd want involvement in creative direction.

Between 2017 and 2024, Salah would emerge as an icon for the whole of the Arab-speaking world, a region with a huge population and a matching interest in Premier League football. Over the course of seven years, he would reach a point where he made more money from his activities off the pitch than he did on it. The documents revealed by Harvard showed that if Salah did well in a Liverpool shirt, he would earn nearly £400,000 a week. When his image rights and commercial earnings were added to that, the overall income approached £1 million a week.

Any attempt to engage Salah on an economic level involves Abbas as the point of contact. It is his responsibility to protect the business and financial interests of his client. This includes contacts relating to his sporting future as well as sponsorship and commercial agreements.

Sometimes, a person or a company might think they are getting closer to Salah when, in reality, Abbas is merely vetting the player's options. On one occasion, in 2022, around the time Abbas was negotiating Salah's new deal at Liverpool, a television network from the Middle East proposed a documentary series, having attempted to get Salah and therefore Abbas to the table for nearly two years.

In this case, Abbas eventually responded to a WhatsApp message and for nearly five months, correspondence went backwards and forwards before it was relayed to the senior management of the company that Abbas was interested. Two meetings were arranged, one in London and a second in Paris.

Earlier that year, a series about Neymar entitled *The Perfect Chaos* had been broadcast in the UK for the first time. The deal for access to the Brazilian, then playing for Paris Saint-Germain, involved between £2 million and £3 million. The network interested in Salah thought he was worth a similar sum, though they argued they would do it better because of the organisation's cultural understanding of the region.

It was an opportunity for Salah to tell the Middle East more about himself. He was viewed as a superhero and this was a chance for him to demonstrate his normality. There was a confidence within the network that the series could be sold to other broadcasters across the world.

What followed, according to someone close to the deal, was a six-month dating process. The network felt as though it had laid out a red carpet just to get in front of Abbas, albeit without Salah, who was not present at any of the meetings. While the TV people spoke enthusiastically about the project, Abbas tended to sit quietly, listening. He was not afraid, however, of speaking his mind when he felt it was necessary. He was viewed as being observant, smart and otherwise incredibly blunt.

The project became the number one aim of the network, which had previously paid over the odds to get other deals over the line with footballers. Yet as discussions dragged on, and the sports documentary market became saturated, discouraging companies from paying so much money for access, appetite cooled on both sides. By the end of the summer of 2022, contact between both parties ceased – and Salah, having signed a new contract with Liverpool, was staying in England.

Was Abbas prepping for a potential exit for Salah? Amidst inevitable discontent amongst Liverpool's fanbase, the documentary would have been a a chance to humanise him and tell his side of the story on his terms. It was clear to some of the people involved in those meetings that Abbas wanted Salah to become a global rather than just a Muslim icon, though it was impossible to know what Salah really thought because they never met him.

In total, the project would have cost nearly £6 million to make because Salah's own fee was just for access to the talent. This was a few years after Michael Jordan's *Last Dance* made it onto Netflix, setting a new standard for sports documentaries. The difference was that the makers of *The Last Dance* had access to nearly everyone who was involved in Jordan's career, whereas any agreement with Salah was only going to cover between twenty and thirty filming days, most likely for two hours a day. There was a concern about locations: his life was a cycle of commute, train, gym and family. Trying to find the sort of variation in settings that usually contribute towards a good documentary would have been a challenge.

Salah's new contract at Liverpool made him the highest-paid player in the club's history. The TV company realised what it was up against: he would earn almost as much in a month at Anfield as he would for any documentary, which in real terms was only as lucrative as any other enhancement or sponsorship deal – and they involved a lot less work.

Such a project was only ultimately beneficial for his vanity, potentially leading to interest in him in parts of the world previously out of reach. Yet the documentary-makers understood that for that to happen, the production values had to be good and with such a narrow timeframe, it was going to be difficult to achieve.

'The figures just didn't stack up at all,' said a source close to the negotiations. Yet the source was satisfied to some degree, believing the network got closer than any of its rivals in its attempts to convince Abbas that a deal was possible.

Though he had made good money representing Colombian players, and he was there in London when Salah signed for Chelsea, Abbas was not a well-known name in the wider football world when he registered with the social media platform formerly known as Twitter in October 2014.

It was only a few years later that he became more active with his views, after his representation of Salah was formalised. In May 2016, he congratulated Leicester City for their improbable Premier League title win, posting a picture of him on graduation day at the city's university. It became clear over time he was against animal cruelty and, steadily, he became more political. When British Airways cabin crew voted to strike in 2016, he suggested, 'We miss Mrs Thatcher,' the Conservative prime minister between 1979 and 1990. Across her three terms, she described 'crushing the unions' as one of her greatest achievements, having made it one of her mission statements upon winning her first election.

Thatcher's ideology centred around privatisation, deregulation, the primacy of the free market, the abdication of societal responsibility and a reduced role for the state. Abbas's apparent warmth for such politics became clearer around the time of the American election in late 2016, won by Donald Trump. A month after his comment about Thatcher, Abbas announced he no longer liked the filmmaker Michael Moore because he had attended an anti-Trump rally. Trump himself targeted the news network CNN for broadcasting what he claimed to be 'fake news' because of its reporting on proven links he had to Russia. Though it was unclear exactly what the biggest news network in the wealthiest country in the world had done to annoy Abbas, two months later, in April 2017, he described the television station as 'unwatchable'.

All of this was before Salah signed for Liverpool, where he smashed all sorts of goalscoring records in his first season, making both himself and his lawyer, albeit to a lesser degree, a name anyone with an appreciation of the world Salah was operating in would be aware of. Towards the end of that campaign, and a year after deriding CNN, Abbas was willing to sanction the network a substantial amount of time with his client. It was the first sign he was prepared to set aside any of his own views if it made his client look good.

It was the first big interview of Salah's career with a Western media outlet. But for a few short conversations with Liverpool's in-house media channels, Salah had barely spoken to anyone from any part of the world about his astonishing achievements at Anfield. For CNN, an interview with him was a spectacular coup.

The organisation's bureau in Abu Dhabi was led by Becky Anderson, a British journalist with a strong interest in football. She was in regular contact with reporters from other parts of the world about potential stories relating to sport. With Salah breaking records and Anderson well positioned in the Middle East, it made sense for her to try and engage Abbas, who now lived nearby in Dubai. For Abbas, the interview was sanctioned because he came to like Anderson, rather than the company she worked for.

Yet to other people involved in the interview process, it became clear that Abbas was well aware of CNN's power and influence. Abbas had spent time across the region in lots of hotel rooms where the television packages nearly always included its international news bulletins. If he still held reservations about the company's editorial line, it never came up in conversations.

The interview ended up being a collaboration between Anderson's *Connect the World* show and CNN Sport. Abbas was keen for sections from the interview to be clipped and distributed across CNN's social media pages. According to someone involved in these discussions, 'CNN offered a reach beyond that of any newspaper.'

By 2019 (a year after Salah's interview), CNN and its breaking news handle @cnnbrk had sixty-one million followers on Twitter, more than any news organisation on the planet, exceeding the *New York Times* by nearly five million users and the BBC by nearly ten million. The gap with other established television networks and newspapers was even greater, with CNN doubling and trebling the reach of organisations like Reuters, the *Washington Post* and the *Wall Street Journal*. A fact sheet distributed by CNN suggested its two dozen branded networks and services were available to more than two billion people across more than two hundred countries and territories. It also had a bureau in Lagos serving most of Africa. Inside journalism, CNN was generally considered to be committed to good storytelling in a part of the world that was neglected by mainstream outlets.

Correspondents who worked in Africa (and the Middle East) were often seen as celebrities themselves, and they got huge television audiences and online responses whenever they interviewed other famous people from the region.

Prominent coverage by CNN gave Abbas and Salah a route into the wider consciousness of Africa as well as North America – this at a time when representatives of his rival Sadio Mané were also considering how best to tell their own client's story.

Like Salah, Mané was attempting to become the best footballer in Africa. Like Salah, he realised his appeal had not really extended that far beyond the boundaries of the continent, or in truth, perhaps even any further than the country he came from.

CNN was the most significant interview of Salah's career to date and, ordinarily, officials from the club he represented would have been involved in the arrangements. Though Liverpool granted use of the Kop grandstand at Anfield for filming, as well as the training ground at Melwood, there was no interference from its press office.

There tends to be a misunderstanding of how Liverpool grants access. Its relationship with the media has changed since 2018, the year Salah's name became really well known and the Liverpool team reached the Champions League final for the first time in eleven years. Previously, the interests of Liverpool and independent media were closer, but their in-house media operation has risen and is keen to drive the clicks that keep sponsors sweet, as well as fulfil commercial agreements with external partners that want to be involved in the successful culture created by players like Salah. The result is that newspapers and non-rights-holding broadcasters have found themselves behind in the queue in terms of who did what with whom.

As the demands on players increased, it helped the press office if a news organisation was able to arrange an interview directly, usually with an agent, because it meant one less favour to ask, allowing the press office to prioritise commitments around the partners who ultimately helped make the club money.

Liverpool's economic world under Fenway Sports Group ownership was a real one, based on profit and loss, and wherever the club thought it could make money, it would try.

After leaving an interview with a player on a club tour, a finance director from Liverpool once suggested to a journalist that he should be paying for the access. The journalist thought he was joking initially, but after a pause it became very clear the director was not.

With or without club involvement, journalists tended to talk to players under strict time limits and certain conditions. It was common for journalists to be informed before meetings about what they could discuss and what they could not. CNN was used to getting ten minutes with celebrities and sportspeople. Yet with Salah, the network spent an evening and then a whole day with the most talked-about player on the planet – without restrictions. It was quite a commitment. Though it became clear Salah was reluctant to discuss his faith and his family on camera, he wasn't in a rush to leave or dodge any questions.

For some of the media people involved, it felt strange to have a run as free as this, especially as the night before Salah had scored his thirty-ninth goal of the season, sending Liverpool through to the semi-finals of the 2018 Champions League with a 2–1 second-leg victory at Manchester City. On colder reflection, they concluded they were fortunate with timing. Salah was hardly a youngster at twenty-four but he seemed green to the interview process and his branding was in its infancy.

There was no sense that Salah saw a purpose behind the interview and he gave no impression that he had an understanding of his own commercial potential or marketability. As boring as it sounds, he appeared to be a young man who just wanted to play football.

Abbas could not have been more helpful or obliging. He could see a wider picture, having identified what his client could become. Over dinner in the restaurant of the £18-million Aloft Liverpool hotel on North John Street in the city centre, Abbas was obsessed with the reach and promotion of the interview on social media, while Salah ate salmon fillet.

Though he was always present when Salah was talking, Abbas never interjected. When clubs were involved in these processes, there was often a PR person sitting next to the player, recording everything that was said, but with Salah there was none of that. It seemed that the pair's trust in one another was total.

Earlier that day, a delegation from CNN had met Salah and his lawyer at Melwood, before they were given a tour of the training ground. In the small talk, it became clear Salah was curious about the reporting. He explained that he'd rarely been in this position before, with so much interest in him. Back at the hotel, he did an interview to camera with Anderson, filming at the Titanic Hotel the next morning by the docks, before walking along the famous Mathew Street, visiting the rebuilt Cavern nightclub which The Beatles made famous.

CNN hired a 4x4 to drive around the city and Anderson wound the windows down. There was carpool karaoke and even some of the Evertonians who spotted him in traffic were generous about his impact at Liverpool.

Salah was more open away from the camera but both he and Abbas were happy with the production values when it was broadcast the following week. Later that summer, this led to CNN breaking stories about Salah's new five-year contract at Liverpool and him potentially retiring from international duty due to his latest feud with the Egyptian Football Association.

Two weeks after Salah fired a penalty kick past the Tottenham Hotspur goalkeeper to put Liverpool on their way to a sixth Champions League crown in Madrid, *GQ Middle East* published an interview with Abbas. The existing relationship between Abbas and *GQ* meant that in 2021, when the magazine's editorial team in New York City picked the footballer that it felt had made the most impact on the game, it was slightly easier to reach Salah.

This was just before an unprecedented quadruple became part of the possibilities around Liverpool's season. Crucially, Salah's contract impasse with the club was not resolved, and this left *GQ* at an advantage. Having researched, spent time with, and interviewed Abbas, they knew he was a smart strategist. He was cynical but shrewd. Most people who spent any time with him came away thinking he had very little loyalty to Salah's club, yet they also tend to conclude it was actually quite refreshing to hear the representative of a footballer speak so openly and honestly about his role, rather than to try and dress himself as the good guy in an industry of wolves and charlatans.

Everything with Abbas seemed very deliberate. He would use public opportunities, such as an interview with a major international magazine, to exert pressure on other parties. In this case, with *GQ*, that party would be Liverpool, and the club's sporting director – who was now in charge of contract negotiations. Reminding everyone that Salah was a footballer who carried a global interest would strengthen Abbas's hand in negotiations, particularly if image rights were being discussed by both sides. The imagery connected to any meeting with Salah was also important. When he met *GQ's* photographers in the autumn of 2021, he would pose in an Adidas-manufactured Liverpool shirt from the 1993–94 season. To the Liverpool fans keen for him to stay, this showed Salah as a footballer who was ingrained in the club's history.

Time with Salah was now rare. Abbas was exacting in his client's exposure, attempting to keep it to a minimum to reduce the cultural risks associated with the region he came from, where holding celebrity status was fraught and the relationship between its sports stars and the media was impacted by the political climate.

Egypt's status in the World Press Freedom Index tumbled dramatically between 2019 and 2024, from forty-three points out of a hundred to twenty-five. The country ranked below Iraq, Cuba and Saudi Arabia, and was only just above China. This made it one of the worst places in the world for press freedoms.

In the same period, the USA fell from seventy-four points to sixty-six. Yet the culture of its sports coverage remained the same, with journalists permitted to enter the locker room and speak to players after fixtures. This simply did not exist in Egypt, but nor did it in England, where journalists were restricted to mixed-zone access after matches and players only stopped if they wanted to. Salah had only done that twice and on each occasion he left reporters thinking that either he wasn't the most loquacious person in the world or he was choosing his words very carefully. Clearly, he was not interested in sharing his innermost feelings but that was also clear to many of the people he worked with at Liverpool over many years, leading to some of them wondering whether he had any feelings at all.

Those at Liverpool who were closer to him, however, began to understand that everything Salah said, even from the safety of England, had an impact back home, where his every move and utterance were examined by the state. In some ways it was much easier for everyone if he simply did not talk, but he also knew that saying nothing harmed his image because Egyptians would think he was aloof.

'I cannot win,' he told one member of staff at Liverpool. He would prefer it if he could just play football and be judged on that, quietly donating to causes in Egypt that needed it. Yet Egypt wanted to see evidence of the quality Muslims especially tend to look for in a notable person. A big interview and a fancy photoshoot did not necessarily make him look 'humble' but it did show he was present in their lives, at least thinking about some of the issues Egyptians were facing.

Salah and Abbas were always wary of the final outcome of any interview. In 2012, GQ was only the eighty-second bestselling magazine in the USA. Yet its global publication model meant they could put Salah on the front of newsstands across more than thirty countries. With its focus on fashion and culture, it could also offer Abbas the chance to include Salah's commercial partners like Gucci, as it later did. Though Abbas was very aware of Salah's popularity and saw his own role as not letting him do or say anything stupid that diluted his value, he knew when to act on an opportunity, even if it came with some risks.

Though it was a challenge, in persuading him to surrender control around the publication of quotes, as well as creative direction in terms of what he wore when he was photographed, Salah was interested in *GQ* and, when it came to it, both the player and the lawyer seemed happy to be led by experts who knew more than they about photography and fashion.

GQ were aware that Abbas had also granted sixty minutes to a Middle Eastern broadcaster, with the player rumoured to be earning more than half a million pounds for his commitment. What would Salah's priority be, if he chose to give something up about himself? *GQ*'s Oli Franklin-Wallis, an award-winning magazine journalist, was due to meet Salah. He was a few months away from being appointed features editor, having previously written for the *Guardian*, the *New York Times* (*NYT*) and *The Times* and *Sunday Times* magazines. Franklin-Wallis had met Salah's teammate Trent Alexander-Arnold and had focused his interview on the art of becoming a free-kick taker. He would discuss how he positioned himself, how he struck the ball and what it sounded like when the ball hit the back of the net. Did Alexander-Arnold know he was gifted at this from an early age or was it more down to practice once he'd discovered his talent?

Franklin-Wallis would later find Manchester City's Erling Haaland easier to write about, mainly because he was so misunderstood: fans saw him as a big target man who was stronger and quicker than everyone else, like the bully in the schoolyard. Yet Haaland's game was very different. He could read what was going on around him and choose his moments to get involved. Haaland was supremely intelligent, even though he was not associated with intelligence.

Footballers are not always willing to discuss their failures publicly but Salah was different. He spoke at length about what had happened at Chelsea. It was the writer's conclusion that Salah was defined by his competitive drive and a superhuman focus to better himself. He often read books about American billionaires and how they made their wealth and this approach to money was not unique amongst footballers from poor backgrounds. Salah was aware that his time was limited as a player, especially at the top.

Salah did not seem to relish the creative part of football, or want or really know how to discuss it. He was a competitor rather than an artist. He was more like Novak Djokovic than Roger Federer. Salah was successful because he was an instrument of will.

By 2024, more than £25 million ($32 million) was on the balance sheet of the privately registered company Salah had set up to manage his image rights in the UK. This figure had increased across the previous twelve months by more than £5 million after tax.

It was only a snapshot of the economic world Salah had created for himself. Abroad, the first deal Abbas brokered for the player had been with Pepsi, when he was still at Roma. This led to commercials being filmed with Lionel Messi. Agreements with Adidas, Vodafone, Uber and the Bank of Alexandria would follow. The lawyer would tell Harvard that each of these deals was worth between £3.5 million and £6 million a year to his client.

Another Arab player, Riyad Mahrez, would earn more than Salah by agreeing to move to Al-Ahli, where he was paid north of £850,000 a week by a club owned by Saudi Arabia's Public Investment Fund. But this sum comprised of wages alone: the Algerian international, who was born in France, did not have the same commercial potential as Salah.

By the summer of 2024, Salah was close to having nineteen million followers on the social media platform Twitter, or X. Mahrez, by comparison, had just four million. Meanwhile, Erling Haaland was arguably the best player in the Premier League and his following was six million.

While these figures are not an exact reflection of popularity they do suggest Salah had tapped into markets that were beyond the reach of most Europe-based footballers. In total, the number of followers across all his social media platforms was close to a hundred million – Haaland was the nearest Premier League player, with thirty-nine million followers.

More than four years would separate Salah's interviews with CNN and GQ. The permission for each, as well as the delivery, revealed a lot about the position of Salah's career at the time. While CNN's broad appeal brought a sense of seriousness to his story and, by extension, the sort of respectability very few Arab footballers reach amongst Western broadcasters, GQ revealed he was now on a different level altogether. If these kind of fashion shoots were good enough for David Beckham twenty years earlier, they were good enough for Salah – who was not only the most famous footballer from the Arab world, but arguably its most famous sportsman overall.

★　　★　　★

The key for Salah was achieving this success while seeming as though he remained in touch with his roots. When *GQ* later interviewed him again, under the headline A HERO'S STORY, the story told was a little thin on detail but amidst mentions of Nagrig, there was a collaboration with clothing supplied by his boot maker, Adidas and the luxury Italian brand Gucci.

Abbas ensured Salah kept only a few sponsors, with each of them respectable brands paying a premium. He was conscious of giving critics the room to claim that Salah was only involved because he was being remunerated handsomely. This meant Abbas had been very careful around hard advertising. He did not want to put his client in a position where he was directly telling consumers to buy something. Nor did he want him belittled because a contract said he had to do a song or a dance, as Cristiano Ronaldo did when he advertised the Singaporean e-commerce platform Shopee. The brand had to be established, it had to be in demand, and it had to make Salah look good, not provoke someone to ask, 'Can you believe what he's done?'

It was also an unwritten rule that Salah did not work with partners who wanted to sign him because of his faith. Abbas could bring balance to conversations with the player because, while Salah was a practising Muslim, Abbas was not religious in any way, despite a surname that might suggest they shared the same faith. Abbas, in fact, was raised in Colombia as a Catholic, but as he got older he drifted away from God. Rather than being an atheist, which simply means an absence of belief in any higher spirit, Abbas identified as being antitheist, which meant he was consciously and deliberately opposed to the concept of a god.

Abbas did not want to make Salah a diversity signing and he turned down several lucrative deals because he felt a box was being ticked. Instead, he was clear that any agreement should be based on the player's individuality, as an international icon.

For Abbas, being slapped with an identity was also bad for business. While an issue around race or religion might occupy a space in the media for a short period of time, he believed that people got tired of it eventually. It was his view that the public was increasingly looking at celebrities in only one of two ways: those who elicit sympathy and those who claim invincibility. Being felt sorry for wasn't particularly exciting. Abbas and Salah instead decided to leave sympathy for those who were really struggling: for people who didn't have enough to eat or were sick.

It meant that while Salah might confront an issue, he has never complained about anything, even the occasions where fans of Liverpool's rivals have called him a 'bomber'. It was his conclusion that they'd prefer it if he showed he was annoyed but he did not want to give them the satisfaction. While Salah understood why other sportspeople got upset if they were targeted for abuse, and felt bad for them, if it happened to him he thought the only way to respond was through performance. The best way of achieving that was to score a goal.

Abbas knew that some critics thought that Salah should speak out more about issues such as racism but he believed that his responses achieved more. Abbas was delighted to hear that Islamophobia decreased in Liverpool following the player's surge of goals in 2017, when he didn't do anything other than play football and do well for the team. He did not say a single word about anything during the period. It was purely organic.

At the end of one season when Salah won an award from football writers, among many other accolades, he spoke at the

Landmark London hotel. He was clearly comfortable telling people about what they could achieve with hard work. He liked to think of himself as an inspiration but this was where his and Abbas's opinions diverged; while Salah asked people to follow their dreams, and generally wanted other Egyptians to succeed, Abbas thought the message belittled Salah's own achievements and that only he has been able to get to where he is – because of who he is.

For selfish reasons, Abbas did not want anyone to succeed as much as his client, but he also did not think it was very probable. Even if he were only a centre forward scoring fifteen goals a season at a mid-table Premier League club, he'd be doing something no Egyptian had ever done. Instead, by 2024, Salah had scored twenty or more goals for seven years in a row playing as a winger at one of the most famous clubs in the world, during one of the most intriguing periods in its history.

If Muslims, especially, wanted to identify with Salah, then they were welcome, but it was not something either the player or his lawyer actively pursued. Salah did not want to be defined by his religion, or by anything else he believed in. Religion was a part of who he was but Abbas was wary of forces beyond their control dictating the conversation around him.

On one occasion, a magazine approached Abbas about putting Salah on the front cover and he was curious to learn the headline. When the magazine resisted sharing, Abbas told them there was no shoot. Eventually, they relented and said the headline was going to be: THE WORLD'S FAVOURITE MUSLIM. Abbas declined, just as he turned down an article that focused on the Manchester Arena attack of 2017 – when an Islamic terrorist's bomb killed twenty-two and injured more than a thousand.

The article was to centre on the theme of Muslims not being terrorists but Abbas was furious that Salah was being linked – even in the contrary – to something so violent. Why should he occupy the same space as an extremist?

While Abbas thought that some Western media outlets wanted to use Salah to promote a supposed diversity in its own politics, publicly, at least, Salah remained apolitical. While he read a lot, and might see something on the news and comment on it, he had lived in Europe for a greater proportion of his football career than he had spent in Egypt. Meanwhile, his first daughter was born in England, he was unable to return home much, and his assets were abroad. If anything, he would have more of an understanding about British or even American politics where – unlike in Egypt – more than one party has a chance of making an impact.

Salah still loves living in England, where he, his wife and his daughters enjoy freedoms they would not have if they lived in Cairo or Nagrig. Many Egyptians got annoyed when he posted Instagram photographs of himself celebrating Christmas, seeing it as blasphemous. The posts drew a visceral reaction, some even asking whether he had turned to Christianity. Alternatively, was he just trying too hard to assimilate, being a good little Muslim?

Yet the fact remained that he kept doing it. Having lived in England for so long, a nation which has become more secular, he thought of the festive period as simply an opportunity to spend time with his family. Despite the landslide of criticism that came his way, he made the same post each year, and the same Egyptians used it as evidence of his pulling away from the culture he once knew. Though some defended him by saying it showed the confidence he had in himself, he lost a minority of people who believed he thought he was better than anyone else.

A similar reaction was provoked in 2022 in the wake of the death of Queen Elizabeth II. Salah released a post that reflected his condolences to the British head of state. In the minds of some, it was another sign he was more connected to Europe than Africa, but it was one of the few occasions Salah acted on instinct. When he was injured at Wembley a few months earlier in the FA Cup final against Chelsea, Prince William checked on him after the match. In Salah's view, it was only right that he should try and show that he was thinking about him following the death of his grandmother, without explicitly suggesting they were somehow familiar with one another.

Salah rarely took sides on the issues where he was expected to and he was especially reluctant to offer opinion on complicated matters. While it may have been easy for him to raise awareness about stray cats being exported from Egypt to another country to be eaten, it meant that, whenever Egyptians or Muslims in other parts of the world passed away without him responding, he would be told that he was indifferent to human suffering and he cared more about animals than people.

The conflict that started between Isreal and Palestine in October 2023 was one such example. After several days, he was cited for not releasing a statement about Muslim deaths. Quietly, he'd made a substantial donation to the Red Crescent charity which was trying to get aid into Gaza. But even when this became known, and after he'd released a video calling for an end to the bloodshed, receiving two hundred million views, it still wasn't enough for some sections of the Muslim population, who wanted the messaging to be more decisive.

Neither Salah nor Abbas took advice from specialists over their PR strategy. When they met, it was usually in Dubai, where they ate in Salah's favourite Japanese restaurant which had fresh fish flown in from Tokyo each morning. They discussed Salah's investments. He owned four Banksy paintings, along with an apartment in the Emirate where he was one of Abbas's neighbours, a thirty-five-floor tower that stands in the shadow of the Burj Khalifa, the world's tallest building.

Yet whenever Salah visited Dubai, he had to cover his head to go unrecognised. He considered Abbas a friend and like all true friends, they did not agree about everything. On one occasion, Salah had been out with some Egyptians and it was late when he knocked on Abbas's door to see if he was still awake. The topic of religion came up and the debate went on until 4 a.m.

Chapter 11

Big deal

Ahead of the 2022 Champions League final in Paris, Liverpool's principal owner, John W. Henry, checked into the five-star Cheval Blanc hotel, near the banks of the River Seine. Ramy Abbas had also booked one of the art-deco building's seventy-two rooms, and it amused the lawyer that Henry did not recognise him as they ate at nearby tables at the Le Tout rooftop bar, overlooking the Pont Neuf bridge and the sprawl of the Latin Quarter.

Abbas remained a kingpin in contract talks over the star player at the club Henry owned, though the billionaire had no direct involvement. That responsibility was left to Mike Gordon who, five months earlier, in December 2021, had said farewell to Abbas in Miami, Florida, following a meeting that ended with neither party close to a resolution.

Liverpool would narrowly lose the final to Real Madrid at the Stade de France, after which Salah returned to Merseyside with the squad for a parade to mark cups won earlier in the season, where he was in no mood to celebrate, before boarding a private jet at Manchester Airport that landed in Hurghada on Egypt's Red Sea. At a resort just up the coast in El Gouna, he went sea fishing and kitesurfing. One evening, Abbas called him from Dubai, saying, 'I am starting to fear that we may not be able to come to an agreement on a new contract, Mohamed – their latest offer is still very far from what we want.'

Talks had stopped altogether and Salah was now nearly a year out from being able to move to another club on a free transfer. It was ultimately Abbas's job to present every possibility to his client. At the time, he told some people that the destination could be another Premier League club. The only person he was loyal to was the player himself. Salah wanted to remain at Anfield but the decision would come down to respect and, by extension, money, though Salah insisted in January 2022 what he was asking for wasn't 'crazy stuff'.

When Abbas revealed details of what happened next in an academic paper released by Harvard Business School, he suggested the player's priority was to remain in England rather than explicitly at Liverpool. This was because of how settled Salah and his family were. 'Starting a new life somewhere else is hard,' Abbas noted. Salah, indeed, was adamant that he was not thinking about playing anywhere else, and he wanted to remain at Liverpool. 'But the club needs to show that they want me to stay as well.'

Abbas had examined what other elite players were earning and Salah was nowhere near the top. City's influential Belgian midfielder Kevin de Bruyne was earning £375,000 a week. Meanwhile, Liverpool valued Salah in the region of £150 million. In 2021, Jack Grealish had left Aston Villa for City for a fee of nearly £100 million and his contract was worth £300,000 a week.

The offer on the table from Liverpool would have given Salah a 15 per cent pay rise on his £200,000 a week contract but that would have made him only the fifteenth best-paid player in the world after bonuses. This, agreed Salah and Abbas, undervalued his status in football. In Miami, Abbas reflected expectations from his client that would have instead made him the sixth highest-paid player. Though Abbas subsequently sent Gordon a revised set of demands by email after returning from Florida, a deadlock remained across the first half of 2022.

Gordon wanted to retain Salah but not at any price. He was prepared to make him the highest-paid player in the club's history but only without demolishing a wage structure that was manageable and kept everyone happy, including the other highest-paid players, Virgil van Dijk and Alisson Becker.

Gordon's Brookline mansion was just around the corner from John W. Henry's even bigger mansion. Henry had developed a rather curious, close working relationship with Manchester United's chief executive Ed Woodward over Project Big Picture, a plan hatched by the owners of Liverpool and United to shake up how money was redistributed across English football clubs. Woodward had told Henry that goalkeeper David de Gea's 2019 contract at Old Trafford had changed the expectation of United's players.

Gordon was wary of making the same mistakes. Even when Liverpool's legendary captain Steven Gerrard asked for an extra year on a new deal in 2015, Gordon baulked. In the summer of 2021, he contributed towards the decision that led to cutting off a £25 million investment in Georginio Wijnaldum when he asked for too much money in wages. The hugely popular Dutchman was a fine player and a hard worker in Liverpool's midfield but sporting director Michael Edwards advised that approaching thirty, it was possible to replace his output.

Salah was a different story. By the end of the 2021–22 campaign, he had finished as the Premier League's top scorer in three of the previous five seasons. If the hardest thing to do in football is put the ball in the back of the net, Salah was invaluable. As the impasse rumbled on, he was on course to equal his second-best return over a single season with thirty-one goals across all competitions – this in a campaign in which he had also won the award for the most assists in the Premier League by creating thirteen goals. If Salah was selfish, he had a funny way of showing it. 'Single-minded' would be a better description. This would all add up to him winning the PFA Player of the Year award as well as the Football Writers' Association Footballer of the Year accolade. Just as crucial was his availability. Across his five years at Liverpool, he had averaged more than fifty appearances a season.

Salah appreciated his own value. Yet he also knew that if he went elsewhere, he probably would not be the main man, as he was at Liverpool – a role which made him feel confident, helping him to perform to his best. Since early 2021, Abbas had developed a curious friendship with Liverpool's all-time leading goalscorer, Ian Rush, who had worked a lot in Dubai, helping the club he used to represent in its commercial partnerships. Rush's 346 goals in 660 games made him a legend but, in the middle of his career, he left Liverpool briefly for Juventus in Italy, where he did not feel the same way about himself, or play with the same ease. Rush had told Abbas and Salah about the perils of moving, and Salah especially listened, realising the value of preserving his legacy.

Yet he still wanted to know how highly the club valued him and he was getting the feeling it wasn't particularly high. In early June 2022, the telephone conversations between Abbas and Salah were long. It wasn't simply a case of them making demands and expecting Liverpool to meet them. They realised that some flexibility was needed on their part as well. Salah was also turning thirty that summer, an age at which the length of contracts footballers sign tend to be shorter and certainly less lavish. This followed a history of Premier League superstar footballers being handed lucrative contracts beyond their peak, and subsequently becoming a burden for their clubs financially.

Upon buying Liverpool, FSG had been admirers of Arsenal's model of buying players young and selling them for huge profits when they were much older. From afar, they had seen the damaging consequences for the club when it acted on impulse, renewing deals for those players who were popular but ultimately past their best. At Arsenal there had been a succession of them: Alexis Sanchez, Mesut Özil and Pierre-Emerick Aubameyang. All of this meant Salah was pushing against FSG convention. To get roughly what he wanted, he would have to be open to receiving a mix of fixed and variable pay, while also potentially feeding some of his image rights into a new deal.

If Salah agreed to stay, it would be his third contract with Liverpool. Though it had been suggested numerous times that Liverpool was the only club interested in signing him from Roma in 2017, Salah was insistent five years later that 'we had some good offers at the time' but he wanted to go back to England because of his love of the Premier League, which he'd watched from afar while he was living in Rome.

'The football in England is faster than that in Italy, and I felt I could express myself better in England,' Salah told Harvard. 'So when Ramy told me that Liverpool was among the clubs interested in signing me, I said, "Let's try to make that happen."'

The player's achievements in his first season at Anfield led to Abbas approaching Edwards about an improved contract in March 2018. It would take three months to agree new terms and, in that period, Salah did the interview with CNN that helped remind everyone – including Edwards – of his increasing importance on the global stage.

Partway through the 2017–18 season, Virgil van Dijk's arrival at Liverpool from Southampton for £75 million – then a world record for a defender – made him the highest earner at the club, on close to £200,000 a week depending on how he performed. Abbas was acutely aware of this development and, in securing a new five-year deal for Salah, he gave Van Dijk a partner at the top of the club's pay scale.

Liverpool were also satisfied with the agreement. Edwards had brokered a contract which did not have a release clause, putting the club in a strong position if a rival suitor like Real Madrid stepped up their interest in the future. For so long, Liverpool had lost its best players in such situations but in getting Van Dijk, who chose Liverpool ahead of Manchester City, and then persuading Salah to stay, there was a residual benefit because it said to players at other clubs that Liverpool was a place to be, potentially strengthening the club's hand at the negotiating table.

Salah's trust in Abbas was total. 'He is always very clear with me,' said Salah. 'He'll say, "You will get this much, and I will get this much – are you OK with that, or not?" If I am not happy with how much his share is, I know he would reduce it. But I never felt that way – if anything, I feel he should be getting more.'

★   ★   ★

Salah's five-year contract, signed in 2018, was three years away from expiring when the campaign to explore what his future might look like began in the summer of 2020. Yet with so much time left on the deal, and Liverpool's matchday revenues disappearing because of Covid-19, the club was not in a rush to improve Salah's terms, or those of any other player on a long-term contract.

Liverpool may have topped the Premier League table as Christmas approached in December 2020 but most fans were still locked out of stadiums, and nobody quite sure when they would all return. The hole in the club's finances would eventually amount to a pre-tax loss of £46 million. A year earlier Liverpool had recorded a profit of more than £43 million, so the swing was approaching £90 million – the value of one or maybe two influential new signings, never mind the costs involved in retaining those stars already attached.

Some of Liverpool's players were concerned how deeply this situation would impact on the club's effort to compete. FSG were cutting its cloth accordingly and this meant pulling out of deals with players who Klopp thought would improve the squad. This included Timo Werner, the German international forward, from Red Bull Leipzig, who Klopp had convinced to join Liverpool before the owners intervened. Instead, Werner went to Chelsea, where he struggled for goals – but, as Salah had proven, just because a player struggled at Chelsea, it might be different in an environment like Liverpool.

Salah was happy at Liverpool because his family were settled in Cheshire but his competitive spirit dictated that he knew he might not feel quite the same way if Liverpool were suddenly unable to attract the talent that kept them competing for trophies. He was also twenty-eight years old – though Abbas later suggested that he could play at the highest level until his forties, Salah appreciated that not everyone would share his representative's optimistic view of the future. If Real Madrid or Barcelona were going to act, it was probably now or never, though the pandemic was also impacting on each club's ability to throw its weight about in the transfer market.

Real would lose close to €300 million (£235 million) due to the pandemic but still registered a narrow pre-tax profit, mainly because they did not sign any players during the 2020–21 season. They also sold one of their brightest young talents in Achraf Hakimi and allowed a high earner in James Rodriguez to leave for nothing, shedding the Colombian's significant wages. In 2021, the club's financial report suggested it 'will continue in its effort so far to contain spending'.

Meanwhile, Barcelona's accounts revealed overall revenues across two seasons between 2019 and 2021 dropped by a quarter, plunging the club into a debt of €1.35 billion (£1.15 billion). Though it continued to approach the transfer market aggressively, it was not with the abandon of earlier years, which had included the deal for the Liverpool forward Philippe Coutinho, for a British record fee. Catalonia would go on to think of him not only as a monumental waste of money but also one of the causes of the club's financial meltdown.

It would take a brave Barcelona director to commit a similar fee for an older player like Salah from the same club. Liverpool, initially steered from the front by Edwards, and from the rear by Gordon, appreciated this: for all the noise that Salah made, there wasn't really an interested party to apply the pressure that was needed to make a quick decision. The club's transfer strategists knew the market. In 2020 the biggest transfer deal of the summer was agreed, before the pandemic, between Chelsea and Bayer Leverkusen for Kai Havertz at £80 million. In 2021 there was the Jack Grealish deal but nobody was willing to pay whatever the going rate for Salah was.

There was interest from Paris Saint-Germain, but Salah wanted to win the Ballon d'Or, and only one player in the award's history (Jean-Pierre Papin in 1991 with Olympique Marseille) had been stationed in France at the point of being a recipient. Manchester City? That would have to be forced, and it would mangle his legacy at Anfield. Liverpool thought they were in a strong position, stronger than the player realised at times.

Salah, therefore, was an extraordinary footballer found waiting in exactly the wrong moment to try and start a bidding war for his talent. Real, Barcelona, City and Chelsea had proven themselves as the only clubs capable of signing Liverpool's best players but now each of them was out of that market for different reasons.

It seemed to Liverpool's directors and money men that Salah had nowhere to go although some in Liverpool's transfer sphere believed the club would have considered selling Salah at any point from the pandemic onwards had the money been right. Yet there was also an understanding that any argument about the merits of this would have been hard to make with a twitchy fanbase, increasingly wary of how the club was operating after leaving Werner to Chelsea.

At Anfield, on 16 December 2020, Salah scored a deflected opening goal against Tottenham Hotspur in front of just two thousand fans permitted to sit on the Kop as pandemic restrictions were lifted. Roberto Firmino's thumping injury-time header secured a victory which saw Liverpool pull away at the top of the table. The following morning, Salah greeted two reporters from one of Spain's bestselling newspapers, *AS*, at a secure location on Merseyside, where he flirted with the company's branded microphone in front of a Christmas tree.

The interview was published in question-and-answer format and was broadly not particularly illuminating but for a few of Salah's responses, which seemed planned as they were so sudden, jumping off the page. One was the revelation that he was 'very disappointed' at being overlooked for the role of stand-in captain when Liverpool played a dead-rubber fixture with Midtjylland in the Champions League at the start of the same month. He also described Real and Barcelona as 'top clubs', suggesting a new deal at Anfield was in the 'hands' of the decision-makers at Liverpool. Though roles and responsibilities would change over the next eighteen months, at the time, these were Edwards (the negotiator), Gordon (financial sign-off) and Jürgen Klopp, the manager who was responsible for choosing Trent Alexander-Arnold as captain when Salah was instead 'expecting' the role, having emerged as one of the best footballers in the world.

Though Salah answered a question nervously about where he stood in relation to players like Cristiano Ronaldo and Lionel Messi, he nevertheless provided a firm response when he was asked whether he was in the same league as these legends.

Inside Liverpool's dressing room, some of the players felt Salah's comments were disrespectful to Alexander-Arnold. Meanwhile, directors at Liverpool interpreted Salah's interview with *AS* as a deliberate attempt to connect with a Spanish audience, driving up interest and strengthening his hand when it eventually came to discussions that might start the following summer, two years ahead of the expiration of his contract.

Merseyside-based officials at Liverpool did not know the interview was landing until it appeared online just before the team travelled to London for a Premier League fixture with Crystal Palace. In front of the broadcast media at Selhurst Park, Klopp chortled at the suggestion the interview was a distraction for either himself or any of his players. Yet he was ruthless in what he did next. He suggested he had already decided to rest Salah for the Palace fixture ahead of Liverpool's game with Spurs: 'Mo missed only seven minutes from the last four games,' he reasoned. 'It is a massively intense period, so it was clear it would be him. Bringing him in for the last half an hour, I thought it was a good idea.'

Yet the data relating to the player's physical condition did not support any such requirement. Salah had started every game he was available for that season and he did not feel as though he was in need of a rest even though Liverpool's fixture schedule had been gruelling. Some of Liverpool's more curious players recognised the decision as Klopp's way of reminding everyone who was in charge and that his authority should never be questioned publicly.

Klopp came out of the situation looking stronger. A subsequent 7–0 filleting of Palace included two Salah goals, one of them spectacular, a curling effort into the top corner. The margin of the victory, as well as Salah's positive involvement as a substitute reduced the noise about his future at the club, while appearing to justify Klopp's decision to leave him out.

It was noted by other players that, as Klopp debriefed the team inside the dressing room, however, Salah was barely listening to what the manager was saying, instead quietly ready-ing himself for a departure from the stadium. It was a subtle show of defiance, but if it annoyed Klopp he did not show it. Though Liverpool were cruising at the point of Salah's intro-duction, the ease at which he helped finish off the opponent reminded everyone of his class, as well as his attitude. If he was annoyed, he did not sulk on the pitch.

Some of Liverpool's staff believed that Salah's relationship with Klopp shifted further apart that day, though it was only obvious to those who really knew about the dynamic between the pair. Until that point, their contact had always been correct and respectful but no more than that. Klopp's reputation as an everyman tended to make everyone outside of Liverpool's dress-ing room believe that he was close with all of the club's players, especially the senior ones. Yet this was never the case, certainly not with Salah.

In March 2021, Salah would describe their understanding in an interview with Spanish daily *Marca* ahead of Liverpool's Champions League tie with Real Madrid as a 'normal relation-ship between two professionals'. Meanwhile, he was more effu-sive for the leader in the opposing dugout, Zinedine Zidane: 'a great coach . . . one of my idols when I was little'.

Klopp tended to get through more to those with greater inse-curities. Footballers who lacked father figures in their lives, for example, tended to respond better to Klopp's paternal approach, at least away from training sessions where he was hard on every-one. He was closer to these types of players, including Virgil van Dijk and Salah's old rival, Sadio Mané. While Mané had lost his dad at an early age, Van Dijk preferred to wear the name 'Virgil' on the back of his shirt after his parents separated when he was twelve years old. From time to time, they needed guidance and Klopp was happy to help with that.

Salah's father had played a prominent role in his early life but the player developed an independence due to the circumstances of his rise. Only he really knew what it was like to travel long hours alone between the Nile Delta and Cairo as a teenager. Though he had to figure a lot out for himself, there was always family at home he could return to, even if it was just over the phone. He was a willing learner and would listen to any guidance that might help him as a player, but he did not expect a manager to help develop him as a person. There was, therefore, a gap between the best instincts of Klopp and what Salah felt he really needed.

In the summer of 2021, six Liverpool players signed new, long-term contracts, though Salah was not one of them. They were Virgil van Dijk, Alisson Becker, Trent Alexander-Arnold, Andrew Robertson, Fabinho and Jordan Henderson, whose deal was the most controversial, as his future could have gone the same as Wijnaldum's had it not been for the intervention of Klopp.

Between 2021 and 2022, Salah received three proposals from Liverpool but none of them met his expectations and he was becoming more public with his frustrations. By this point, Julian Ward had taken over most of Edwards' responsibilities. Though Liverpool's season was going well on the pitch, fans were curious to find out how Ward would handle the challenge – especially dealing with a tough negotiator like Abbas. Yet really, Gordon was the point of contact over contract negotiations and, though Abbas liked Ward, he knew that Gordon was the person he'd have to shake down if he were to get the deal that he wanted.

In 2021–22, Salah was enjoying another fine season, and by January 2022 he was positioned as the most effective forward in Europe's top five leagues, with sixteen goals, nine assists and forty-one chances created. His stock, therefore, was incredibly high when he told *GQ* that he wanted to remain at the club, but he underlined that it was not his decision: 'It's in their hands,' he said. 'They know what I want. I'm not asking for crazy stuff . . . I've been here for my fifth year now. I know the club very well. I love the fans. The fans love me . . . But with the administration, they have [been] told the situation.'

When Salah used the word 'their', he meant FSG – not the sporting director, Ward, or the club's manager, Klopp. Frustratingly for Klopp, he was the only one with the public-facing role and the interview meant he could not avoid speaking about Salah's future ahead of Liverpool's next game, a Carabao Cup semi-final tie with Arsenal. For the first time, Liverpool's manager spoke at reasonable length about what was happening, suggesting that the club and the player had held 'good conversations', though he appeared to claim the challenge of convincing Abbas that Salah should stay was as significant as talking with the player himself. 'There are so many things you have to do in these negotiations and there is, by the way, a third party: the agent is there as well,' Klopp said.

Abbas reacted to that by posting a photograph on social media of him lurking behind Salah, fiddling on his phone, while the player laughed. Two months later, Abbas returned to the same social media page to post seven emojis of a face crying after Klopp insisted it was Salah's decision to stay or leave, as the club had done 'what the club can do'.

If Klopp was trying to diffuse the conversation around Salah, it did not work. Previously, he had vowed publicly to 'get sorted' a new contract for his captain Henderson, yet with Salah, he claimed he was 'not involved' with negotiations. In his *Daily Telegraph* column, the legendary Liverpool defender-turned-Sky Sports pundit Jamie Carragher had previously spotted the disconnect: 'If there is a sound reason for not resolving the Salah contract situation with the same urgency, it is yet to be satisfactorily explained,' he wrote.

Klopp saw a difference between the two situations, however. While there was less will on the club's part to renew on Henderson, they were much keener on Salah – albeit not at all costs. This contributed to him being more relaxed about the situation for a long time. There was also the issue of him being angry at losing Wijnaldum. With Henderson, ego kicked in. He was ultimately the manager and he felt he had a better understanding of what the team and dressing room needed. Henderson was his leader. He could not let the same result happen twice.

Carragher believed that Salah's name would feature in the all-time greatest Liverpool XI, stressing that unless he suffered from a serious injury, he was in such perfect physical shape that he could continue producing for Liverpool until he was thirty-three at the earliest, 'and probably for a couple of years beyond that'. It was his view that Cristiano Ronaldo and Lionel Messi were an inspiration to their peers, 'showing how the early thirties are no barrier to enduring excellence'.

In the subsequent furore, Klopp's complimentary observations about Salah's potential longevity were largely lost. Though he did not appear to be willing to involve himself in contract talks relating to Salah, he backed the suggestion his player would emerge like Ronaldo and Messi. He described Salah as 'the best sort of greedy' because he was greedy for himself as well as the team.

'It's his character, his determination, the way he trains, his attitude, work rate. It's incredible, 'Klopp said. 'He is the first in, last out, doing the right stuff. You can do some not-so-good things when you spend so long in the gym and the training ground, but he knows his body, he knows what to do. He listens to the experts here and tries to improve all the time. He tries to improve for the situation he is in now, and he will not waste it by doing less. I am as convinced as you can be.'

Though Abbas ended up creating more headlines for his client and was vilified for his response to Klopp's suggestion that the future was in Salah's hands, it made both him and his client even more determined to stick to their position. Besides, most of the fans were on Salah's side: FSG were regularly accused of penny pinching, but Salah was doing his talking on the pitch.

Liverpool went to Brighton, where Salah climbed to ninth in the list of the club's all-time top scorers, only nineteen adrift of one of the club's greatest players, Sir Kenny Dalglish. By this point, only one of the other greatest players – Steven Gerrard – had direct involvement in more Premier League goals for Liverpool than Salah. While Gerrard's record stood at 120 goals and ninety-two assists, Salah was on 115 goals and forty-three assists.

The latter metric helped him answer claims that he was self-ish, especially in a period where he was testing Liverpool's financial limits. At Brighton, his goal from the penalty spot meant he joined another elite club. In Premier League history, only Alan Shearer, Sergio Agüero, Thierry Henry, Ruud van Nistelrooy and Harry Kane had scored twenty or more league goals in four different seasons. Now in his fifth campaign, Salah had fallen short of this milestone only once, when instead he registered nineteen goals.

The excitement Liverpool delivered on the pitch as a team distracted from the uncertainty around Salah's future. They would win the Carabao Cup and the FA Cup, beating Chelsea on penalties twice in gruelling games at Wembley. In the latter, Salah needed to be substituted early with a groin injury, which Klopp described as a 'precaution' due to the impending assaults on the Premier League title and the Champions League.

Liverpool would miss out on both. After departing Paris with no progression made on his contract, Salah was seriously contemplating leaving the club. Though Salah felt deep down Liverpool wanted him to stay, reaching an agreement was difficult. 'We are still very far apart,' noted Abbas when he spoke to Harvard. 'Mohamed isn't going to throw away his contract because of a five per cent difference in what we are asking for and what they are willing to give – it is much more than that.'

One thing each party could agree on was the length of a new deal. Another three years would potentially see Salah remain at Liverpool until he was thirty-three. The main sticking point was the balance between fixed pay and bonuses. Liverpool wanted to weigh a deal more in favour of Salah's performance while the player and his agent wanted greater guarantees. Abbas was adamant that any variable agreement should be based on his output over the previous seasons rather than any expected decline because of his age. This would see the total value of his contract increase 'significantly', making Salah the highest-paid player in Liverpool's history.

It was the player and his representative's view that, ultimately, Liverpool's insistence on the contract being weighted heavily on incentives made any deal more complex, contributing towards the whole process dragging on. Abbas and Salah came up with a strategy to move it along and to react to certain events taking place in any subsequent negotiations. The discussions between Dubai and El Gouna involved consideration as to whether or not Salah's remuneration for goals and assists should be capped, and whether these bonuses should be paid as they happened on the pitch or as a lump sum when milestones were passed. Abbas also knew that Ward was keen to ensure that certain team-related performance bonuses were dependent on Salah's contributions. Abbas calculated Liverpool would be interested in seizing some of the player's image rights. His projected earnings over the next few seasons were between €54 million (£45 million) and €62 million (£52 million) per year. If the club could benefit from using Salah's name and face financially, it might prompt them to drive up their own offer to the player.

Abbas knew he was taking a risk. What if Liverpool stalled or walked away from the table entirely, then Salah got injured the following season? He spoke to the player about taking out extra medical insurance, though it was the lawyer's view that a long-term playing contract was the 'best insurance you can have'.

For Abbas, it was the toughest deal of his career. It would have been easier for Salah to move on and join another club. Yet he fired off an email with the player's final proposals to Gordon and waited.

★　　★　　★

Re-signing Salah ended up costing Liverpool nearly £55 million. His three-year contract was worth £350,000 per week basic. If he did well for Liverpool, that figure would be pushed towards £400,000. It easily made him the highest-paid player in the club's history. Mike Gordon had steered the negotiations entirely but Julian Ward was pictured on the photographs when Salah signed the deal beside Ramy Abbas on the Greek island of Mykonos, where he was enjoying another holiday.

Deep down, Abbas had been wondering whether or not Liverpool really wanted to do the deal because of their reluctance. When the offer came through that clinched an agreement, he even sensed that Liverpool secretly hoped they might reject it. Klopp, meanwhile, was relieved the saga was over. 'It's the best decision for us and best decision for him,' he said. 'He belongs with us I think. This is his club now.'

Klopp understood that Salah was one of the best players in the world and this meant negotiations were always going to be far from straightforward.

'I have no doubt Mo's best years are still to come,' he added. 'And that's saying something, because the first five seasons here have been the stuff of legend. Fitness-wise, he's a machine – in the most incredible shape. He works hard on it and he gets his rewards. His ability and his skill level get higher each season, and his decision making has gone to another level also. He is adored by his teammates. As coaches we know we work with someone special. It means we can achieve more together.'

Salah's willingness to commit to a variety of performance-related bonuses relating to goals and assists was a sign of the confidence in himself. 'I feel great and I am excited to win trophies with the club,' he said. 'It's a happy day for everyone. We are in a good position to fight for everything.'

Except, Salah was largely unaware of an upheaval behind the scenes at Liverpool that would impact upon the way the club recruited its players over the next two seasons and would have a major bearing on the team's output.

After barely six months as sporting director, Ward was beginning to feel that the balance of power at Liverpool was tilting further towards Klopp. Rather than reaching decisions by consensus, the manager and the owners were increasingly working things out between themselves, with Ward acting on instruction. Other departments were left in the dark over key decisions. This contributed to the departure of Ian Graham, the club's head of research, who handed in his notice soon after a recruitment meeting in the summer of 2022 that lasted barely ninety minutes. At the end of the meeting – which also involved Klopp and the owners – everyone outside the inner circle was informed that Liverpool were signing Darwin Núñez from Benfica for what would potentially be a record transfer fee of £85 million, if the Uruguayan forward hit certain milestones.

Members of Liverpool's data team had looked at Núñez and were uncertain that he would fit the team's style. While Sadio Mané was replaced by Luis Díaz earlier that year, with Ward taking much of the credit for getting the deal over the line despite competition from Tottenham Hotspur, Núñez was essentially coming in to succeed Roberto Firmino. Both Núñez and Firmino were willing runners, but they were effective in different areas of the pitch, with Firmino often dropping deeper and Núñez more dangerous higher up. Firmino was a play-maker, bringing others into the game, while Núñez was viewed as more of an individual whose game needed rounding off.

Klopp became convinced Núñez offered Liverpool the chance to evolve after examining his performances in both legs of Liverpool's Champions League quarter-final tie with Benfica in the previous season. Klopp had prepared for those ties by watching videos of Benfica's games in earlier stages of the competition where Núñez scored against Bayern Munich and Barcelona, as well as the winner against Ajax in the round of sixteen. His blistering pace was devastating and Klopp believed the player would strike fear into opponents because he was so direct. Klopp was willing to tweak his team's approach to accommodate Núñez, whose £140,000-a-week wage over the course of a six-year contract equated to another £43.7 million on top of the transfer fee, which was slightly less than the figure Liverpool were paying to keep Salah for half of the time.

Klopp and Ward worked closely together to ensure Núñez went to Liverpool rather than Manchester United, who were also interested. Ward's experience dealing with Portuguese agents and club representatives in the past helped. Previously, he had been Liverpool's scouting manager for the Iberian Peninsula and, before that, he was the head of analysis and technical scouting for the Portuguese national team. Most importantly, he was now established with Jorge Mendes, the country's super-agent, whose influence seemed to be everywhere.

When the data team were breezily told of Núñez's impending arrival, it felt like a fait accompli. Graham had been one of the influences behind not only the appointment of Klopp, but the recruitment of Salah. Graham had never had much interaction with Klopp over the previous seven years. Yet Klopp was impressed by the work of Graham's department, and in most cases understood it. By 2022, the dynamic had shifted.

Edwards, of course, had already departed Liverpool after finding out, as would Ward, that Klopp's instincts were being followed more than ever. Graham, a Welsh Liverpool supporter, had been hired by the club he loved because of Edwards as his own power grew. He had been promised that data would not just be a consideration in recruitment, but a leading part of the review process.

Edwards was still just about a Liverpool employee when he watched the Champions League final in Paris, wearing non-club attire and away from the official travelling party, having already handed over his responsibilities to Ward at the end of 2021. With him leaving, and the era of collaboration between departments at Liverpool, especially over transfers, being treated less seriously or quite possibly coming to an end altogether, Graham concluded it was also time for him to move on. He handed in his notice in June 2022 but this development only became a public matter in November, before he finally departed officially in May 2023. Then he set up a data consultancy business called Ludonautics with his old friend Edwards.

Liverpool would begin the 2022–23 season with a fixture at Fulham, who had been promoted three months earlier from the Championship. The midfield that afternoon was ageing, with Fabinho at its base (almost twenty-nine), Thiago Alcântara (thirty-one) and captain, Jordan Henderson (thirty-two). Though the trio had made an enormous contribution to the previous campaign, where Liverpool went so close to winning a quadruple, each player appeared exhausted as Liverpool toiled to a 2–2 draw, thanks to an eightieth-minute equaliser from Salah.

Klopp knew that this area of the pitch would need remodelling and he had nearly four weeks to do something about it. This was a reminder of the separation from the model that had made Liverpool successful under him. Fabinho, for example, had arrived by stealth at the start of the summer of 2018, within twenty-four hours of the Champions League final defeat to Real Madrid in Kyiv.

Klopp was desperate to sign Jude Bellingham from Borussia Dortmund but the German club had told Liverpool that he would spend another season in the Bundesliga. This left Klopp in a difficult position because he did not want to sign another player from the same pool pot, ruining the chances of him getting the one he really wanted.

Different options were presented. The club's South American scouts had flown to Merseyside with a dossier including detailed reports on João Gomes from Flamengo, as well as the more attacking Facundo Buonanotte from Rosario Central. On Merseyside, they initially met Klopp's assistant, Pep Lijnders, who was not keen on any of the recommendations. Later, Ward took the scouts out for a meal to explain why the coaching staff had reservations. Ultimately, it came down to the same old problem of the jump between Brazil or Argentina being too great.

Both Ward and his predecessor, Edwards, agreed that it would be smart for FSG to buy a second club, ideally somewhere warm in southern Europe, where Liverpool could acclimatise such players in the future. Had that been possible when Edwards and chief scout Barry Hunter tried to recruit Rodrygo from Santos in 2018, then maybe the Brazilian would have ended up playing for Liverpool rather than Real Madrid.

The other serious option in the summer of 2022 was Matheus Nunes from Sporting Lisbon, whose release clause was set at £38 million. The money for the Brazilian-born midfielder, who had lived in Portugal since he was twelve, was ready to be sent to a Lisbon bank account when Klopp concluded the player needed Premier League experience before committing to him. Instead, he joined Wolverhampton Wanderers for the same figure, on the condition he could leave for Liverpool for a bigger sum if they came up with the cash.

In the end, Liverpool agreed a loan deal with Arthur from Juventus on the last day of the transfer window. By then, the team's injury problems were concentrated in the midfield and Klopp felt as though he had to act, despite Arthur's own problems with injuries. He would play only thirteen minutes for Liverpool, as a substitute in a crushing 4–0 defeat away to Napoli, a result which exposed the team's frailties and pointed towards the long, hard season that would follow.

Though Salah thought Liverpool were in a 'good position to fight for everything' they were not even capable of qualifying for the Champions League. Someone who was close to each of the departments at Liverpool suggested too many influential figures had left too quickly because of the strain of working with Klopp. 'I just don't know how you regain control,' the contact said. 'Julian [Ward] had deals for midfielders and Klopp kept saying, "No." These midfielders then went elsewhere before Klopp decided he needed one with a few days to go. I don't see how anyone can work in such an environment or why they would want to, given they get the blame for it by the fanbase, while Klopp is regarded as a loveable rogue not supported as he should be by owners when really they were prepared to back him.'

Just five weeks after losing the 2022 Champions League final in Paris, Liverpool's preparations for the next season were already well under way with a friendly against Manchester United in the rains of Bangkok.

A monsoon and heavy traffic meant the Rajamangala National Stadium was not full when the game that involved three halves of thirty minutes kicked off. It was Erik ten Hag's first in charge of United following his hiring from Ajax, where he had taken the team to the brink of the Champions League final in 2019 where they would have faced Liverpool had it not been for late Tottenham goals. Four months earlier in 2022, Liverpool had completed a 9–0 aggregate victory over their greatest rivals across two Premier League fixtures, but in Bangkok, ten Hag started with a much stronger team than Klopp and this contributed towards a 4–0 thrashing.

Klopp conceded that the game came 'a bit too early' for his squad, after less than a week's training for many of the experienced players, including Salah. Klopp did not like the scheduling of these Far East tours because they placed commercial gain over preparation but he understood their importance, in theory creating a better economic environment for him to work in.

This trip helped Liverpool's commercial revenue rise by £25 million to £272 million. When the club released its financial results in May 2023, a statement suggested the 'success was achieved due to a strong growth in partnerships and a hugely successful pre-season tour, playing games in Thailand and Singapore.'

Klopp, however, saw very little sporting value in these excursions. It had been five years since the club's last trip to the region, though this was explained by the Covid-19 pandemic getting in the way of a planned visit in 2020.

In 2017, Klopp saw training sessions cancelled due to the weather. He also thought the pitches Liverpool had access to in Hong Kong were not up to scratch. As he waited in his room at the Ritz-Carlton hotel in Kowloon for the clouds to clear, his frustrations festered and this even led to a heated argument with members of the club's in-house media operation when they tried to make light of the situation.

Klopp preferred the USA, where the weather and facilities were more reliable and schedules involved a more reasonable commercial commitment for both him and his players, even if they were still demanding. 'The Far East was the last place he wanted to go,' said a member of staff who served under him, 'because it was the one place where he did not have control, including the conditions.'

After Thailand in the summer of 2022, the Liverpool squad flew to Singapore for another friendly, this time with Crystal Palace. A better performance and result followed, albeit Liverpool won 2–0 against a Palace squad that only involved ten senior players due to injuries and failures to meet the country's strict entry requirements around Covid-19.

In a restaurant of another Ritz-Carlton hotel, this time the Millenia, which overlooks Singapore's famous marina, another argument blew up, one which had consequences for the start of the season because it meant Liverpool started the campaign without a club doctor.

A profile on Liverpool's website had described Andy Massey as the club's 'master of medicine', before it was announced that the Northern Irishman, who'd played for Bangor and Linfield, was going to leave his position as the head of medicine for a similar role with FIFA in March 2020. According to a member of Massey's staff, it had been his job to 'reduce the number of injuries' at the club during the average working week, though on a matchday, he sat on the bench monitoring what was happening on an iPad. Whenever a player required assistance, he would enter the pitch and try to help the physio.

It was reported that Massey was leaving Liverpool in December 2019 but he had handed his notice in several months earlier. It became Edwards' responsibility to source his replacement and by New Year 2020, he thought he'd done enough to convince Arsenal's head of medical to move to Liverpool. Gary O'Driscoll had joined Arsenal in 2009, earning the promotion that would see him run the club's medical department in 2017, replacing Gary Lewin, who had also worked with England.

Manchester-born O'Driscoll, however, began to have second thoughts after discussions with Mikel Arteta, Arsenal's first team manager, who was fresh into the job having been appointed in December 2020. O'Driscoll, the cousin of the legendary Irish rugby player Brian O'Driscoll, had also done his homework on the environment at Liverpool, where he learned out about the challenges of working with Klopp, who was impulsive and did not always react with reason when he heard bad news about a player's injury status.

In 2023, O'Driscoll joined Manchester United in the same role he had interviewed for at Liverpool. Three years earlier, however, he had decided to stay in London. This created a problem for Liverpool because in the same month Massey left the club, just as Liverpool were closing in on their first domestic title for thirty years, the football calendar was paused due to the pandemic, with nobody knowing when it would return. Suddenly, player welfare became an even bigger issue for football clubs. Liverpool were unable to recruit anyone to replace Massey for a significant time because of lockdown restrictions.

Liverpool also needed a quick decision. This left them with no alternative but to promote from within, initially on a temporary basis. Jim Moxon, a doctor who worked at the club's academy, was asked by Edwards to fill the space left by Massey. He took the job at an unprecedented time, under pressure to meet the government rules and regulations that would allow players to return to a training bubble and eventually return to the pitch, where Liverpool won the title in front of an empty stadium.

It was an exhausting period to be a Liverpool doctor. As defending champions, the 2020–21 season did not go well for the club and, with a couple of months of the campaign to go, it seemed as though the team, unable to feed off the energy from a crowd, would miss out on Champions League football altogether after six successive home defeats in a row at a spectatorless Anfield.

This slump had followed the 7–0 thrashing of Palace, the one in which Salah responded to being dropped or rested – depending on who you speak to – by scoring twice as a substitute. Over the next sixty-seven days, the team's season imploded. After topping the Premier League table at the start of January, by mid-March they were closer to the relegation zone than leaders Manchester City. Having failed to score in eleven of the next fourteen fixtures, they had also conceded more goals than any other side in the top half of the division.

Klopp had previously turned Anfield into a fortress, in which Liverpool had not lost in sixty-eight Premier League fixtures. The six defeats in a row (to Burnley, Brighton, City, Everton, Chelsea and Fulham) formed a first in the club's history, representing the highest number of home losses in any season since 1953–54, when Liverpool were relegated. The slump was staggering and Jamie Carragher, the club's defensive icon, described the descent as a team turning from 'mentality monsters' to 'mentality midgets'.

With ten matches remaining, Liverpool were eighth in the table and seven points away from the top four positions. Amidst all of this, Klopp's mother Elisabeth had died in Germany at the age of eighty-one and he was unable to attend the funeral because of Covid-19 travel restrictions. Meanwhile, goalkeeper Alisson Becker's father had died in Brazil after drowning near a waterfall.

Incredibly, Alisson would become the first goalkeeper in Liverpool's history to score a goal when his injury-time header defeated West Bromwich Albion in May, a result that pushed Liverpool into fifth and within touching distance of redemption. It would all come down to a home fixture with Crystal Palace, ahead of which tensions were inflamed between Liverpool's mild-mannered doctor Moxon and a brooding Klopp.

Liverpool's entire campaign had been undermined by a defensive crisis, which left Klopp relying on the inexperienced and previously untested duo of Nat Phillips and Rhys Williams at centre back. Ahead of the Palace game, Williams reported a thigh strain and Moxon asked how he was feeling. This made Klopp furious, believing that Moxon had given the player the opportunity to develop doubts about his availability when the injury was not serious enough for him to miss such an important fixture. Williams played, and Liverpool won, qualifying for the Champions League.

Moxon was well liked by other staff members but over the season that followed the availability of players became more crucial than ever as Liverpool attempted to win four trophies. The strain between medical and football departments grew worse.

Moxon's departure from Liverpool was confirmed by a brief statement on the club's website, published on 1 August 2022, just five days before the start of the Premier League season at Fulham. 'During his tenure, Dr Moxon has devoted himself to the club, none more so than in recent years when he led the club's response to the Covid-19 pandemic,' the statement read. 'He has also made a major contribution to the team's success, through his excellent work in the field of sports medicine.' The doctor's exit had been triggered by a clash in Singapore over a sickness bug affecting some of Liverpool's players.

Ward was now acting as sporting director and was keen to hire a Portuguese doctor, with the support of Pep Lijnders, who had spent an earlier part of his coaching career in Portugal. The reputations of the medical departments at Benfica, Sporting Lisbon and FC Porto were renowned across Europe but employment restrictions following Brexit meant Ward was unable to make the hires.

Liverpool explored the possibility of rehiring staff who had worked with Klopp, only to leave, feeling burnt out by the experience – albeit also for better-paid jobs. While Ward and Klopp figured out what to do, current staff from the club's academy temporarily filled in, stretching resources at the junior levels.

With expectations as high as ever after the unprecedented possibilities that Klopp's team had created only a few months earlier, the 2022–23 season began badly, with two draws to opponents expected to struggle in Fulham and Crystal Palace, and then a chastening defeat at Old Trafford to Manchester United.

Liverpool's chances of silverware were once again undermined by injuries. By the turn of the year, Liverpool had played twenty-six games and twenty-one different players had missed matches through injury. This meant by the end of the season only six players in the senior squad had been available throughout and one of those was Salah, who had played more minutes than anyone else.

The unavailability of others brought concerns amongst the staff at Liverpool that Salah would eventually break down because he was playing too much. Privately, Salah confided in the people around him at the club that he was becoming concerned about what seemed to him to be a trend.

Eventually, Moxon was replaced by Jonathan Power, a Merseysider who had applied for different roles at the club before. His most recent position was, curiously, in Bermuda. 'The medical staff that we've got are at the highest, highest level and hopefully I can add value to the department and make it even better than it is,' he suggested.

A feature of the Klopp era had been the practice matches the day before a weekend game. These were treated seriously by the players, as if points were at stake. It was Klopp's view that the intensity of these encounters would prepare them better than anything for what was to follow. The players tended to agree. It was an old-school approach, one that Sir Alex Ferguson followed during the glory years at Manchester United. Yet as players continued to get injured, and his selection options narrowed, Klopp was persuaded to scale back these games to stem the list of absentees.

Klopp took some convincing and though he relented, Liverpool's fortunes did not exactly improve. A 3–0 defeat at Molineux to Wolverhampton Wanderers in February 2023 would see Liverpool fall to tenth in the table, the team's lowest position at that stage of the season in the Klopp era. Though Liverpool regained some control of their season, Klopp was becoming more combative. After one victory, when it was half-jokingly suggested by a former employee now working for another club that Klopp's team had experienced a stroke of luck, onlookers saw the Liverpool manager react indignantly, making a hand gesture that implied the old colleague had suddenly found the testicular fortitude to stand up to him.

The pressure on Klopp was cranking up because Liverpool were in danger again of missing out on a place in the following season's Champions League. Not only would this blot Klopp's record going back to 2017, it would cost the club as much as £50 million in prize money and participation fees.

If a famous 7–0 filleting of United at Anfield, with Salah scoring twice, seemed like the moment that would prompt Liverpool to turn a corner, it was not. The result heaved the team up to fifth and another victory at Bournemouth the following week could have seen them rise into the top four.

The midfield that helped destroy United included Fabinho, Henderson and Harvey Elliott. At Bournemouth, Klopp replaced Henderson with eighteen-year-old Stefan Bajcetic. The Spaniard had earned his opportunity in the first team earlier in the season due to Liverpool's injury problems. Though he had impressed through what was a difficult few months for the team, it was felt at Bournemouth by several players that Klopp had misjudged his selection and should have tried to build on the confidence taken from the previous week by choosing the same XI.

Klopp had an eye on the second leg of Liverpool's Champions League tie with Real Madrid, but they were already facing elimination following a 5–2 humbling at Anfield. It was felt that Bournemouth should have instead been the priority. Liverpool could have secured a draw, but Salah's penalty miss led to another defeat. Trent Alexander-Arnold described the performance as, 'Not acceptable – it can't happen again.' In the post-match inquest amongst the players and the staff, some of Klopp's decisions became the focus of the conversation, and some of the players openly questioned his role in the outcome for the first time.

Salah started to speak his mind more in the months that followed, both on the training field and following matches. He was concerned by the club's position in the table and he wanted to compete in the Champions League. Liverpool would lose just one more league game in the remaining twelve, to champions Manchester City, yet they would also draw four. For the first time in the Klopp era, the final game of the season counted for nothing, and a chaotic 4–4 draw at already relegated Southampton summed up a campaign that would be the last at the club for Roberto Firmino, James Milner, Alex Oxlade-Chamberlain and Naby Keita.

Liverpool's remaining senior players were concerned about how the club would find new experience. 'We have to replace them,' Ibrahima Konaté said, when he returned to France for international duty in June. 'If not, what do we do? Do we play with an understaffed squad lacking in quality? You can't rely on youth at this level. I'm sure the boss and the recruitment team know we need new players.'

The quotes barely made a mark back in the UK, but for those who knew about the resistance Klopp was facing, according to one source, Konate had 'let the cat out of the bag' by being so explicit about Liverpool's problems.

Chapter 12

There will be fire

When Mino Raiola brokered the transfer that took Paul Pogba back to Manchester United from Juventus for a world record £89 million in 2016, Ramy Abbas could not but help admire his work. Reports suggest Raiola took home with him between a quarter and half of the fee, money which allowed him to buy the former Miami home of Chicago gangster Al Capone for £7 million.

Abbas did not consider himself an agent like Raiola. He did not really like agents at all. Law, after all, is a slightly more respectable-sounding profession. Yet, he came to respect Raiola above other agents because, like him, he was direct with high-and-mighty club employees and was thought of as an outlier in an industry dominated by agencies, too many clients, and conflicts of interests everywhere.

It would irk Abbas somewhat that, when Mohamed Salah signed a new contract at Liverpool in the summer of 2022, much of the focus in the British press was on his basic wage. Three-hundred-and-fifty thousand pounds a week was a lot of money but in reality, after achievable bonuses and endorsements, he was regularly earning somewhere in the region of a million pounds a week. This not only made him by far the highest-paid player at Liverpool but also placed him amongst the highest-paid players in the world.

Instead, the attention in the UK focused on the much lower figure. This allowed Liverpool to keep the rest of the squad sweet – sure, most of his teammates appreciated Salah deserved more, but how much more? Ultimately, the player's earnings were enough to allow Abbas to make the decision to represent only Salah. From 2022 onwards he did not take on new clients. Raiola, before his death in 2023, had a significant stable of footballers to look out for and, despite his reputation, he often had to deal with interference from parents and extended family. Abbas had none of these problems. It was just him and Salah.

Yet had he and Salah delayed agreeing to the new Liverpool contract, perhaps the pair would have been in an even better financial position. But they were not to know that within six months of the new Liverpool deal being signed off, the Saudi Arabian government would change the financial landscape of football through its investments in the game.

This was all part of the country's Vision 2030 plan to diversify its economy by ensuring a sustainable future when its oil resources finally run out. Initially, four Saudi Arabian Premier League clubs were taken over by its Public Investment Fund (PIF) in the spring of 2023, just around the time Salah's old contract would have been running out had he decided not to renew the summer before. Al-Ittihad was one of those clubs, just so happening to be the one that Abbas brokered his first deal with as a lawyer-agent many years earlier.

The forces around Al-Ittihad had since changed yet, when Abbas was approached to see whether Salah was interested in leaving his lucrative Liverpool contract for an even more lucrative contract in Jeddah, he considered it to be his responsibility to find out what numbers were potentially going to be involved.

A snapshot of the economic environment in Saudi Arabian football in the summer of 2023 could be found on the other side of the country, where Al-Ettifaq were connected to the state through the ministry of sports, if not being one of the PIF-owned clubs. It was thought a petrochemical company called SABIC was quietly bankrolling the club. SABIC had been a part of PIF before the majority of its shares were taken by the state oil firm, Aramco.

Liverpool's Roberto Firmino would take Saudi money by joining the PIF-owned Al-Ahli, while Jordan Henderson would go to Al-Ettifaq. Though his representatives would later deny he was earning £700,000 a week, let's just say he was for a moment, because roughly that would equate to £36.2 million a year: a huge sum of money for a midfielder arguably past his best, but not a particularly lavish investment when you consider Aramco's profits in 2022 alone were reported as being £126 billion. Henderson would have to represent his new club at that notional figure for another four millennia before earning the profits Aramco posted in a single year.

Al-Ittihad would come for Salah, offering Liverpool £150 million at the end of the summer transfer window. By then, although both the player and his lawyer were well aware of the interest, Salah was keen on staying, provided he was still wanted, which, as it turned out, he was – in no small part because of the timing. Any deal would have left Liverpool short on the pitch for at least six months, with no way of replacing a player who had scored twenty goals or more in each of the last six seasons.

Besides, the transfer fee that Liverpool would have received to some degree narrowed the potential for Salah's own earnings. If the Saudis were still investing in two years' time (and this is where the lawyer and the agent gambled because geopolitics were at play), Salah would potentially be in a position to command bigger wages and, crucially, most certainly a much bigger personal signing-on fee. Salah would be a few years older by 2025 but the sum of money Al-Ittihad were willing to give to Liverpool in the summer of 2023 gave an indication of the figures they might be able to trouser. The well-advertised sum also invited a potential residual advantage with any new partners, by showing them how much he was worth.

The strategy of Vision 2030, followed by the country hosting the World Cup four years later indicated Saudi Arabia was going to continue with its interest in football. Though Abbas was keen for Salah to be defined as one of the world's best footballers rather than the world's best Muslim footballer, he understood that Salah's religion would always create interest in an Islamic country that was spending cash like a startup company.

In the West, it was assumed that a Muslim footballer would be delighted to become the poster boy of an Islamic league, yet Salah had come to appreciate his English lifestyle, where his children could go to school without anyone recognising them, and the family could live quietly in the Cheshire countryside. That would all potentially end in a city like Jeddah, where his superstar status could invite the sort of intrusion he'd complained about on trips back to Egypt. He was also obsessed by professional standards and, despite the money being thrown about in Saudi Arabia, the country was still playing catchup with Europe, where Salah appreciated he played his best football because of the game's long-established structures. There were regular reminders of this dynamic whenever he returned to Egypt.

Saudi Arabia and Egypt were almost neighbours, separated by the Gulf of Aqba to the north and the Red Sea to the south. In theory, Salah might take with him the interest of more than a hundred million Egyptians. It was a point Abbas could try and make in any future discussions, but it wasn't a particularly scientific or accurate one. While the countries' interests overlapped, they were not exactly good friends.

Egypt considered itself to be the cradle of civilisation, viewing Saudi Arabia as the crass interloper: a place with new money and less culture, attempting to dislodge Egypt from its position at the pinnacle of Islamic society. Considering Abbas and Salah had spent six years attempting to maintain the player's sense of independence, there was no getting away from the fact that Saudi Arabia saw his potential signing as a political move. Egypt, after all, would never have the financial muscle to bring him back home.

As ever the tentacles of Egypt's authoritarian leader President Sisi were not far away. When he gained power in 2013, it was believed that the Egyptian army was being funded by Saudi Arabia and militarily as well as economically, the countries would become closer over the years that followed. While Saudi Arabia recognised Egypt's large military force was useful in protecting its own interests in the Red Sea, Saudi Arabia had the biggest Egyptian expatriate community anywhere in the world, with 2.5 million foreign workers boosting Saudi's labour force.

With the Egyptian economy struggling, Saudi provided significant financial support, but that relationship was tested when Crown Prince Mohammed bin Salman rose to power in Riyadh and withdrew the country's unconditional support.

Now, Saudi Arabia wanted something in return. Though Sisi was a strongman at home, he was willing to cede territory to Saudi Arabia in 2016 by the transfer of two Red Sea islands.

After a Saudi finance minister announced the era of help for Egypt 'without strings attached' was over, a cabal of Saudi commentators with links to the monarchy targeted Egypt for its 'failure' since the 1952 revolution, as well as the continued prominence of the military at the centre of its government. The criticism was met with a ferocious response in Egypt, where the state-owned newspaper *Al-Gomhuria* reminded readers of the country's historical superiority by claiming, 'Barefooted scoundrels and the nouveau-riche have no right to insult their masters.'

The gap between Egypt and Saudi Arabia was also apparent on the football pitch. Egyptian fans, of course, were furious with Salah when he did not celebrate the team's opening goal against Saudi Arabia at the 2018 World Cup, a fixture which may have meant little in terms of the competition but everything to Egyptians who thought regularly about the past.

Across North Africa and the Middle East, it tended to be accepted that the Cairo derby between Al Ahly and Zamalek was the biggest rivalry in the region. Prominent Saudi Arabian sports presenter Walid Al-Faraj decreed in August 2023, just a few months after the country had started ploughing money into the game, that Riyadh's Al-Nassr and Al-Hilal clubs were now ahead due to the numerous broadcasters across the planet signing up to deals with the Saudi Arabian Premier League. According to him, the Cairo derby 'lacked an international audience'.

It was another attack on the status quo. Egyptians were proud of their country but the majority were not exactly feeling great about themselves after decades spent in poverty, unable to do

THERE WILL BE FIRE

anything about their position because of societal controls. If Salah went to Saudi Arabia, potentially, such a move would act as another reminder of the country's sense of lost value. Meanwhile, Salah made a trip to London in his hoodie, visiting an Egyptian exhibition at the British Museum and posting a selfie. Maybe he was reminding anyone who followed his Instagram of Egypt's place in the world. The question was, did he really appreciate what had been lost, and what it would mean if he returned to the region but not home?

Salah, as ever, would not speak about what was happening, and the photos taken in the museum would only add to the sense of ambiguity. What was certain, he had spent his career carefully protecting his image while attempting to remain independent of the significant forces operating in his world. Moving to Saudi Arabia would render him the apparatus of a state other than his own, placing his future in the hands of those responsible for creating relationships with the rest of the world. He would not be his own man.

From time to time, Salah uploaded shots of the latest material he was reading and most of it was self-improvement. In January 2024, as he was preparing to travel to Ivory Coast from Egypt for the delayed 2023 Africa Cup of Nations, he shared a verse from a passage of a text without a title. 'They want to see you as the normal one, the same as them,' it read. 'Don't ask, don't think, don't feel; doesn't take risks, gives up, fake, and empty from the inside. The price was mutilation: making you give up your nature, changing your culture. To be fake but adapted: to walk in the planned path, which is created to be fit for your size.'

Posted in Arabic, the message received virtually no attention in Europe. Yet it gave an insight into Salah's thinking at the time. He was doing rather well in a Liverpool team that was suddenly threatening to win its second league title in four years, contributing eighteen goals across all competitions by the time he flew to Cairo to begin Africa Cup of Nations preparations.

Yet it felt like he was gearing himself up for a challenge that involved a different type of pressure. He was a key player at Liverpool, but it never felt as though the team relied entirely on his performances. The dynamic was different in Egypt, where the country's focus and expectations were all on him. Ferociously independent, Salah was reminding himself of who he was – as well as those critics who seemed to relish defining his legendary status by the fact he'd never won an AFCON title.

Since Egypt last won in 2010, Salah had become a corporate machine, a person whose story and achievements appealed to people beyond the border of his country. Though he was a first in Egyptian football history, he had not played domestically in Egypt for nearly twelve years, having never represented either of the country's two biggest clubs. Many Egyptians were more likely to see Salah on a billboard than a football pitch.

The seeds of the national side's failures may have been planted at home but it was much easier to blame a high-profile foot-baller who lived abroad rather than domestic figures with powerful friends. Whereas federations like those in Morocco and Senegal had successfully separated themselves from the impulses of government administrators, relationships in Egypt remained tangled. Those with any understanding of how foot-ball worked (or didn't work) in Egypt appreciated that the organisation running the national team did not have the experience or the funding to unlock the potential of a team led by the most famous player the country had ever produced.

Salah believed in the power of his achievements on the football pitch but there was one problem. If he was going to be judged only on sporting reasons, any gap in his CV was always going to receive focus, especially one as significant as the AFCON title.

In Ivory Coast, the team's group games were taking place in the centre of Abidjan and the squad was staying in the Tiama, a hotel just over the road from the Felix Houphouet Boigny stadium. While fans could come and go as they pleased at the nearby Pullman hotel, shared by the Nigerian and Ghanaian squads, the security operation at the Tiama was more stringent: partly because it was hosting one of the world's most famous players.

In the lobby, Salah's role as captain and leader of the team was visible a few hours before their opening game with Mozambique. Ahead of a team meeting in the facility's Restaurant l'Ambassadeur, most of the players waited, filling the time by playing table football. Salah, however, in his shower slippers, had set himself to one side, leaning alone against the glass window of one of the hotel's shops. It seemed as though he was focusing on what was to come, the latest opportunity to change the conversation around him. When it was time to go, he signalled and everyone followed.

Unfortunately for Salah, the same connection among the team did not exist on the football pitch. Egypt started their AFCON campaign with a 2–2 draw, only Salah's penalty in the seventh minute of injury time preventing a loss. That he did not celebrate reflected both his and Egypt's disappointment. It would prove to be his only goal of the tournament. In the second group fixture against Ghana, Salah's hamstring injury led to his substitution and yet another moment at which his commitment to the national team would be questioned by some of the country's most prominent commentators.

Another 2–2 draw with Ghana meant Egypt could not afford to lose to Cape Verde. Salah was already ruled out of that game, but uncertainty remained about the extent of his injury. What followed was a curious sequence of events which started in the lecture theatre of Abidjan's Palace de Culture. Salah, as Egypt's captain, took part in a pre-match press conference even though he knew he wasn't playing.

Salah had not previously taken on any media duties and Egyptian journalists had been frustrated with the lack of access they enjoyed after training sessions. For Salah, it would be a bad look if he had not spoken at all to the press before Egypt went out. Ibrahim Said, a two-time AFCON winner, claimed from a studio back in Cairo that Salah cared more about Liverpool than he did his country because of the lack of intensity in his performances.

'When we lose a match people are very critical,' Salah responded. 'It is true that I am the captain, but I wish people would be more flexible and realise players are giving their best, even if the outcome is different to what is expected. I ask the supporters to get behind the team. Football is not easy. We have some players participating in the tournament for the first time. Pressure is not on the supporters but it is on us as players.'

By Salah's standards, his words represented an impassioned defence. Yet in the hours that followed, the focus on him sharpened. Thousands of miles away, Liverpool were trouncing Bournemouth 4–0 and, when asked about Salah's condition after the final whistle, Jürgen Klopp revealed that he was more than likely to be travelling back to the club to receive treatment. His injury was worse than first feared and only with an intense rehabilitation programme might he be able to return to Ivory Coast to complete the tournament.

Klopp's words enticed Mohamed El-Wafa, a member of the Egyptian Football Association (EFA), to a magazine show, where he told viewers that Salah's injury was not as bad as Klopp was claiming, and there was no plan to fly him to Merseyside. Just as that interview was happening, the EFA itself released a statement that contradicted him: Salah was, after all, leaving camp. This prompted an embarrassed El-Wafa to attempt an about-turn, emphasising the decision was being made by officials on the other side of the continent.

The EFA had wanted to make this announcement after Egypt's game with Cape Verde and the organisation was angry with Klopp for going public before they were ready. Now, the EFA's competence was being questioned again and ahead of a game that would dictate whether or not the country would make it out of the group stages. The pressure was increasing on the players because of the attention on their captain.

It was unclear how transparently the EFA had communicated with Liverpool, and whether Klopp, if he knew about it, was paying attention. The EFA claimed at least one person at Liverpool knew was happening because of the level of consultation over the weekend. As many as five conversations took place a day, each lasting as long as an hour, according to the national team's doctor, Mohamed Abou Elela.

Klopp was ultimately only looking after his own interests, but if he had been fully aware and thought hard, he'd have realised he had caused a problem for Salah, who was staying with Egypt for the Cape Verde game anyway. Had Egypt lost, he could have returned to Merseyside without anyone knowing about his intentions. Instead, an early exit from the competition would potentially lay the blame at his door, while progression would harden the edge of arguments that the team was better off without the distraction created by its best player.

Ahead of Liverpool's first game after the injury, the club's assistant coach Pep Lijnders suggested he did not recognise the claims against Salah that were being made in his own country. 'I never met a guy, and also a human being, who is more committed to the life of being a professional football player,' he said.

In the past, Liverpool had sent doctors to Africa to monitor its players. The club had a good relationship especially with Senegal, whose star Sadio Mané had pushed against medical advice and signed a waiver absolving doctors in order to play. Senegal defeated Burkina Faso and progressed to the final, where they beat Egypt on the final on penalties.

Salah was reminded of Mané's commitment levels in the criticism that followed his own departure from Abidjan. One of the loudest voices was that of Hossam Hassan, the all-time leading scorer for Egypt, with 69 goals in 177 appearances. For years, as Egypt struggled to match the achievements of the past, Hassan, along with his brother, Ibrahim, had been amongst the team's most ferocious critics. Egyptians would listen because like Salah, he'd played at a World Cup (in 1990), but unlike Salah he'd won the AFCON – and not just once, but three times.

Hassan, a bullet-headed centre forward, was considered a throw-back but he was popular and his supporters questioned why he was constantly overlooked for a coaching role with the national team. Regularly, it was speculated that this was because of his criticism of Salah, who was not involved in any decision, but was recognised as one of the most influential people in Egypt. Neither the government nor the EFA wanted to be in the middle of any tension between two of the country's most famous players, one which might shine a light on the mistakes of the authorities around them.

When it was announced that Salah was leaving Abidjan, both Hassan and his brother went mad, with Hassan suggesting he should never return to Ivory Coast if he made the trip to Liverpool. 'Back here, we have men to do the job,' insisted Hassan, whose sense of masculinity had been proven in the eyes of Egyptian males many years before. He was said to have been in the living room of a coach who dared to drop him from the national side because of a personal issue. After an alleged fight, Hassan returned to the team.

Egypt would draw 2–2 for a third time in Abidjan, making it through to the knockout stages where yet another draw, this time with DR Congo, led to a shattering penalty-shootout loss. This led to the sacking of the Portuguese coach Rui Vitoria, who Salah had previously defended. Though the EFA wanted to replace him with another foreigner, Egypt's economic problems were deepening and, with the devaluation of the Egyptian pound, the country would struggle to afford a top foreign coach.

Meanwhile, Hassan was leading in the opinion polls as the domestic alternative. It was claimed in Egyptian state media that once again Sisi listened to the people and in the press conference that followed his appointment, Hassan tried to diffuse any tension with Salah by suggesting he remained the most important player in the country.

By the middle of February, Salah had returned to the Liverpool team and the club was concerned about him playing too often, too quickly. When Liverpool requested his withdrawal from Hassan's first squad, it was reported in Egypt that Salah ignored his calls. Salah did not respond publicly to those claims, though it was around this time he'd changed his number again, after suspecting a leak following Egypt's failure at AFCON.

Hassan was insistent on Salah travelling to Egypt because he'd been able to return to the Liverpool team, where he played two games in four days. But Salah would get his way after the government confirmed he was exempt from being called up, sports minister Ashraf Sobhy speaking to the player and wishing him well on making a 'full recovery'.

Hassan later suggested that problems with Salah were 'fabricated' but after Egypt lost to Croatia in the second of his first two games in charge, with Salah training with Liverpool, the new coach cited the absence of several key players through injury or other reasons as contributing factors to the 4–2 defeat. He made no mention of Salah. Meanwhile, although Mohamed Elneny had been left out, Hassan thanked Arsenal's midfielder for his understanding, and for 'answering me', which said to those with suspicious minds that Salah had not picked up his call.

In Egypt, Salah's supporters reasoned that he was trying to remind Hassan he could not simply say whatever he wished, even though it had not stopped him from getting the job of coach. Salah wasn't used to getting pushed around and on 4 February, a month after he set off for Ivory Coast hoping to avoid repeating an unwanted piece of personal history, he released another anonymous text in Arabic, reminding the world that he was still trying to be his own person. 'Be yourself, never be like anyone else,' it read. 'Never let other opinions be like a prison for you. Never be a size which fits for others . . . Just be yourself.'

Earlier on in the same season, Salah registered his two-hundredth goal in English football against Brentford at Anfield. He'd either scored or assisted for the fifteenth home fixture in a row. In Premier League history, the feat had only been bettered by Alan Shearer (eighteen and seventeen matches) and Thierry Henry (seventeen). In Liverpool's history, Salah had also become the first player to score in his first six home games of the season.

Liverpool were in a familiar position, chasing Manchester City at the top of the league table. After the 3–0 victory, Brentford's manager suggested that Liverpool were capable of running their rivals down, but he also eulogised the team's star player, suggesting he was underrated and not mentioned enough in conversations about the best players on the planet. 'Mo Salah – I don't know if he gets enough praise; what a level,' said Thomas Frank. 'He must be in the top three players in the world. When you have a player of that quality . . . his first goal is a signature Liverpool move.'

In fairness to Jürgen Klopp, he'd faced questions about Salah's ability so many times over the previous six years that there was very little new he could offer. 'The composure for the first goal is insane,' he said, reflecting on his movement: warping into a position he was so familiar with, cutting infield on his left foot. 'There is no doubt when the ball is in that area you will see him on the scoresheet.'

By now, Salah's status at Liverpool was so secure that he was able to develop routines without being challenged. Like, for example, the one ahead of games, as the players waited in the tunnel before warming up, like eager schoolchildren poised to enter the dinner hall. He casually leaned on one shoulder on the opposite wall to his teammates. Liverpool's players noticed this but they would never question him: all footballers have curious rituals that inform their preparation. Some of the more confident players saw this as Salah's way of reminding himself who he was performing with. To more cynical minds, this was Salah's way of reminding everyone how different he was. Normally, only Klopp would stand on the same side of the corridor as him. No other player was bold enough to position himself near the manager. Meanwhile, it showed that Klopp, who always embraced him forcefully rather than lovingly in these moments, was subtly willing to give him a special status. In the tunnel, nobody else was afforded the same freedom.

Klopp realised Salah trained and performed at his best when he felt as though he was important. Though he was socially quite reserved, he seemed to like it when others gravitated towards him. According to staff, Salah was the sort of guy who would walk into a busy room and find his own table. In the canteen at Melwood and later the AXA training centre, he would happily greet teammates wanting to sit next to him. Yet it was clear he was not at Liverpool to build deep, meaningful friendships. While he was close enough to Dejan Lovren, he also gravitated towards Xherdan Shaqiri partly because he was the richest footballer that Swizterland had ever produced and he'd invested his money well. Salah was always a keen learner but winning meant more to him than anything – even at chess. His desire contributed towards him being on the fringes of the main social groups, aligning himself with some of the more unusual characters in the dressing room. As time went on, though he enjoyed arguing about physical prowess with Andy Robertson, the team's Scottish left back, he was more likely to be found with another left back, Kostas Tsimikas, who was the only Greek player in the squad, and did not fit into any natural circle

Salah would give very little away about himself. Having attempted to create his own sense of independence for so long, he had come to think that being distant and remaining inaccessible was a strength. The less people knew about him, the more he was in control. To some extent, this also explained why he never really opened up to Klopp, with whom his relationship was never as close as many assume, and Liverpool fans broadly would probably prefer to think.

Klopp trusted his instinct about players and he was reluctant to give up on them. He also found saying 'goodbye' difficult. Some players in the squad would get close to Klopp before they were suddenly told they were being moved on despite not being keen to leave. For those watching the fallout from a safe distance, it led them to thinking Klopp was only really interested in their welfare while they were useful to him. He tended only to deal with any of the personal issues players were experiencing as soon as he felt they were affecting a player's performance in training; if they were still doing well, it tended to be the coaches in his inner circle acting as conduits of information.

Salah never worshipped at the altar of the messiah. Some Liverpool players spoke positively in public about Klopp even though privately they talked about him differently. Klopp would scream at some players and in the same week, they would describe him generously as a father figure in interviews. It seemed they were petrified about what would happen if they said what they really thought. As someone whose contact extended to both the coaching staff and the squad said, 'A part of the problem was, so much of the media wanted to paint him in a certain way, these players could not exactly say, "Can I just stop you there?"'

Klopp was not disliked but he certainly wasn't loved in the same way he was loved by the fans. For some, he could be ferociously unreasonable. For others, at times, he was caring. Though Salah quietly enjoyed having a sense of place, he did not need a coach holding his hand. He did not require an arm around the shoulder. His relationship, to some extent, was only as strong as the team's results.

When one notable reporter implied Klopp had helped resolve Salah's contract issues in 2022, he was promptly informed by Abbas that this was not the case. After all, it had been the club recruitment team's determination that led Salah to Liverpool and he felt as though he'd since built his own reputation, evidenced by the fact that he scored on his debut and did not stop. It was not as if Klopp had been patient with him, waiting for him to deliver. It would be understandable if Salah felt as though he did as much for Klopp as Klopp did for him. Until his arrival, Liverpool were a promising team but Salah's goals made it seem as though Liverpool could beat anyone and achieve anything.

Salah would tell friends that he learned more from Luciano Spalletti at Roma, especially about the defensive side of the game. Spalletti, he thought, was the best coach he'd worked for, and the one he developed the quickest under. Though he was more prolific in front of the goal, he continued at Liverpool what he was already doing in Rome. Spalletti, a bald-headed Tuscan – who later achieved with Napoli what Klopp did at Liverpool by helping the club win its first domestic title in three decades – had helped prepare Salah to return to the Premier League, where he hit the ground running. If anyone else deserved credit for his performances at Liverpool, it was the teammates he shared a pitch with rather than a manager whom he respected but felt as though he did not owe him the whole world.

Salah's first three seasons at Liverpool were defined by outrageous promise and the delivery of success. After forty-four goals and a Champions League final at the end of his first season, he became the first Egyptian to win the competition in his second, scoring in the final before the World Club Championship and the Premier League title followed in his third. Between 2020 and 2024, Salah kept on scoring but Liverpool would win the League Cup twice (Salah did not play on the second occasion because of injury), as well as the FA Cup, when he was substituted early, again because of injury.

The period would be remembered differently had Liverpool taken another Premier League title and the Champions League as they threatened to in 2022, but in the end those crowns went to Manchester City and Real Madrid. In Paris, Liverpool could have won the Champions League for the seventh time. They had reached the final with a fortuitous draw, beating Benfica and Villarreal en route but Salah believed Liverpool had a stronger team than Real, who edged past them with a 1–0 victory. Salah was distraught, telling friends he was reluctant to join the parade back on Merseyside the following day. Unlike Kyiv four years earlier, there had not been a great gulf in class between the sides on the night but it was Salah's view that in small moments, Liverpool had been undone tactically, while the substitutions had not worked for the team. The players were not to blame for that.

He had never felt so deflated in his career. Over the next eighteen months, as Liverpool fell out of the Champions League picture altogether, and several of the key players in the squad started to move on, Salah started to openly question the environment he was working in, including Klopp and his methods. He was not the only player to voice his concerns.

Bit by bit, the structure behind Klopp that had supported him on Liverpool's rise to the top of the European game had been broken up. While two sporting directors had left in quick succession, so had a host of medical staff. In addition, some sources were suggesting that Mike Gordon, the FSG president running Liverpool, was under internal pressure from other members of the organisation for the dismantling. Gordon and Klopp were so close that in 2022, when Klopp renewed his contract, a break clause dictated that he could leave if Gordon were ever to make the same decision before him. Amidst all of this, Liverpool were put up for sale, and when Gordon temporarily stepped away from daily duties, Klopp started to think about his own future.

Though he'd decided ahead of the 2023–24 season that it would be his last at Liverpool, Klopp did not reveal his impending departure until January 2024, just around the time Salah was beginning his rehabilitation programme following the hamstring injury sustained at AFCON. Salah had seen Klopp's agent Marc Kosicke at Liverpool's training facility in Kirkby earlier that morning and assumed Klopp was signing a new contract. The only player Klopp told ahead of the announce-ment, made in front of the players only ten minutes before it became public, was his captain, Virgil van Dijk. He was wait-ing next to Salah for the unscheduled meeting to start when he nudged him, saying: 'Do you know what this is about? The boss is leaving.'

Salah later said, 'It was a weird day for us and for football,' but it was hardly an emotional response considering how much success they'd shared together. Liverpool were still in the running for four trophies and, initially, it seemed Klopp's impending exit had inspired the players to give him a grand send-off, winning ten of the next twelve games, a run which included the League Cup final victory over Chelsea at Wembley despite the squad being decimated by injuries, including one to Salah.

It was another improbable feat secured by Klopp trusting a team of kids which left fans dreaming of the impossible again. Yet as some of the senior players, including Salah, returned to the team, they could not find their rhythm and by the middle of April, Liverpool had tumbled from the top of the league to third, and were out of the FA Cup and the Europa League. Some of the players questioned Klopp's team selections in both ties.

While Salah had been injured on international duty, other key players suffered setbacks during training sessions at Liverpool. One such example was the goalkeeper, Alisson Becker, who pulled up with a hamstring strain the day before a game at Brentford after joining a sprint drill. Some of Liverpool's more analytical players and staff members saw this as another example of the training load under Klopp carrying too many risks.

While Klopp was temporarily able to get more than anyone expected out of a few untested academy players, Liverpool's pursuit of another league title was undermined by absenteeism. By the end of March 2024, only five players in the first team squad had not missed a game through injury. Though most of the injured players were available to him by the end of the season, none of them were able to find their form. It was especially hard as many were being reintroduced at roughly the same time.

After Liverpool's first defeat of the Klopp era in the Merseyside derby against Everton at Goodison Park, Liverpool's title challenge was in tatters. Klopp reacted by making a raft of changes to the starting XI in the next game and Salah was left on the bench. Another deflating performance and result in London followed, with West Ham equalising to make it 2–2 just as Klopp was preparing to make a triple substitution, including the introduction of Salah. Klopp, in a bad moment, reacted to West Ham's goal by saying a few words to Salah, and teammates intervened to hold the player back.

If Salah had viewed Klopp as a figure of authority, it was clear he did not any more – although surely Salah would not have reacted in the same way if Klopp was staying on as Liverpool's manager. Only a few people were close enough to the pair to know exactly what was said and a variety of accounts subsequently circulated out of Liverpool's dressing room. The most believable account involved Klopp's fury at the amount of time it had taken Salah to get ready, only for the player to tell him he could not be responsible for West Ham's goal because he was not on the pitch. That, ultimately, was Klopp's decision. Salah, after seven years' service, felt as if he'd been ditched by a manager at the very end of their working relationship, scolding him in public for his own mistakes.

Klopp had been a great manager for Liverpool but he was not always a joy to be around, even in the good times. This was him finishing the season as he had done the last: drained, brittle and snarky. He would try to suggest after the final whistle that the problem with his player had been diffused in the dressing room. Liverpool's title race was over and Klopp was also now protecting his own reputation to some extent. He had always been regarded as a manager players liked to play for, but the incident showed he did not always choose his words carefully.

Klopp had instigated the altercation but Salah was condemned for retaliating, which violated an unwritten law in football: the manager is always right, even when there's a chance he might not be. From a studio in Qatar, Mohamed Aboutrika weighed in, suggesting, 'Salah is wrong, this is your coach. You and he have succeeded in building a relationship that people dream of. The disagreement should not appear in public and in front of the fans.'

Confusingly, nobody seemed to want to ask if this was a consequence of Klopp's approach over the previous months when, like him, his team seemed distracted and exhausted. Salah was not in a mood to apologise. He would march out of the Olympic Stadium, having calmed down, declining requests for interviews as he always did, warning: 'If I speak, there will be fire.'

Lots of people find it hard to believe that football teams achieve things while simultaneously the individuals involved do not necessarily get on and that training grounds can be vipers' nests. It is not unusual for anyone to feel threatened by the slightest thing and politics play a big role in how problems are addressed.

Salah, unsurprisingly, was unhappy about being a substitute as it was not a role he was familiar with. Yet he was more annoyed about the way another season of promise fizzled away to nothing. Of the two trophies Liverpool had collected over the previous four seasons, he had started in only two of the games, making it into the second half in only one.

When it ends like this, with a petulant scene involving a hugely popular manager, when you are thirty-two years old, and it starts to get said you are not the same player as you once were, it might be tempting to believe it yourself, but Salah can at least look to the data for reassurance.

He has constantly been judged against his first season at Liverpool when he scored thirty-two Premier League goals and four-four in all competitions. This meant he was on a chart all by himself. Seven years later, Salah finished the campaign with a yield that broadly followed everything that came after 2017–18. The only difference was, he dipped below his expected goal total for the first time, but in fairness, his teammates might have impacted his decision making. There was the likes of Darwin Núñez playing alongside him – who generously could be called unpredictable or, somewhat less generously, erratic.

Though Salah's role in the team had more often pulled him into a wider position, with the once marauding full-back Trent Alexander-Arnold now tucking infield and becoming more of a ball player, Salah was often further away from the goal than before. He was still around, however, to try and convert some of those chances.

There has perhaps been less focus on Salah's willingness to adapt his game. In 2023–24, he created more chances for other players than at any other point in his Liverpool career. No other Premier League player created more clear-cut opportunities than Salah.

From here, the contract both he and his lawyer fought so hard to get from Liverpool has a year left to run. A romantic would say he should stay at the club for ever and try and break the goalscoring records that younger fans have been told will never be broken. At the time of writing, the start of the 2024–25 season, Salah is 135 goals away from the club's all-time leading scorer, Ian Rush, so the chances of that happening do indeed seem unlikely – unless, as Abbas continued to claim, he plays at the highest level until he is forty years old. Salah is already, however, beating Rush on one front, whose goal-to-game ratio is lower than Salah's. He stands only behind South African-born Gordon Hodgson on that list, a player whose Liverpool career finished in 1935.

Klopp's replacement, Arne Slot, is a Dutchman who won the Eredevisie against the odds with Feyenoord. He judges his wide players by what they create as a first point of reference rather than how many they score. Given there have been refinements from Salah on that front, he should easily fit into a system where the team looks to slowly wear down the opposition through its domination of the ball.

Those close to Salah insist he has no axe to grind at all with Klopp but it motivates him to prove the team can be successful without the manager who helped the club almost deliver everything.

As Liverpool toured the USA in 2024 ahead of the start of another campaign that will involve the Champions League once again, Salah would spend his evenings bunkered in his hotel room re-watching his performances in the friendly matches. His quest for self-improvement is not over.

And neither was the respect he commanded from his teammates. Over the summer of 2024, a coffee bar was installed at the club's training centre just outside the dressing room. It quickly became a place where staff relaxed. In between Salah's breakfast, which usually consisted of fruit, and his salad lunch, he would enjoy a hit of caffeine — one of his few vices. When other players latched on to what he was drinking, the two baristas got used to serving up espresso macchiatos.

Acknowledgements

I owe a particular debt to David Luxton, the literary agent, whose idea spawned the process that followed. During that time, my wife Rosalind let me get on with it. Thank you also to my kids, Celeste and Vincent, for not making me feel too guilty when I was locked away researching and writing, and my father Peter for his understanding throughout.

I appreciated Andreas Campomar's enthusiasm at the beginning of all this, and Holly Blood's patience towards the end.

I am grateful for the support from my colleagues at *The Athletic*, both old and current. Thank you to Alex Kay-Jelski for backing me at the start of this project, as well as Andrew Fifield, as it progressed.

Neil Jones acted as a bridge, while Tony Evans was willing to share, and Tim Abraham, as always, listened. There are lots of people I'd like to thank in Egypt but it's probably safer for them if I do that in person at some point. Equally, there are contacts closer to Merseyside who agreed to be interviewed but only on the condition of anonymity, protecting their working relationships. They know who they are and without them, I don't think I'd have been able to write the story.

Elsewhere, Maher Mezahi, as ever, was full of ideas and always pointed me in the right direction. Lastly, thank you to the lads: Mark, Andy, Matt, Ian, Jay, Howie and even Billy (sorry Billy). You all have to read this now.